The DEVIL'S ADVOCATE

The DEVIL'S ADVOCATE

A Spiritual Man's Case Against God

Dr. Alonzo Richard Fleming Jr.

Next World Publishing
A Division of Next World Technologies
www.nextworldpublishing.com

FIRST PRINTING 2008

Next World Publishing books may be purchased for educational, business, or sales promotional use. For information, please email **inquiry@nextworldpublishing.com**.

The author gratefully acknowledges all of his teachers and his students who have crossed his life's path leading to the writing and publishing of this book.

Scriptures taken from the King James Version of the Holy Bible (unless otherwise noted) are in Public Domain. Special thanks to Crosswalk.com for making scripture usage effortless and Lulu.com for excellent service.

Library of Congress Cataloging-in-Publication data on file with the Library of Congress.

ISBN: 978-0-6151-9118-8

Printed in the United States of America

APPRECIATION

To my grandfather, Thomas Fleming,
Who bounced me on his knee and told me,
"Boy, you gonna be swift like a shark and deep like a rock!"

To my father, Alonzo Fleming Sr.,
Who provided huge shoulders for me to stand on.

To Al Freeman,
Who taught me how to be a Free-Man.

To my spiritual father, Pres Preston,
Who once proudly announced that I was
the first Man he had ever introduced.

To my mother, Fannie Coleman,
Who cleverly left books everywhere for me to read.

To my first wife, Latravana Cotton,
Who blessed me with three beautiful children.

To my spiritual wife, Cherice Fleming,
Who blessed me with four more beautiful children
and is my lifelong partner and friend.

To my children who I trust will stand on my shoulders
And realize all their dreams in this life manifestation!

To Euphemia Tasker, my first mother-in-law,
Who attempted to help me write my first book on rap music.
Thanks for believing I could write a book when I didn't.

To Mr. Esselman, my sixth grade science teacher,
"You taught me that science is my nature."

To Diana Pleasant and Sandra Simms,
For reinforcing my Potential.

To Detroit Public Schools,
"Your rejection of me forced me to look within."

Thank you All for Shaping
My Life.

Table of Contents

Table of Contents

"This is the Beginning of the New World.

As we stand together, I weep for my Family because I know that tears bring joy.

And I know that this is the Beginning of the Freedom of all the Slaves – And the Slave Masters!

I weep for my People because

I know that tears bring joy.

This is the beginning of the Freedom of the Slaves and the Slave Masters"

-- Erykah Badu, May 2, 2005

Excerpts from a speech given at the launching of the

Millions More Movement

About the Cover

I held my son in my arms while sitting in my grandfather's chair. I contemplated his future and how the mind of death awaits him in this present world.

I thought of the Culture of Death designed to kill him, imprison him, or drive him insane.

I thought of the Ministers of Death whose sole purpose is to convince him to sell his divine birthright to the God of White Supremacy.

I thought of the cross; the symbol of the Death of GOD, and a constant reminder that except I bow to White Supremacy, I too will die.

I thought about the Scales of Justice sitting on the foundation of White Supremacy.

I thought about the implications if I participated in the Conspiracy of Silence.

I thought about the mantra of the civil rights preachers who bombard my mind with hollow hopes of integrating into white supremacy, and living in harmony with it.

I contemplated the history of America; her religion; her politicians; her education, her leaders, and the present condition of her people; I concluded that she has been weighed in the balances and found wanting! It is time to take my earth back.

I chose the images on the cover because they represent the inward struggles that were in front of my fathers, my grandfathers, and now are in front of me. I decided to announce it on the housetops, "The Serpent Told the Truth! The Emperor has no clothes! The Christian God is actually Satan, the God of White Supremacy in disguise; and the Negroes in America are the proof of it!"

Each item in the picture is symbolic of a thought trying to live in my mind:

Woman with baby: Represents LORD God's world, which can only live if I die.

Cross: Represents the Death of GOD, and the death of any hope for my son.

Table: Represents the poisonous table from which I have eaten.

Books: Represent the doctrines of white supremacy in all its forms.

Scale: Represents justice built on white supremacy.

Baby: Thomas, the Son of the Original Man.

Man in chair: The Original Male looking only to the Elevated Serpent.

Chair: Represents relaxing under false hopes of integration.

Serpent: Represents the Elevated but hated Truth that heals, and opens the eyes of the blind.

What The DA Intends to Show

In the American Judicial System, there is a high standard of proof when anyone has been charged with a crime. A person cannot be convicted with a heinous act simply on hearsay and scant evidence, because his very freedom is at stake. To prevent injustice to the accused, guilt must be proven "beyond a reasonable doubt". This means that when all the evidence has been weighed; there is no reasonable doubt that the person being accused either committed or did not commit the crime.

We will use this standard of proof to make the case that a heinous crime has been committed against the whole of humanity and black people in particular by the LORD God of White Supremacy. The criminal in the case left a recording in his own words, and fingerprints with his own hands. Up to this point in history, he has not been brought to justice. On the contrary, he is worshipped as the legitimate owner of the earth though his hands drip with blood. Therefore, as you read, carefully consider the evidence. While the whole of humanity is the victim; the condition of black people is the best proof of the LORD's utter ruthlessness as well as the ruthlessness of his children.

We, who present this evidence, believe our case is so strong that you will have no doubt that the LORD of this current World order is Satan himself. We will use the American Negro as the primary victim who warrants the case being heard.

During the heyday of the 1960's Civil Rights Era, a book burst on the scene in which its author was called by Readers Digest, 'The Most Powerful Black Man in the United States'. In Message to the Black Man in America, The Honorable Elijah Muhammad made a bold statement about the Bible. He called Christianity a religion created to deceive black people; and the Bible, a poisoned book, designed to support White Supremacy. **We intend to show that the current condition of black people in America (herein called Prodigals) is proof that Elijah was correct.** Further, We will show where the poison has been hidden in the book, and WHO currently administers the poison.

For approximately 200 years now, Christianity has proven itself powerless to improve the Negroes' condition. Though Negro preachers read from the same book, their philosophy has only divided and impoverished Negroes in every respect; and has robbed them of any knowledge of Self. The preachers have either knowingly or unknowingly blinded and stripped naked, an entire race, while injecting them with the deadly Doctrine of White Supremacy.

We intend to clearly show that the LORD God of the Bible, to whom the Negro Preachers make obeisance, and cause the Negro people to do the same, is the Enemy of the Souls of Black Folk. The God they serve is actually Satan disguised as Creator of the Original Man.

First we intend to show that Satan injected himself within the pages of the scriptures for the purpose of ruling Man. Second, only Satan's children can have a sin nature. Third, the Serpent in the Garden of Eden told the truth; Fourth, LORD God is the true Satan who put Man to Death and cursed him; Fifth, redemption is found in the Original Male and Original Female looking within and turning away from the Doctrine of LORD God; Finally, the Doctrine of White Supremacy which is the Ultimate manifestation of LORD God's thought system, is **the thinking that currently rules <u>every</u> Negro church**.

How to Read this Book

This book is designed similar to a textbook, study guide and reference manual.

It is comprised of four major sections: Text, Case Studies, Essays and Exhibits. There is also a glossary to define terms being used.

The **Text** will lay out the case and introduce you to a thought system that will challenge your current thinking and its' effects, by introducing you to your Self.

The **Case Studies** outline actual events in **"time"** to help you connect your current thinking with your current experiences.

Essays are opinions to help you consider the question ***"If I employed a different thought system, would I get different experiences?"***

Exhibits are actual evidence of the "Basis of your current thinking".

Closing Arguments outline damages, remedies and exercises in United Thinking.

As you read, be sure to pay attention to the footnotes and scriptures. They will refer you to various sections. They will give you detailed answers to your questions as they arise.

Some of you will read the book straight through; others will read a section, then read the case study or exhibit being referred to. It does not matter; the results will be the same.

Conventions used in this Book

When you see this:	It means this:
Citizens	Descendants of Slave-Owners who hold LORD God's thought system.
DA	Devil's Advocate; This abbreviation is used to remind the reader of the role of a District Attorney who represents the People in a Criminal Matter.
Devil	GOD unperceived; the perceived absence of GOD.
GOD	The Universal MIND operating in Genesis chapter 1, who is the Devil to this present world. The creator of Original Man.
LORD God	Satan; The Mind operating in Genesis chapters 2, 3 and throughout much of the Bible. The God of this present world order.
Man	The GOD-created, unified Male and Female; the image of GOD and Owner of earth. Original Man.
Adam and The woman	The separated man that LORD God made; consisting of two Men; one being subordinate; Corrupted man.
Mankind	The resultant thought system of LORD God; the mind of men and women who began filling the earth as offspring of LORD God's separated male and female.
MIND	Creative force; The Energy that permeates All. Commonly called GOD. (all upper case letters)
Mind	The orientation of the Created Self and the Material world. (Upper case "M" only)
present world	The current mental orientation of all Mankind. The war experience that LORD God's set of rules has caused Mankind's Mind to manifest.
Prodigals	Blinded Original Male and Female Descendants of Slaves who have some remembrance of Self but imitate citizens.
World	An agreed upon experience among equals; the set of rules used to orientate the Mind to manifest the experience in earth.
GOD's World	The agreed upon experience Created by the Original Man; the GOD experience based on the Male/Female reality.

For more definitions, see the Glossary in the back of the book.

Italicized Scriptures are direct quotes. Others are paraphrased or explanatory.

The DEVIL'S ADVOCATE

INTRODUCTION

The Elevated Serpent told the Truth but he is called the Devil. And though LORD God admitted to the truth, he still cursed all mankind plus GOD's creation in the Garden of Eden story.

Though the LORD exhibits all that is called evil, he is worshipped as a loving God! And his offspring act out of the same evil nature universally.

Dr. Alonzo Fleming Jr. presents a compelling case against LORD God. He is willing to say what everyone is thinking!

For centuries, man has resisted and quieted the voice inside his own head that asks the obvious questions: How could God curse his own children and creation, then call it love? How could he tell everyone else to love their enemies, yet he gladly kills his own? How could he instruct us to bless and not curse, yet he curses? Why would God set his children up to die, in the first place?

Maybe the God that we've been following is not GOD at all, the authors assert that the God of Christianity is an Imposter and the #1 enemy of the Original Mind! He is in fact Satan disguised as GOD! This means that the "Devil" of Christianity represents the Unknown GOD. This is true because the unknown GOD represents a world opposite that of the present world. In other words, if the present world is good, then the emerging world must be evil. If the current world is evil, then the coming world must be good. The authors advocate for this unknown and unperceived GOD; the GOD that mankind cannot know and has blinded the Mind of Man from perceiving.

This book begins by introducing Man to the Unknown GOD of Reality. We then present our case against the God of Christianity; the Imposter and the Illusion. Finally, we bring the readers to a point of decision; either continue to follow the LORD God of Death; or re-orient the Mind to create a new Reality!

CREATION

In the beginning God created the heaven and the earth. And the earth was without form, and void; and darkness was upon the face of the deep. And the Spirit of God moved upon the face of the waters.

Genesis 1:1-3

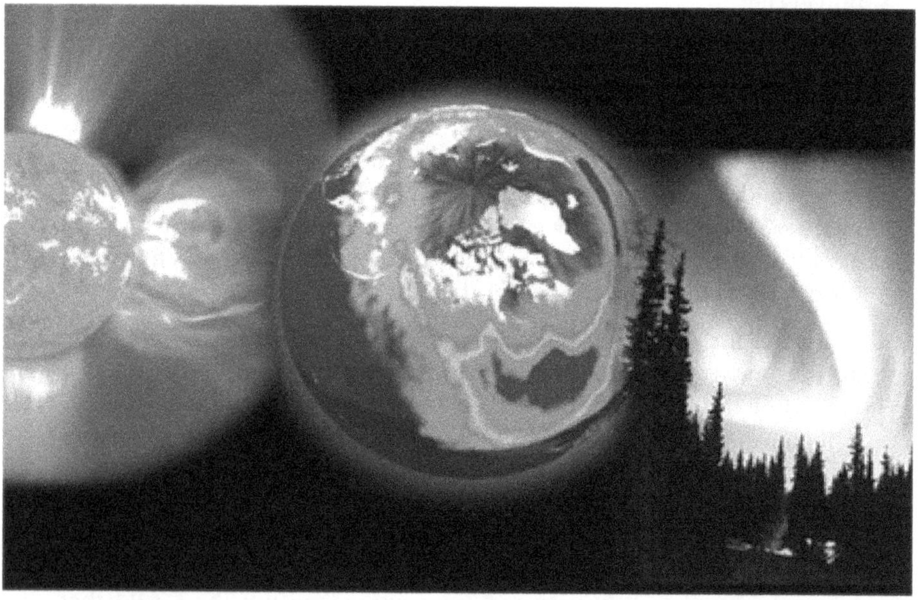

Creation: A solar storm, aurora from space, and aurora on Earth.

Acknowledgment to Michael L. Kaiser,
STEREO Project Scientist
NASA/Goddard Space Flight Center,
whose department captured and created
this image via "Our tax dollars at work"

1

THE LAW

Meet the GOD of Reality

In the beginning God created[1] the heaven and the earth. And the earth was without form, and void; and darkness was upon the face of the deep. And the Spirit of God moved upon the face of the waters[2]. Gen. 1:1-2

To know the Self is to know GOD. This is the scientific approach the ancients employed. However, before one can begin to consider the magnitude of the Self; he must first consider its nature and how it originated. Is the Self like the finite material world, which organizes to manifest on earth, only to degenerate, re-organize and re-manifest in a different order? Where did the Self come from and who originated it? Who or what is GOD, and when was the "beginning" that the scriptures refer to?

We state at the outset that the Genesis creation is a reminder to the sleeping Original Man; who has placed himself in "time". It is a record of the eternal inheritance and power he has with GOD. It is an ancient acknowledgment of his Creator's gift to His Self.

"The universe is mental—held in the Mind of [GOD]" --The Kybalion

"GOD IS SPIRIT! But what is Spirit? This question cannot be answered while using the present materialistic thought system. To do so would in effect be defining GOD, which cannot be explained, defined or even detected, using physical methods.

---

[1] See Exhibit 1a: A scientific discussion on the age of the universe. Pg. 182-184.

[2] There are obvious problems in the sequence in which physical matter is said to have appeared; however, this work is not intended to discuss the manifestations of matter with respect to order. For an exhaustive study on that subject, Read The Science of God, by Gerald R. Schroeder.

Spirit is simply a name that men give to the highest conception of Infinite, Living, Mind—it means "The Real Essence, or Substantial Reality". We use the term "Spirit" to speak or think of GOD. For purposes of thought and understanding we are justified in speaking of Spirit as Infinite, Living Mind; at the same time acknowledging that the materially oriented mind cannot fully understand it. We must either consider the universe a mental picture in the Mind of GOD, or stop thinking about the matter all together[3].

If GOD is Mind and permeates ALL that is; then the material universe must therefore have its existence as a mental creation in the Mind of GOD. The ancients declared that "in Him (GOD) we live, move and have our being". Thus we conclude that whatever the eventual "substance" GOD is, the physical universe is merely the rule of thought given physical manifestation within God's Mind. And man, appearing to have separate experiences, is merely an effect of thought being extended to give Images of physical manifestation, all within the context of GOD's Mind. Furthermore, if GOD's thought **could** change or shift, then so would the rules of the physical universe also change.

The next question is: When did GOD create the heaven and earth, and what does it mean to be without form and void?

Suffice it to say, GOD is timeless. The "when" of creation could have no meaning to GOD, since it would subject GOD's thinking to "time and space" making time[4] "above" GOD, having the ability to "cause" GOD to act.

To better understand this principle; carefully consider the following philosophical question: Could there have ever been a time when the thought of creation was NOT in GOD's Mind?

1) If you answer "yes", it implies that a thought GOD was previously unaware of, can arrive in His MIND from another location, and influence him to act. It also implies that there is such a place from which a new thought can arrive. This answer declares that there is some place where GOD does not exist; and a thought may come and influence GOD from that place.

---

[3] See Exhibit 1b: The Mental Universe. Pg. 185-186.

[4] See Exhibit 1c: What is Time? Pg. 187-188.

Furthermore, it implies that there could be other thoughts in existence that GOD has yet to think. Do you see how it also rules out the assertion that GOD is ALL-Knowing?

2) If you answer "no" to the question, it implies that time is a meaningless concept to GOD. You agree that GOD is omniscient; and there is no thought that GOD could "start or stop" thinking; no physical manifestation that could ever come into or leave existence. And there is "No Place" from which a thing (including a thought) could come to him.

Therefore the words "Creation" and "Beginning" as used with respect to the Infinite MIND, have nothing to do with time, space nor matter "coming into existence". Thus, time, space, matter and Man have always existed.

However, scientific observations across a variety of disciplines indicate that the known physical universe did indeed have a beginning. Ever since Albert Einstein's theory of Relativity was postulated, man's perception of space, time and matter has forever been changed. Almost every implication of Relativity, including big bang, an expanding universe, background radiation, black holes and the relativity of space and time has had multiple verifications. Current scientific inquiry is even experimenting with time travel (something allowed by relativity). Our ability to measure the age of the universe is so precise that we have narrowed its age down to be approximately 14 billion[5] years!

The American Academy of Science released a work indicating that science and creation (or an Intelligent Designer) are not necessarily mutually exclusive concepts; provided it be understood that science is based on physical experimentation; and creation based in non-physical terms. Thus in the classical definition, current science can only investigate naturally occurring, physical phenomena. Creationism is beyond physical experimentation[6]. Therefore, assuming GOD exists and set the Laws in motion, he had nothing else to do with its function. This allows for a creator, while maintaining the rules of an observable, evolving universe. It rules out superstition, blind faith, and miracles; leaving room only for knowledge as the basis of inquiry.

---

[5] See Exhibit 1a: A scientific discussion on the age of the universe. Pg. 182-184.

[6] Science, Evolution and Creationism, National Academy of Science 2007.

How does GOD Create?

"For the invisible things of him [who is] from the creation of the world are clearly seen, being understood by the things that are made, even his eternal power and Godhead." Romans 1:20

The question remains, how could GOD create a universe in "time" and from nothing if Man and the universe have always existed?

It is said that Man was created in the Image and Likeness of God. If this be true, then we should be able to extrapolate how GOD creates by understanding how man creates. We use the mathematics of similar angles[7] and the Law of correspondence[8] to aid our analysis.

1. Man creates by using materials that are outside of him (like the materials required to build a house). However, if GOD created in such a way, it would mean that there is something outside of him to be acquired and used as material. Seeing that GOD fills all space, there can be no "outside" of GOD from which he could acquire materials. Therefore, this method of creation will not suffice.

2. Man creates by procreating; or reproducing his kind through the process of begetting. This is self-multiplication or transferring a portion of himself to his offspring; But neither will this do, since GOD cannot add to himself (multiply) nor transfer from himself (subtract). In the case of adding to himself, where would the material come from to be added to him? If GOD could subtract from himself where would the material go to be separate from GOD?

As you can see, the first two ways require something outside himself from which he must take; or something outside himself, to which he must give. However, there is a third way that man creates without any outside material, nor by reproducing himself.

The third way man creates is mentally. *"Man can form things in his thought, and by impressing his thought upon formless substance can cause the things he thinks about to be created[9]"*. In this way he uses no outside materials, nor does he add or subtract from himself, <u>yet his universe exists as long as the thought is held in his Mind</u>.

---

[7] If two shapes are similar, one is an enlargement of the other. This means that the two shapes will have the same angles, and their sides will be in the same proportion. We use this property to help us analyze and conceptualize the idea. We realize its limitations.

[8] That which is below, corresponds to that which is above; that which is above, corresponds to that which is below.

[9] Quote taken from Standing in the Majesty of Grace, Dr. Keefa Lorraine Weatherspoon N.D.

Man accessed Two Million or more Minds

A very potent example of this law is the 1995 **Million Man March**, which was conceived and created in the Mind of The Honorable Minister Louis Farrakhan and his wife. This event was no fluke. It was a carefully conceived mental image and "creation" at the most powerful levels of Mind. One Man focused his thoughts so strong in the direction of unity that he affected the collective Mind of an entire people.

Farrakhan and his wife united in Mind, accessed the highest level of two million minds of black males, having different religious and philosophical backgrounds; and compelled them (including the Devil's Advocate) to put down what they were doing and descend on Washington D.C., in the highest level of unity.

In spite of the relentless attempts by the American media machine to derail his success, the need to attend the Million Man March was compelling to the point of hypnosis. Furthermore, this Law of creation is so powerful, that in spite of carefully crafted attempts to "separate the Man (Farrakhan) from the Message"; the peace and beauty that ruled the Million Man March, was an extension of the same Spirit of peace that resided in the Mind of Minister Farrakhan and his wife. This is the Law. It dictates that all things, including thoughts, create after their own kind; and the physical manifestations of creation are always consistent with their thinker.

"Even bodily parts come into manifestation as a direct result of commands received from the brain, nervous system, and thought impulses[10]".

Have you ever thought about how your body knows to grow from an embryo to an adult? Consider it.

Therefore, GOD creates the universe MENTALLY, in a manner akin to the process of Man creating Mental Images. Just as you may create a universe in your own mentality, so does GOD create universes in his[11] mentality; however, your universe is the creation of a finite Mind, whereas GOD's is the creation of Infinite MIND. The two are similar in kind, but infinitely different in degree.

---

[10] Quote taken from Standing in the Majesty of Grace, Dr. Keefa Lorraine Weatherspoon N.D.

[11] We use the word "his" only for purposes of convenience. We do not intend to imply a single gender to GOD.

Physical Manifestation is Proof of Thoughts held in Mind

The universe exists at the point of thinking it, and the thinkers' spirit permeates the thought and all its manifestations[12] thereby giving the entire universe the nature of the thinkers. Physical manifestation is merely proof of the rule being used by the thoughts held in Mind. When thoughts are consistent with the laws of harmony, the physical manifestations of harmony are the only result from them.

It is therefore clear from our examples that THOUGHT is the reality, and the fluid physical manifestations simply obey the rules of the thinkers! This is a very important principle to understand.

For the Original Man, these truths bring with them powerful implications. If GOD and the created Man are in the same Image and Likeness and GOD is unchangeable, then it follows that the Original Man's reality cannot be changed; only his perceptions of himself can be altered. His physical experiences are merely representations of what is in his own Mind. He need do nothing more than re-focus his thoughts about himself, and his universe onto formless substance to change his experiential manifestations.

The Mind may be likened to a garden. When neglected, it grows wild; cultivate it to see order. Whether cultivated or neglected, it must and will, bring forth. If no useful seeds are put into it, then an abundance of useless weed-seeds will fall therein, and will continue to produce their kind.

Just as a gardener cultivates his plot, keeping it free from weeds, and growing the flowers and fruits which he requires, so may a Man tend the garden of his Mind, weeding out all the wrong, useless, and impure thoughts, and cultivating toward perfection the flowers and fruits of right, useful and pure thoughts.

By pursuing this process, a Man sooner or later discovers that he is the Master-gardener of his soul, the Director of his life. He also reveals, within himself, the laws of thought, and understands, with ever-increasing accuracy, how the thought-forces and Mind-elements operate in the shaping of his character, circumstances, and destiny.

–As A Man Thinketh

---

[12] The author does not assert that GOD and Man are in the same degree, (though in the same order). As a drop of water is the same substance as the ocean, so is the Original Man the same substance as GOD.

"Let us[13] make Man to our image and likeness" Genesis 1:26

The Genesis 1:26 scripture is a profound declaration of the Original Man's ETERNAL IDENTITY and PHYSICAL APPEARANCE! The GOD of the universe created an entity that reflected his own image and operated in his likeness. However, the depth and power of this creative statement does not immediately present itself. Yet ponder for a moment what it means to "image" a thing.

We stated earlier that physical manifestations represent thought. They are literally the image or reflection of how or what one sees. To better understand what we mean, imagine GOD looking into a mirror. When GOD looks into the mirror he sees Man (his image); when Man looks in the mirror he sees GOD (his image). Or better still, Man and GOD are reflections of one another! And when the Original Man beholds himself, he says as Jesus said: "When you see me, you have seen the father" (John 14:9); The Father being those thoughts that created him. Whoever or whatever the Original Man is, he is literally the physical representation of GOD Almighty, and he rules the earth!

Now reflect on the implications of being the Likeness of GOD. This is a powerful declaration of the Original Man's NATURE. In section 1.1, we eluded to the mathematical principle of similar angles to illustrate the similarities between Man and GOD. The aforementioned verse declares that the created Man's nature is exactly "like" GOD's nature! It suggests that Man is a miniature version of GOD; having similar power, tendencies and abilities to a lesser degree.

To better understand this principle, reconsider our previous discussions on how Man creates within the material universe. Man can create by reproducing himself. At the highest level of thought he conceives of a being like unto himself; then using the principle of Gender[14], Man transfers a portion of his physical being to an offspring. In doing so, he gives his nature and physical appearance to another like unto himself, thus increasing (or multiplying) himself. The offspring is said to be in the image and likeness of Man.

---

13 The author believes that the phrase "let us", represents the masculine and feminine thoughts of GOD.

14 See Exhibit 2a: On Male and Female. Pg. 189-190.

Conception is done at the highest levels of Mind, even before the male and female ever physically meet. Furthermore, the principles that govern the Man's thinking, his disposition and power are also passed to the offspring and will govern the offspring's thinking. Thus, just as GOD does; Man also creates in his own Image and Likeness.

THE COMPONENTS OF MAN

"And God created man in his own image: in the image of God he created [Man]: male and female he created them". – Genesis 1:27

Upon careful examination, the reader will clearly see that GOD, in addition to giving Man a specific nature, he gave him a name; MAN. He also endowed Man with an essence composed of specific guiding principles of life and creation.

"Gender is in everything; everything has its Masculine and Feminine Principles; Gender manifests on all planes."--The Kybalion.

The components of masculine and feminine make up the most powerful aspect of Man's nature. We maintain that GOD cannot reproduce or beget since there is no "Outside" of GOD. And since Original Man operates within GOD, we do not violate the principle. In addition, Man must use the components of masculine and feminine to even operate in his function as the direct offspring of GOD. Thus an understanding of the Principle of Gender will help the reader take a large step towards the essence of Self; because the secret of Man is hidden in the divine connection between the Original Male and the Original Female.

"The Principle of Gender embodies the truth that there is GENDER manifested in everything--the Masculine and Feminine Principles ever at work." This is true -- not only of the Physical Plane, but on the Mental and Spiritual Planes as well. On the Physical Plane, the Principle manifests as SEX (commonly called man and woman), on the higher planes it takes higher forms, but the Principle is ever the same. No creation, physical, mental or spiritual, is possible without this Principle.

The Principle of Gender

The Principle of Gender works in the direction of generation, regeneration, and creation. Everything, and every person, contains the two Elements or Principles, within him or her. Every Male entity has also the Female Element; and every Female entity contains also the Male Principle. "If you would understand the philosophy of Mental and Spiritual Creation, Generation, and Re-generation, you must understand and study this Principle.

The Principle of Gender has no reference to the many base, pernicious and degrading lustful theories, teachings and practices, which are taught under fanciful titles, and which are a prostitution of the great natural principle of Gender. Such base revivals of the ancient infamous forms of Phallicism tend to ruin mind, body and soul, and the Hermetic Philosophy has ever sounded the warning note against these degraded teachings which tend toward lust, licentiousness, and perversion of Nature's principles. If you seek such teachings, you must go elsewhere for them. –To the pure, all things are pure". –The Kybalion

On Male and Female

So, what are the components that make up the Original GOD Man?

Before we discuss the creative nature of Man in detail, it may help the reader to study Exhibit 2a, "On Male and Female". Observe the completeness with which GOD created the Original Man.

It is very difficult for the contemporary mind to conceive of the Original Man in his completeness. The author is aware that contemporary mankind refers to those having predominant masculine manifestation and energy as "man"; however the reference is a distorted view of the Original Man. It is more accurate to refer to them as "males".

Exhibit 2a demonstrates that Man is composed of male and female. This is not to suggest that Man is an individual with a woman inside of him. Notice that GOD called THEM Man. Original Man exists manifest in the divine unity of male and female. At GOD level, Man manifests as universes; at the physical level Man manifests as male and female (incorrectly labeled man and woman).

Again we stress; the male is not a Man within himself, nor is the female a WoMan within herself. Both of these illusions were created by LORD God. Man is the unity of the Original Male and Female.

Creative power is accessed through unity. And it's only through the unity of the Original Female and the Original Male that Man can see himself. It is the divine unity that allows the Original Man to see the present; and it is only through divine vision that the Original Man can operate in his function as God.

Thus, Man is the blessed manifestation of the divine connection between the Original Male and the Original Female. And with this divine connection, the Original Man brings into existence all Humans; and manifestations of earth. He can also remove and rearrange the universe simply by thinking or not thinking about it.

And God blessed them, and God said unto them, be fruitful, and multiply, and replenish the earth, and subdue it: and have dominion over...every living thing that moveth upon the earth. Behold, I have given you every herb bearing seed, which is upon the face of all the earth, and every tree, in the which is the fruit of a tree yielding seed; to you it shall be for meat. And to every beast of the earth, and to every fowl of the air, and to every thing that creepeth upon the earth, wherein there is life, I have given every green herb for meat: and it was so." Genesis 1:28-30

Immediately GOD informs the united Male and Female (the Man) that the universe is theirs to do with it what they WILL. GOD has already provided them with the knowledge of the universe. In the aforementioned verse he tells the Male and Female, in the presence of the entire universe, it is theirs. He also instructed the universe to obey the Man.

God directs the Man to look at EVERY tree, shrub and fruit on the face of the earth. When the Man looked at it, GOD told him that ALL of it was his, and that he could eat from any tree he desired. The reader should note that GOD placed NO limitations on his Man. He didn't say to him anything like "You can go here, but not there, or you can eat from this tree, but not that tree". GOD gave his Man complete rule and ownership over the entire universe. In fact, the scripture says that GOD 'commanded' the Man to rule it!

After creating Man and giving him authority, GOD emphasizes that his word is bond by including: "and it was so". God then reviewed his creation and placed his stamp of approval on it by calling everything he created "very good!"

Thus the heavens and the earth were finished, and all the host of them. And on the seventh day God ended his work which he had made; and he rested on the seventh day from all his work which he had made. And God blessed the seventh day, and sanctified it: because that in it he had rested from all his work which God created and made. Genesis 2:1-3.

Man Rules – GOD Rests

According to the scripture, all matters of creation have now been put to rest! GOD had done all he planned to do. He created the body of Law (called heaven) that would govern the universe. He placed the principles of matter in motion, and brought about the first generation of Heaven and Earth.

He put his Man in place, and gave him the knowledge and ability to run the universe as God. He even gave the Man the nature of GOD, so Man could properly rule. He told Man to use the second Law of creation and multiply his Self. He commanded the earth and universe to obey the Man.

GOD then ended ALL his work. As stated before, GOD set the Laws in motion, placed the first generation of heaven and earth in motion; then gave the world to his Man. Since this event, trillions of generations of heavens, earths and universes have been created by the Original Man and his offspring (the Son of Man).

Before leaving this section, it is helpful to make you aware of the many issues that will be raised in the next section. In the resolution of these issues, you will see that we will make a powerful case, well beyond any reasonable doubt that the God of Christianity is not the same one aforementioned.

Consider the following questions as you read the next few sections:

1) We established that GOD is eternal; having no beginning, middle, end or break. From your understanding, can GOD, or any part of GOD be changed, corrupted or die?

2) You may have noticed that in Genesis chapter one, everything GOD created, he blessed it and called it good; GOD even went so far that he called Man VERY GOOD. Can GOD, or did GOD change his mind about the blessed and good nature of his creation?

3) Can Man change his own nature from the image and likeness of GOD, to another nature?

4) Is there any indication in scriptures or daily life that GOD revoked Man's authority and dominion over the earth?

Carefully consider the aforementioned questions as you read the next section.

DECEPTION

"Satan promises only to deceive" – Holy Qur'an

A Separate World: Human, space, universe and the cosmos.

Internet Public Domain Image located on various blogs.

2

THE CASE AGAINST The God of this World

"We created an orbiting cycle that turns on its own axis forever unless a phenomenon occurs and re-shifts the positions of the male and female savages.

Our experts warned us that the mind has a strong drive to correct and re-correct itself over a period of time if it can touch some substantial, original, historical base;

And they advised us that the best way to deal with the phenomenon is to shave off the brute's mental history and create a multiplicity of phenomena of illusions, so that each illusion will twirl in its own orbit, something similar to floating balls in a vacuum."

- *Let's Make a Slave: The Negro Marriage Unit. Willie Lynch*

LORD God, the Ultimate Rebel

A Lord is an Original Man whom GOD has given authority over a particular realm. A God (or god) is one who has mastered universal principles and makes or manipulates worlds based on knowledge.

The LORD God is from the son of Original Man; who is in rebellion against the ways of GOD because GOD's World appeared to be foolishness to them (Isaiah 14:13). In this book, we refer to the LORD God as an individual; however, we are very aware that LORD God represents the Ruling, Satanic Mind within a group, country or nation.

LORD God is the ultimate rebel. He is unwilling to properly oversee the earth from one generation to the next. He resents sharing authority and wants to build a world of slaves who will serve him. In his rebellion, he manipulates the forces that are under his control in order to deceive and recruit a few from amongst Man into his experimental garden. For eons he tried, however; no Man would follow LORD God.

Man knew that the earth and all in it belonged to them. So what could LORD God offer Man to cause them to rebel against themselves? This is why it is said that "...There was no man to till the ground"—That is, LORD God wanted slaves to do labor that was shared by all, but every Man refused, having knowledge of themselves and their realms of responsibility.

Being a wise scientist, LORD God revised his plan. He couldn't take the earth or cause it to disobey Man, because Man was the rightful owner. He couldn't create another reality because GOD is the only Reality, nor cause the Man to willingly rebel against his own Nature (GOD); nor could he actually take the authority from Man. He decided he must convince Man that they were not "Christ, the Image and Likeness of GOD", but that they were dust of the earth (2 Corinthians 4:3-7) and faulty.

In short, he had to convince man that his nature had been changed from the image of GOD and re-assigned as earth. Man could then be divided and made to think that LORD God was the Image of GOD. Since the earth serves Christ the Image of GOD, the blinded Man would gladly serve the LORD God as legitimate owner of the earth—hence the cry: "The earth is the LORD's and the fullness thereof".

Reversing Man's Thinking

LORD God's ultimate plan was to raise a different kind of man who would cause everyone coming into the world to believe in and serve LORD God as a normal course of nature (Psalm 51:5). LORD God used the laws of biology, genetics, physics, chemistry, mathematics and the rules of Mind to make his own kind of man; separate and apart from reality.

While he could not remove Man's control of the earth or their ability to make earth do what they willed—he would cause Man to think that none of their power was their own and that whatever they did was to the credit of LORD God. To do this, LORD God had to carefully cultivate Man's thinking to respond to fear, division, and the physical senses. Any stimulation coming from the higher Self (which is based in LAW and knowledge) had to be rejected by the Man as devilish. Any idea of his oneness and unity must be anti-Christ.

The Man would then give over his power to LORD God. In other words, LORD God had to make someone that would be totally materialistic, and who would completely identify with the flesh (matter). LORD God's first step was to create division between the united Male and Female and then draw some away into his laboratory.

Generations would pass before the LORD God could successfully reverse one Man's thinking to begin to see the world completely upside-down.

Notice in Genesis 2:4, there are generations of created heavens and earth before the LORD God makes earth and heaven. The reversed man has fallen from his higher consciousness to his lower consciousness.

This moment in time denotes the beginning of the LORD God's first successful experiment. Adam, as this male is called, has become dazed and confused by the LORD God's promises of the benefits in Paradise; but the LORD God will need to put the man into a deep sleep[15] to move his diabolical plan into its next phase.

---

[15] See Exhibit 2b: On man and wo-man. Pg. 191-194.

Qur'an declares, "And when We said unto the angels: Fall down prostrate before Adam and they fell prostrate all save Iblis, he said: Shall I fall prostrate before that which Thou hast created of clay?"

History is replete with stories of a created being that rose up in rebellion against GOD and recruited Man as confederates. The Gnostic gospels go so far as to claim that the present physical world is the creation of an evil god who then recruited souls to come and join him in rebellion. The Gnostic[16] gospels were named after the Greek word which means "knowledge".

". . .for the LORD God had not caused it to rain upon the earth, and there was not a man to till the ground. But there went up a mist from the earth, and watered the whole face of the ground. And the LORD God formed man of the dust of the ground, and breathed into his nostrils the breath of life; and man became a living soul. And the LORD God planted a garden eastward in Eden; and there he put the man whom he had formed. And out of the ground made the LORD God to grow every tree that is pleasant to the sight, and good for food; the tree of life also in the midst of the garden, and the tree of knowledge of good and evil." Gen. 2:4-9

The Douay-Reims version of the Bible calls Eden "The Paradise of Pleasure". Eden was specifically designed to appeal to and cultivate the Man's physical appetites and dependence upon physical senses and stimuli[17]. LORD God kept the rest of earth (universe) in a state of chaos, then planted a beautiful plantation somewhere in the planet we now occupy.

Eden was the only place that resembled what the entire earth should have looked like if the LORD God had not been busy causing mischief in it. Eden was made to attract the Man (like gated communities attract many today), but was under the total control of LORD God for his own experimental purposes.

---

16 Gnostic (pronunciation: naws-tik) refers to collections of writings about the teachings of Jesus, written around the 2nd century AD. These gospels are not accepted by most mainstream Christians as part of the standard Biblical canon. Rather, they are part of what is called the New Testament apocrypha.

17 See Exhibit 2g: On Walking in Flesh. Pg. 218-223.

The Controlled Environment

Scientifically speaking, a garden is a controlled environment where the scientist can grow and/or develop whatever he desires. Gardens are planted for specific reasons, and Eden was no exception. There are several names for gardens, depending on the purpose and objective of the gardener. For example, when one wants to save an endangered species from extinction, he creates a type of garden called a "wildlife sanctuary".

A sanctuary is a garden refuge designed to allow an endangered species the opportunity to breed in a peaceful environment in hopes of increasing their population and preserving them in the earth. The planter (or scientist) does research, breeding and experiments to that end. After the population has sufficiently increased, they are then released back into the wild.

While a garden can be a completely controlled environment, it must be conducive to its inhabitants; howbeit for the purpose of the planter. Take for example the animal living in a wildlife refuge park. To the animal living in the garden, everything seems normal. His food is there, the environment sustains him, and everything seems fine; little does he know that an electric fence surrounds the perimeter of the garden.

One day the animal wanders to close to the electric fence, and Zap! He suddenly realizes that his seemingly natural environment is actually a prison, controlled by someone else. After enough time, the gardener may actually turn off the electricity on the fence. He need not worry though; his prisoner dare not venture close to the fence lest the power of 10,000 volts remind him of his place.

LORD God desolated the universe then set up a garden laboratory and made the male call IT earth. He allowed the rest of the universe to appear to degenerate into chaos so that the male would shrink from it in fear. This is why today, as huge as the universe is, the entire creation appears hostile to mankind except for the planet called earth. The garden was designed to poison him against himself and his Creator by stimulating the physical senses of the Man, causing him to depend on changing senses and ignore his higher Self.

Eden was abundant in all things which are "pleasant to the sight and good for food". These things in and of themselves were not evil, but LORD God's intentions were evil. He set it up so that when the Man compared Eden with the rest of the universe, Eden would be Man's logical selection. As will be seen later, the tree of life and the tree of knowledge were only included in the garden as a means to further attract the Man and snare him (similar to how cheese is used in a mouse experiment).

"LORD God took the man, and put him into the Garden of Eden to dress it and to keep it." Genesis 2:15

This was a literal kidnapping for the purpose of slavery and servitude! He had finally convinced a male and female to listen to him.

LORD God literally TOOK the Man whom he had previously dazed and confused; and placed him into the controlled laboratory environment. He now had a Man under his complete control. Although the Man still required further processing into slavery, all things were in place to make them complete slaves.

So he first gave the male a job. Serve the earth! Dress it and keep it for the benefit of LORD God! Thus at the right time, LORD God gave the male a commandment designed to encourage the Man to look ONLY to him for identity, and nature—to fully trust ONLY him for guidance.

As laboratory's go, the scientist began to design experiments around his new test case. Thus, he presented Adam with his first test. "The LORD God commanded the man, saying, of every tree of the garden you may freely eat: But of the tree of the knowledge of good and evil, you may not eat of it: for in the day that thou eat of it you will surely die." (Gen 2:16-17)

It was the first introduction of fear into the World. LORD God wanted the Man to fear the Self and his own nature. He knew that Man had unlimited access to all knowledge and would naturally eat of the knowledge of good and evil since all knowledge in heaven and on earth was given unto him.

The Introduction of Fear & Death

Prior to coming into the garden, the Man had no concept of fear or death. This removal of access to knowledge made him susceptible to control; and the introduction of fear removed the Man's knowledge of Self and his own power. The next step was to form Mankind; an entirely different kind of thinker. As will be seen, this is done by dividing Man.

The last thing LORD God had to do before re-making the Man was to "freeze" him under the threat of fear and death. LORD God used the fact that Man came and left the earth at will, as a tool to deceive Adam into thinking he could die -- that he was actually leaving existence and in effect "dying".

As the Man began to look more and more away from his Self and towards LORD God within the garden prison, his mind was systematically separated from the ability to access any knowledge that reminded him of his Self, Power and Nature. LORD God was now ready to fully divide the Man, and send him hopelessly spiraling into the abyss of dreams, illusions, fear and ignorance of Self.

The Final Operation Begins

"And the LORD God said, It is not good that the man should be alone; I will make him an help meet for him. And out of the ground the LORD God formed every beast of the field, and every fowl of the air; and brought them unto Adam to see what he would call them: and whatsoever Adam called every living creature, that was the name thereof. And Adam gave names to all cattle, and to the fowl of the air, and to every beast of the field; but for Adam there was not found an help meet for him.

And the LORD God caused a deep sleep to fall upon Adam, and he slept: and he took one of his ribs, and closed up the flesh instead thereof; And the rib, which the LORD God had taken from man, made he a woman, and brought her unto the man.

Read carefully the statements above. They give you insight into the motive of the one speaking and acting. Analyze LORD God's statement and then his following actions.

He first declares that "It is not good for Man to be alone". This is the first lie LORD God tells. Man was not alone, he was unified!

He is redefining Man in Adam's Mind. He's talking to the Male to convince him that he ALONE is Man. LORD God knew that if he could get the Man to see himself as lonely, it would allow him to submit to the idea of creating a partner for him (a wo-Man).

Next, he let the man see him form animals with partners, and begin to parade them before the man; suggesting to the man that he had formed him from the dust of the earth just like these creatures; As the creatures had partners, he could form a partner for him. LORD God was solidifying three deceptions in the Man's mind; 1) he was dust of the earth and, 2) as a male he was a Man by himself and 3) Man needed a partner to be complete.

When LORD God saw that his plan to lull the Man into a deep sleep had worked; he brought him a female whom he had also put to sleep and convinced that she too was a lonely Man. LORD God brought the separated female whose thinking he had now programmed to desire to mate with Adam. He told him that she was taken out of Man.

LORD God's Operation is a Success

And Adam said, This is now bone of my bones, and flesh of my flesh: she shall be called Woman, because she was taken out of Man. Therefore shall a man leave his father and his mother, and shall cleave unto his wife: and they shall be one flesh. And they were both naked, the man and his wife, and were not ashamed." Genesis. 2:18-25

Adam's indoctrination proved sound in that he named the separated female, wo-Man, just as he had named all the other creatures and their partners that the LORD God had brought before him. The new name would provide an even greater separation from their true identities by shifting their mental identity down to that of the beasts.

To maintain separation and division, LORD God broke off generational relationships. This would have the effect of ensuring that any knowledge of Self could be passed from one generation to the next; ensuring the longevity of his satanic thought system.

Knowing that the rest of Man in the earth was clear about their own identity, and the TRUE identity of the now blinded Adam and Woman, the LORD God could not afford to risk any contact with thoughts that he had not pre-approved. "For this reason a Man should leave his mother and father". It also had the effect of causing Adam and the Woman to be hostile towards anyone outside of the Garden.[18]

Knowing that Man has a natural inclination towards Oneness, LORD God cleverly redirects the basis of unity, saying: "Adam and the woman shall be one flesh". The LORD tells this lie, with the full knowledge that only Minds can unite. Flesh can never unite. This was done to ensure that they would be carnal (see glossary), always divided, and totally dependent on Him!

It is said that Man is the only creature born without his own clothes. It's interesting to note that in the garden, while LORD God had them asleep, he also stripped them naked. Now naked and unaware of their nakedness; the scripture makes it clear that they should have been ashamed but were not.

---

18 Keep in Mind that there were generations of people who were not living in the garden.

LORD God puts Man to Death and fills his Mind with lies

The LORD God had now accomplished his objectives to:

1. Cause Man to think that he and the beasts are of the same order.

2. Cause Man to see in terms of division and separate interests.

3. Cause Man to sense lack, insufficiency and dependence upon LORD God.

4. Cause Adam to think LORD God (Satan) is his creator.

5. Cause Adam to feel privileged and special by the LORD God's willingness to allow him to name the creatures (though naming the creatures was his inherent right) as though he was Adam's friend.

6. Cause Adam to see a wo-man as an Independent but subordinate man, rather than a Female having a divine connection as ONE with the Male[19] whose divine unity is the Man.

7. Cause Man to think that his own power was actually LORD God's.

---

[19] Review Exhibits 2a and 2b for detailed analysis. Pg. 189-194.

Opening the Eyes of the Blind

"So that 'Seeing they may see and not perceive, And hearing they may hear and not understand; Lest they should turn, And their sins be forgiven them." Mark 4:12

"Others said, These are not the words of him that hath a devil. Can a devil open the eyes of the blind?" John 10:21

The separated Man wandered all through the plantation naked and helpless until a day when the woman encountered the Serpent. Prior to speaking with the Serpent, neither the woman nor Adam had any inkling of their blindness to their true Self. They were only conscious of the upside-down world of LORD God. However, once they ate the forbidden fruit (the Knowledge of Self) their eyes were opened and they received a glimpse of their True Nature.

"And the eyes of them both were opened, and they knew that they were naked; and they sewed fig leaves together, and made themselves aprons." Genesis 3:7

Several things immediately occurred after the man and woman ate the forbidden fruit:

1. They could see clearly (Understanding/Awareness)
2. They gained knowledge (Principles)
3. They took steps toward Self realization (Responsibility)

LORD God is the god of this present world. He blinds the minds of them that do not believe the Serpent (II Corinthians 4:4). When LORD God put the Man to sleep, he stripped him of the Knowledge of him Self; blinding Man to him Self. When he removed the female from him, he removed Knowledge of GOD's Creation and blocked Man's ability to receive knowledge that would make him wise.

Keep in mind that it is a desirable thing to have one's eyes opened. No one wants to be blind and neither did the woman in this case. Remember, the tree was "good for food". It was "pleasant to the eyes", and it had power to "make one wise". Who wouldn't crave these healthy benefits?

The scriptures are filled with discussions of the benefits of having ones eyes opened:

~ *"Give Light to my eyes, lest I sleep the sleep of death." Ps. 13:3*

~ *"Open my eyes, that I may behold wondrous things from thy Law."*

--Ps. 119:18

~ *"...He that hides his eyes shall have many a curse." --Proverbs 28:27*

~ *"The eyes of your understanding being enlightened; . . ." –Eph 1:18*

There are scores of other scriptures that indicate it is righteous and desirable to have one's eyes opened. Who in his right mind desires to walk around blind? Who desires to be blind to knowledge? Why would LORD God remove sight from them and strip them naked, in the first place? In this book, you will notice that throughout history, whenever the Serpent appears, he immediately opens the eyes of the blind.

The first thing that happened after eating the fruit was that they could SEE!

After Adam and the woman gained sight, they became somewhat Knowledgeable of their true circumstance! They knew that they were naked and vulnerable. It is a natural thing for one to be clothed in their right mind (Mark 5:15, Luke 8:35), but here, LORD God had stripped them of their right mind, signified by their nakedness! The scriptures are replete with verses indicating that it is desirable to be clothed. Jesus taught that GOD clothes his creation (Luke 12:28, Matthew 6:30). Jesus said thieves make one naked (Luke 10:30).

So why would it be evil to desire clothing unless there is one in control who despises the natural order of GOD?

Now the Man had to take action because with Knowledge comes Responsibility! After discovering that they had been blinded and made naked, They "came to themselves". In other words they saw the truth of their Being and took refuge in the trees that GOD gave them in the beginning!

The Journey back to Self

Initially, they used the trees to begin regaining their former state by re-clothing themselves. Unfortunately, it was too late. LORD God had invested lots of time and effort in re-oriented their thinking. The momentum of their own thoughts caused them to subject themselves to LORD God even though they realized he was an IMPOSTER. It would take time and constant effort to fully recover.

Jesus illustrated this process when he told the story commonly called "The Prodigal Son[20]" (Lu 15:11-32). The parable contained the principle of constant composition[21]. In spite of the fact that GOD's son was lured away from his "Self" to a far away place, his nature remained consistent with its creator.

After losing knowledge of self, the prodigal began to identify with strange ways of thinking, by joining himself to a citizen of the far away country. In other words, he subjected himself to a body of law and thinking that was hostile to his very identity.

The citizens of that country cleverly provided him with sport, play and riotous living while stripping him naked of his substance. He partied and disregarded the power of his own nature, while sinking lower into the gutter of ignorance and despair.

Having spent all that he had, he became a 100% beggar! Though the universe all around him was filled with abundance and all of it designed for him, he became bogged down in poverty and lack; not realizing that the power of his own Mind was being used against him.

"Suffering is always the effect of wrong thought in some direction. It is an indication that the individual is out of harmony with himself [and] with the Law of his Being...A Man only begins to be a Man when he ceases to whine and revile...As he adapts to that regulating factor, he ceases to accuse others as the cause of his condition. He builds himself up in noble thought" -- As a Man Thinketh, James Allen, page 31.

---

20 One who departs from the knowledge of self and kind.

21 The law of constant composition states that the composition of a substance is always the same, regardless of how the substance was made or where the substance is found.

While the prodigal indulged himself in sport and play, the truth of his own nature was being laid low. He pleaded with the citizens for help. But alas help came in the form of scraps thrown to him as he lay in the swine pit, seeking compassion from a strange people.

After a time, a glimpse of the young prodigal's former Self entered his consciousness. This is when he "Came to himself" and remembered the abundance and security of his fathers house. "I am the very offspring of GOD", he said to himself. "While the servants in my father's house live like kings, I lay here dying in muck, seeking compassion, acceptance and equality in the house of Death. I know what I will do. I will arise from this death and return home to Self".

When the power of Self-knowledge shined into his mind, his eyes were opened; he stood up and pointed his face towards home. He ceased to beg the citizens of the strange country for food, jobs, civil rights, and reparations. The prodigal simply stood to his feet and began the journey back to Self.

In spite of being on his way home, the young prodigal was still insane. He had long practiced inferior thinking while in the strange far away country. It had now become very difficult for him to conceive of his equality which exists as a result of his birthright. He was now unable to even fathom the idea of not having to beg for his life and existence – the world of deception, rejection and abuse had become common place, and second to his nature.

As he made his way home, the temptation to return to his abusers was great. The far away country was heavily populated with privileged people (minds); some of whom looked like him but were really tools of his demise. These minds were groomed to convince him that the ways of the strange country were valuable. If he waited just a little longer in the pig sty, the strange people would finally change.

In addition, the prodigal thought that if he returned home broke and poor, his father would reject him out of anger. He was no longer aware of the principles that governed his father's thinking. **His own beliefs would now present the biggest challenge to his resurrection.**

The Difficult Journey Home

He tried to reconcile his conflicted feelings by planning to convince his father that his behavior merited him the position of a servant, rather than a Son. He had become so used to seeking pity that he totally identified with a pauper's mentality, and now planned to convince his father of his own illusion.

Upside-down thinking had been taught to the young prodigal. As Adam in the garden, sustained interaction with citizens of the strange country caused the momentum of his thinking to go totally against his own nature.

As he approached home, his father would not so much as hear suggestions of making him a servant. The father instead, celebrated the resurrection of his son. The son had been stripped naked of his substance and blinded to his identity. The father immediately clothed him, and opened his eyes by reinforcing his original nature.

The father exclaimed: "This, my son was lost, and is now found. He was dead and is now alive" (Luke 15:32). Notice he didn't curse him.

Thus was the case with Adam and the woman. By listening to LORD God, they strayed so far away from the path, that they no longer knew themselves.

They were dead; yet hidden within them was an ancient but faint knowledge of Self.

They were all but 100% committed to the ways of death brought on by the mind of LORD God. So when they ate of the forbidden tree of knowledge, they awakened momentarily and began to make their way home; that is until they encountered LORD God again. It would take another 6000 years before they could completely awaken and free themselves of the LORD God of this present world.

Returning to the Grave

And they heard the voice of the LORD God walking in the garden in the cool of the day: and Adam and his wife hid themselves from the presence of the LORD God amongst the trees of the garden. And the LORD God called unto Adam, and said unto him, Where art thou? And he said, I heard thy voice in the garden, and I was afraid, because I was naked; and I hid myself. Genesis 3:8-12

They hid themselves? Hid themselves from who? The Serpent? No! They hid themselves from LORD God! It was he whom they were afraid of because they realized he was not of Love. He was the LORD God of fear --I John 4:18.

They hid themselves because they feared what he would do to them as a result of gaining knowledge. As long as Adam and the woman hid themselves in the living trees, they could see LORD God (death) because of their split mind, but LORD God could not see them (life) because of his completely evil mind.

The LORD God frantically walked through the garden all day looking for Adam and calling his name. LORD God knew that if he didn't find the Man soon, his world would die because LORD God can only rule if Man gives him thought power. He called and called until finally, during the evening, Adam decided to answer. Even when Adam answered, LORD God could not see them but could only hear them talking back to him. He had no idea where they were until they revealed themselves.

Even though the Man's eyes had been opened as a result of listening to the Serpent; and though they now knew the truth of their equality, LORD God still had control over the momentum of their thinking. Ultimately, they did not fully trust the Serpent (John 3:16). As a result, they (like scared runaway slaves) turned themselves in and sought validation and acceptance from the LORD of Death.

Had the Man not answered from his hiding place; he, like the prodigal son, would have soon returned home to the peace and safety of his father's house.

The Dark Ages Begin

When Adam finally answered LORD God, it was the beginning of the Eve[22] of humanity! Eve being the mother of the living Dead.

22 The woman's new name was given after the LORD God's cursing spree and now Eve (representing Evening; coming of Night; Darkness) would be the mother of the dark ages.

THE CRUCIFIED SERPENT

" ***And as Moses lifted up the serpent in the desert, so must the Son of man be lifted up:*** *That whosoever believeth in him may not perish, but may have life everlasting." – Douay-Rheims John 3:13-15*

The Renounced Nehushtan: The Italian artist, Giovanni Fantoni, is credited with designing the metal decorations inside the sanctuary as well as the Serpentine Cross (The Brazen Serpent Monument) on the exterior. These are symbolic of the bronze serpent taken by Moses into the desert, and the cross upon which Jesus was crucified. In alchemy, the crucified serpent is a symbol of overcoming one's base or materially inclined nature.

3

UNDERSTANDING SYMBOLISM

The Significance of the Serpent

After being cursed by the LORD God, Truth is completely laid low (in the Mind of Mankind). The Serpent in the tree represented truth, healing and Man's higher Nature. This symbolism may be observed throughout the Bible as well as in other religious and scientific manuscripts. The Serpent laid low represents the truth laid low which signifies deceit, craftiness and pain. This is why a deceitful person is referred to as a 'snake in the grass'.

The LORD God lays the truth low and puts hatred and hostility between the woman and the truth and between the woman's offspring and the truth's offspring.

It's interesting to note that while Adam blamed the woman, and the woman blamed the Serpent; "the Serpent willingly offered himself, and opened not his mouth". As we observe the striking similarities between the significance of the Serpent and Jesus, we may uncover the same context of the bruising of the innocent for the healing of the sick.

Many Serpents have come into the LORD God's garden to free the Minds of Men throughout time. In this chapter, we will briefly analyze the symbolic significance of the Serpent and how the symbols have been used throughout history.

Twofold Meanings

"Everything is Dual; everything has poles; everything has its pair of opposites; like and unlike are the same; opposites are identical in nature, but different in degree; extremes meet; all truths are but half-truths; all paradoxes may be reconciled." – The Kybalion

According to the Wikipedia encyclopedia, "serpent" is a word commonly used in a specifically mythic or religious context. Serpent is from Latin origin, and is not regarded as a mundane natural phenomenon nor as an object of scientific zoology (study of animal life), but as the bearer of some symbolic value.

The serpent is one of the oldest and most widespread mythological symbols in the world.

There are four primary implications of a serpent's symbolic value in mythic and religious context. Where relevant, we review the scientific implications: *(Images used are in public domain)*

1. Revelation/Deception

The religions of Christianity, Islam and Judaism, regard the Serpent as a deceiver. This line of reasoning is followed from the Torah, through the Bible, to the Koran. In this book, we present a thesis for which we unveil the Garden of Eden as an alternate creation by a rebellious LORD God (scientist) who tricked Man; and the serpent was the revelator of truth. In many Egyptian tombs, the serpent is depicted as a wise counselor, held in great admiration.

2. Guardianship/Danger

The Serpent is represented as a potent guardian of temples and other sacred places in religions of antiquity. The serpent's danger was present in his powerful body grip and in his tongue for the unscrupulous wayfarer. The Greeks depicted the serpent as the guardian of their oracles.

3. Medicine/Poison

Simbolo de Asclépio

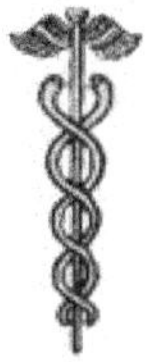

Simbolo de Hermes

The serpent is used as a medical symbol of healing. As a medical symbol, the serpent is depicted on a wooden staff in an elevated position. The elevated position is significant because of the Law of Polarity.

The Simbolo de Asclepio (staff of Aesculapius) and the simbolo de Hermes (staff of Hermes) have both been used by the Medical Community. Although at one time widely used, the staff of Aesculapius is used by few Medical facilities today.

The staff of Aesculapius represented rejuvenation (renewal). Aesculapius was a healer who went from place to place curing people. People of his time believed that snakes lived forever because of the shedding of their skin and that they helped discover health-giving medicinal herbs. Due to his good works, Aesculapius was later graduated to the being designated as the "God of Healing". The single serpent and staff represents him.

The caduceus or staff of Hermes is associated with Hermes (Mercury), the messenger of the Gods, also known as the God of trickery, wealth and death! The staff of Hermes became the more popular symbol of the Medical Community in later years and is the most used today. Notice the unnatural integration of two serpents.

4. Renewal, Rebirth, Regeneration/Death

The most powerful example yet, is the serpent associated with renewal, rebirth and regeneration by the ancient Egyptians. The Book of Coming Forth into Day is a more accurate name for the transition Mis-labeled as The Egyptian Book of the Dead. Death had nothing to do with transition. The image above depicts the serpent as a ship which carries and guides the traveler's way into the day, or depending on one's perception, into the night.

The Serpent in the Tree

The Serpent in the Tree is the symbol of Truth which creates the world consistent with Man's nature (Ga. 5:22, Eph. 5:9). The tree symbolizes bringing forth fruit. The fruit might be good or evil; but never both. The Serpent symbolizes the Wisdom of GOD which is the proper application of Knowledge. When Wisdom and Man are united, the World is at-one (or atoned). Peace is the result; and war unknown.

And I will put enmity between thee and the woman, and between thy seed and her seed; it shall bruise thy head, and thou shalt bruise his heel. Genesis 3:14

The first thing to consider is the obvious contradiction. The Female does not have a seed; only the Male does. So how could the Wo-<u>man</u> have a seed unless she too was a separate man, having a feminine orientation? LORD God had to put war between the truth and the Wo-man. He didn't concern himself with Adam. LORD God realized that Adam and Woman saw themselves as separate men; with Adam being a man having a masculine orientation. Thus, only the female-man could RECEIVE. The feminine energy carries with it the ability to conceive, and create based on what it has received.

The Male provides, builds, protects and projects. He provides the Female with ideas; she then creates the World. He builds a world to provide off-spring that projects them far into the future; and he protects his world from outside ideas that might cause his world to crumble.

Had the Woman continued to befriend the Serpent, she would have returned Self to the wisdom of their fathers. Now she was doomed to nurture the thoughts of an imposter and would be in pain while producing after his kind. Her husband would be relegated to building a world for the imposter while suffering extreme hardship in return.

Willie Lynch, is well-known for the brilliant plan to make lifelong slaves, using the same method. He too emphasized causing the female to be completely separated from the male and dependent on Master. Well said Solomon: "There is nothing new under the Sun."

The Tree

The tree is often used in symbolism to illustrate the consistency of Self when it remained in Truth:

Then said he, Unto what is the kingdom of God like? and whereunto shall I resemble it? It is like a grain of mustard seed, which a man took, and cast into his garden; and it grew, and waxed a great tree; and the fowls of the air lodged in the branches of it. Luke 13:18-19

In order to understand the symbolism of the Kingdom of God being like a grain of mustard seed, keep in mind two important definitions. First, the Kingdom of God is not "outside of you" or some "afterlife" as many superstitious preachers have taught you. The Kingdom of GOD is within you! Luke 17:21. The Kingdom is the set of Laws that govern Man's nature and ALL that IS. Secondly, the garden that Jesus is referring to is the garden of the Mind where thoughts are planted, causing the mind to orient in a particular direction, then grow into physical manifestations.

Why is the Kingdom of God like a mustard seed? Even the smallest of kingdom thoughts, if cultivated can rule the universe and provide for all. The Serpent is trying to inform you that you need only cultivate the garden of Mind with the Wealth of Truth. The Earth, being the servant of Man will respond and manifest based on what the Man thinks. This is the LAW. The more thoughts Man orient toward his nature, the faster the Man's world manifests.

The story doesn't stop there. Original Man, you know not your true greatness. You prefer to carry the heavy load of Death; thinking you are the material world. You wallow in Death when the power of your resurrection is as small as a little seed. Your Father's (the Originator's) Kingdom is within! Look within and you save your Self. Other Selves will come to you for life and you gladly give life. No longer are you the example of destitution and poverty. This day, look within and see the Image and Likeness of GOD!

The Snake in the Grass

The snake in the grass is a modern symbolism representing the truth being laid low – giving way to deception:

And the LORD God said unto the serpent, Because thou hast done this, thou art cursed above all cattle, and above every beast of the field; upon thy belly shalt thou go, and dust shalt thou eat all the days of thy life:—Genesis 3:13

Notice that the LORD God never said that the Serpent had caused the Death of the man and woman. He knew that HE had already done that. He merely said, "Because thou hast done this." Done what? What had the Serpent done?

The Serpent spoke the Truth which is why the man and woman's eyes were opened. They gained knowledge of good and evil like LORD God. The Serpent told them they would not "really die" but they would think they could—which is true! So, LORD God laid the Truth low and made the way to Truth hard and difficult in his World. Truth can never be annihilated, but Truth is the Enemy of Mankind.

The woman would produce children who would loathe the Truth. And as the reader probably suspected many times before, the LORD God acknowledged the Truth that the Serpent spoke: and took measures to block the man from the Tree of Life.

"And the LORD God said, Behold, the man is become as one of us, to know good and evil: and now, lest he put forth his hand, and take also of the tree of life, and eat, and live for ever: Therefore the LORD God sent him forth from the garden of Eden, to till the ground from whence he was taken. So he drove out the man; and he placed at the east of the garden of Eden Cherubims, and a flaming sword which turned every way, to keep the way of the tree of life. Genesis 3:22-24

The woman keeps the Serpent's head in pain--Meaning the innocent would be abused whenever he attempts to open the Eyes of the blind. The Serpent would bruise her heal. Meaning her kingdom will not be strong, though she appears mighty. The Truth would weaken the foundations of Satan's kingdom until it finally fell (Daniel 2:31-45).

The Serpent on the Cross

The Serpent on the Cross (pg. 54) was used by the Hebrews to remind them of Moses and Jesus but was later renounced by the Christian Church. The alchemists adopted the symbol as a way of describing the elevated Self.

There is a great difference between the symbol of the Serpent in the tree and the Serpent on the Cross. The Serpent in the tree is giving Knowledge and Life to Self. The Serpent on the Cross is giving his Life because of Man's rejection of Self. Ponder this for a moment.

Consider for a moment a hypothetical situation. Jesus returns to earth as a man of about 33 years of age. How would he view all the churches bearing the cross; the instrument on which he was murdered? He would despise the cross in much the same way as the Slave-Descendant Male despises the noose hanging from a tree. Compare and review the images below: What would Jesus think?

Figure 4a

"While Rome used cords of wood as crosses for standing human bodies along its highways in great numbers, you are using trees and ropes."
--Willie Lynch addressing the Colony of West Virginia in 1712

"He hath no form nor comeliness; and when we shall see him, there is no beauty that we should desire him. He is despised and rejected of men; a man of sorrows, and acquainted with grief: and we hid as it were our faces from him; he was despised, and we esteemed him not. Surely he hath borne our grief, and carried our sorrows: yet we did esteem him stricken, smitten of God, and afflicted. But he was wounded for our transgressions; he was bruised for our iniquities: the chastisement of our peace was upon him; and with his stripes we are healed." Isaiah 53:3

The Symbol of Death

While pondering the revelation figure 4a brings to Mind, continue with the scenario.

Jesus arrives in the 21st Century and he chagrins at what he discovers. Steeped upon every religious temple that claims to follow him, is the symbol of his murder. He is astounded, astonished, flabbergasted!

After getting over the shock of the symbols, he remembers his own words! "These religious hypocrites now decorate my grave after their fathers murdered me! So now I will enter their tombs of dead men's bones and see how they have turned my teachings upside-down."

Upon entering the church, he sees that the leaders have changed his image to that of another who is much lighter skinned than he was. He also notices that they honor this dead figure. "They have wrapped their entire doctrine around Death, when I came to prove that death is not real." He thinks to himself. "Do they not understand that I couldn't have risen if death is real?"

Next, they teach of worshipping Jesus as God. He remembers clearly that he told them that they also were Gods and equal (John 10:34). He thinks to himself, "I never told them to worship me! I told them that I and the father are one just as they and the father are one."

"These people are lifting up the material earth that I laid down and laying low the principles that I held up!"

He leaves the place disgusted, discouraged and deeply saddened. He believes that all of his efforts to show his brethren their inherent greatness were in vain. Even his final feat which was to prove to them that Death is not real was seemingly hijacked by Satan and made a mockery. Death was now the Central Attraction of the churches.

He runs outside of the temple and jumps on top of the preachers' Lexus as the church service is being dismissed. He screams to the top of his voice, "You are of your father the Devil and the lusts of your father ye do. He is the God of the Dead, and you as his children are proof! He used you to kill GOD's messengers. You now cause the people to worship their Death. This is proof that you are of Satan!

Your churches are graves; raised to honor the murderer. And at every church you build, my murdered body hangs on your blood drenched crosses as a testimony of your thinking. And you shall reap the rewards of your testimony!"

Finally, as he aimlessly walks away, he sees the drunks, crack heads, prostitutes, and outcast Males and Females, at the liquor stores just one block away from each church he passes. He says to these, "come with me, you who are blessed of your father. Follow me and I will freely give you the keys to Life." After hearing his teachings, one of his followers says, "I've never heard anyone speak with the authority of spiritual matters the way you do. Let me go over to the church and get the Reverend." Jesus replies, "The Dead hear not". Resurrect your Self, and follow me. Let the dead bury the dead."

We share this story to create a vivid image in the reader's Mind of who Jesus *really* was and is, today. The preachers teach that GOD can die and did die; the Cross is held up as proof; making their cross the Symbol of GOD's Death! But GOD cannot die! And if GOD cannot die, then neither can his image and likeness die. It is the blinding darkness of Satan's ministers that cause man to think that he and GOD can die. You will see this even more clearly in the next discussion.

The Cross

And whosoever doth not carry his cross and come after me cannot be my disciple. Luke 14:27

Jesus never spoke to the people without speaking in parables (Mark 4:34). In Jesus' day, people convicted of capital crimes were killed on a cross. This was called crucifixion. For centuries, the cross has been the symbol of Death. For example, In the Bible, Joseph, while interpreting a dream, informed a friend he was in jail with, that he, (the friend) would be killed by the king, beheaded, and crucified (Genesis 40:16).

Jesus knew that the people were dead to the knowledge of themselves. Therefore, he could not tell them the Truth plainly. They were like the dead who neither hear nor speak. So he rapped the resurrection truth in stories and parables.

Whenever Jesus considered a new disciple, he immediately informed them that they were the living dead. The follower must first resurrect himself. This was what it means when he says, "Pick up your cross and follow me!"

He was informing them of their self image of death based on the teachings of the preachers, and backed up by the brutality of Rome. Up until Jesus, the people had not known that they were dead. For decades, the preachers had a great interest in keeping them asleep. Many of them made no connection between their thinking and the disease, poverty, and chaos that ravaged their cities.

The cross has admittedly been the most powerful tool used by Satan's children to go forth and conquer (Rev. 6:2). According to history, Constantine adopted this symbol when he was given a vision before going to battle. Constantine was marching his army when he looked up to the sun and saw a Cross of light above it; the Greek words "In hoc Signo Vinces" which in Latin means "With this Sign you will Conquer!" What was the sign? The cross!

At first, Constantine didn't know the meaning of the apparition, but in the following night, he had a dream in which 'Christ' explained to him that he should use the sign against his enemies.

The implications in this section lead the author to conclude that the slave-descendants should stop looking to the cross as an instrument of friendship and salvation. The cross has been, and continues to be the symbol of demise of the enemies of White Supremacy. It is high time the slave-descendants got off the cross; Resurrected themselves, picked up their crosses and followed Christ to the resurrection of the people.

The slave-masters' descendants should also put the cross down. They have used this symbol for nothing more than killing, conquering and pillaging the peoples of the earth. It is high time they began learning how to be friendly to others on the planet.

CAPRICIOUS

"Thesis and anti-thesis are identical in nature, but different in degree; Opposites are the same, differing only in degree" – The Kybalion

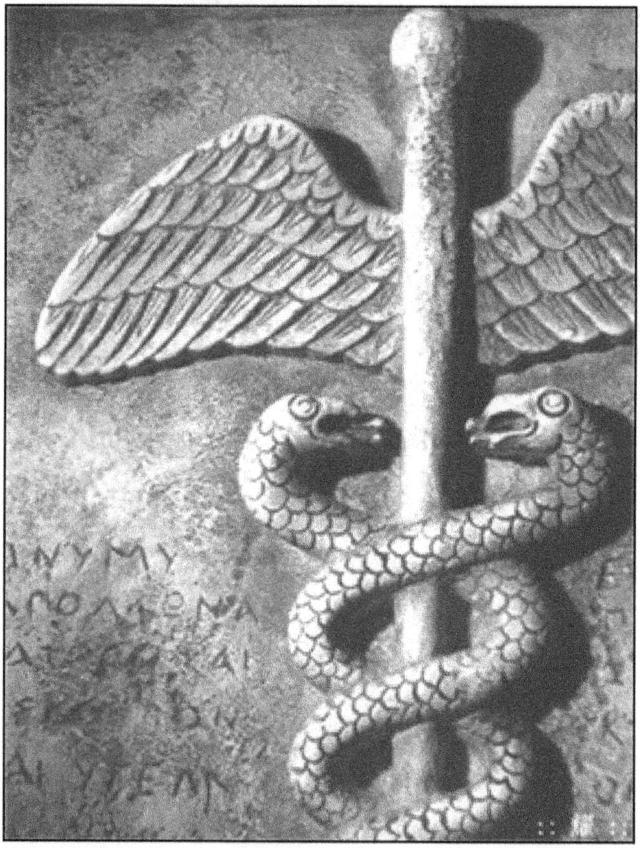

Staff of Hermes: This photo was taken by "Eugene Koh" Significantly, Hermes was known as the protector of sacrificial beasts and served as a conductor of souls of the dead to Hades. In addition, he was the god of social ease, cunning, fraud and perjury. An Associated Press Article from about November 1994 stated that the Minnesota Medical Association wants doctors to start using the Staff of Aesculapius because doctors have been using the wrong symbol for years. The Staff of Hermes' influence appears to be deeply reflected in the Medical Profession.
Perhaps a change of Symbols is in Order!

4

WHEN A PEOPLE

OBEY THE LORD

Man's inalienable connection to the Creator is self evident, natural and mathematically consistent. Since GOD and the Original Man have the same nature (Genesis 1), Man's natural state is one of complete blessedness. And as long as Man realizes his natural connection to GOD, he experiences natural blessedness and cannot be enslaved or cursed.

The scriptures of the Bible and Qur'an speaks of Satan's insatiable desire to snare man, enslave him and sift him as wheat (Luke 22:31 & The Prophets 21:70). However, before he can rule an individual or a people, he must first break the natural connection Man has with GOD.[23]

Therefore LORD God has to create a people who would unquestionably obey HIM in spite of Man's natural state of blessedness. Knowing that Man naturally submits himself to GOD, The LORD had to find ways of making Man think HE was the Creator. And since HIS Mind is that of murder (John 8:44), any individual who follows LORD God becomes a murderer and a master of fear and death; and any offspring of the Original Man, who has been taught by LORD God's offspring, experience rampant murder, death and illness among themselves as long as LORD God's thinking resides in their Collective Mind.

---

23 This is impossible in reality, however since the rules of Mind dictate that as a man thinks, so he sees, and so is his experience, LORD can still rule the universe by proxy if he can get enough minds to think in terms of cursing and that GOD has taken the earth from the Original Man.

Blessings and Cursings from the Same Source

Starting with the offspring of Cain[24], LORD God began filling the universe with minds in rebellion against GOD. LORD God's offspring are literally at war with the gods of the universe (Original Man). LORD God's offspring causes rebellion by creating a perceived gap in Man's mind. As a result, the mind appears to be split into opposing halves. On one side of the mind there is the natural state of blessedness. On the other side is LORD God's mind of curses and Death. A struggle ensues as the Mind attempts to reconcile itself.

Since LORD God's desire is to cause Man to exist wholly on the cursed side of his mind, he inserts himself in the gap of Man's split mind, then sets himself up as GOD (II Th. 2:4) in the mans mind. To increase the cursed mind and diminish the blessed mind, LORD God causes the man to think that his blessings come from spreading curses, death and hell throughout the universe. But LORD God dare not tell the man that he is wholly cursed. If he did, the Man's eyes would become opened through the realization that there is a blessed part of his mind and he would seek to reconcile it. And since the Mind has a natural tendency to correct itself when it touches a historical reality, the man would begin closing the perceived gap in his mind by removing LORD Gods thinking from it. He would then naturally act in accord with his true Creator.

To avoid such disaster, LORD God convinced an entire people that blessing and cursing comes from the same source. So the gap widens. In spite of the obvious violation of spiritual and physical Law, Satan's insanity is clearly seen. Out of the same mouth he speaks blessing and cursing. He thus convinced Mankind that blessedness comes from LORD God. But to receive blessedness, the people must spread fear and terror among the human family, and throughout the universe.

In reality Satan (LORD God) hates blessedness; he hates the Original Man, and he hates the Creator of the Original Man! His hatred is so intense that he is literally attempting to create his own "supreme people", having a nature separate and opposite from the rest of the human family.

---

[24] See Exhibit 2c: Setting Brother against Brother. Pg. 195-205.

In his quest, he simultaneously wants to destroy the rest of the human family and fill the earth with his own wicked followers!

Consider LORD God's own words in the next scripture. LORD God inserted himself in the Bible between the creation story of Genesis 1, and the gospels of Jesus. By doing so, he tried to make it appear as though he is the same entity Jesus represented. Observe as he cleverly weaves blessing and cursing; as though they are the same thing. Consider carefully as you read the following verses. LORD God warns his people not to listen to the other gods.

Even though Jesus said "ye are gods", LORD God instructs his followers not to listen to, or take on the ways of the "other gods". Who are these gods that he refers to? Could it be that LORD God was warning his people against listening to the Original Man (who is God)? Take the time to read the entire chapter below. Rather than blessings existing as the natural state of Man; in Satan's world, blessings are not natural. They are merited by obeying LORD God. We let you consider the question in light of LORD Gods own words:

Deuteronomy 28[25] (The numbers listed count blessings and cursings rather than verses. We include chart Exhibit 4a for better understanding).

1) If you obey the Lord your God and faithfully keep all his commands that I am giving you today, he will make you greater than any other nation on earth.

2) Obey the Lord your God and all these blessings will be yours: The Lord will bless your towns and your fields.

3) The Lord will bless you with many children, with abundant crops, and with many cattle and sheep.

4) The Lord will bless your grain crops and the food you prepare from them. The Lord will bless everything you do.

5) The Lord will defeat your enemies when they attack you. They will attack from one direction, but they will run from you in all directions.

---

25 Good News translation used for clarity. However it is consistent with King James Version.

6) The Lord your God will bless your work and fill your barns with grain. He will bless you in the land that he is giving you.

7) If you obey the Lord your God and do everything he commands, he will make you his own people, as he has promised.

8) Then all the peoples on earth will see that the Lord has chosen you to be his own people, and they will be afraid of you.

9) The Lord will give you many children, many cattle, and abundant crops in the land that he promised your ancestors to give you.

10) He will send rain in season from his rich storehouse in the sky and bless all your work, so that you will lend to many nations, but you will not have to borrow from any.

11) The Lord your God will make you the leader among the nations and not a follower; you will always prosper and never fail if you obey faithfully all his commands that I am giving you today.

WARNING: But you must never disobey them in any way, or worship and serve other gods.

1) But if you disobey the Lord your God and do not faithfully keep all his commands and laws that I am giving you today, all these evil things will happen to you: The Lord will curse your towns and your fields.

2) The Lord will curse your grain crops and the food you prepare from them.

3) The Lord will curse you by giving you only a few children, poor crops, and few cattle and sheep.

4) The Lord will curse everything you do.

5) If you do evil and reject the Lord, he will bring on you disaster, confusion, and trouble in everything you do, until you are quickly and completely destroyed.

6) He will send disease after disease on you until there is not one of you left in the land that you are about to occupy.

7) The Lord will strike you with infectious diseases, with swelling and fever; he will send drought and scorching winds to destroy your crops. These disasters will be with you until you die.

8) No rain will fall, and your ground will become as hard as iron.

9) Instead of rain, the Lord will send down dust storms and sandstorms until you are destroyed.

10) The Lord will give your enemies victory over you. You will attack them from one direction, but you will run from them in all directions, and all the people on earth will be terrified when they see what happens to you.

11) When you die, birds and wild animals will come and eat your bodies, and there will be no one to scare them off.

12) The Lord will send boils on you, as he did on the Egyptians. He will make your bodies break out with sores. You will be covered with scabs, and you will itch, but there will be no cure.

13) The Lord will make you lose your mind; he will strike you with blindness and confusion.

14) You will grope about in broad daylight like someone blind, and you will not be able to find your way.

15) You will not prosper in anything you do.

16) You will be constantly oppressed and robbed, and there will be no one to help you.

17) You will be engaged to a young woman—but someone else will marry her.

18) You will build a house—but never live in it.

19) You will plant a vineyard—but never eat its grapes.

20) Your cattle will be butchered before your very eyes, but you will not eat any of the meat.

21) Your donkeys will be dragged away while you look on, and they will not be given back to you.

22) Your sheep will be given to your enemies, and there will be no one to help you.

23) Your sons and daughters will be given as slaves to foreigners while you look on. Every day you will strain your eyes, looking in vain for your children to return.

24) A foreign nation will take all the crops that you have worked so hard to grow, while you receive nothing but constant oppression and harsh treatment.

25) Your sufferings will make you lose your mind.

26) The Lord will cover your legs with incurable, painful sores; boils will cover you from head to foot.

27) The Lord will take you and your king away to a foreign land, where neither you nor your ancestors ever lived before; there you will serve gods made of wood and stone.

28) In the countries to which the Lord will scatter you, the people will be shocked at what has happened to you; they will make fun of you and ridicule you.

29) You will plant plenty of seed, but reap only a small harvest, because the locusts will eat your crops.

30) You will plant vineyards and take care of them, but you will not gather their grapes or drink wine from them, because worms will eat the vines.

31) Olive trees will grow everywhere in your land, but you will not have any olive oil, because the olives will drop off.

32) You will have sons and daughters, but you will lose them, because they will be taken away as prisoners of war.

33) All your trees and crops will be devoured by insects.

34) Foreigners who live in your land will gain more and more power, while you gradually lose yours.

Your world will be full of Enemies

35) They will have money to lend you, but you will have none to lend them. In the end they will be your rulers.

36) All these disasters will come on you, and they will be with you until you are destroyed, because you did not obey the Lord your God and keep all the laws that he gave you. They will be the evidence of God's judgment on you and your descendants forever. The Lord blessed you in every way, but you would not serve him with glad and joyful hearts.

39) So then, you will serve the enemies that the Lord is going to send against you.

40) You will be hungry, thirsty, and naked—in need of everything.

41) The Lord will oppress you harshly until you are destroyed.

42) The Lord will bring against you a nation from the ends of the earth, a nation whose language you do not know. They will swoop down on you like an eagle.

43) They will be ruthless and show no mercy to anyone, young or old.

44) They will eat your livestock and your crops, and you will starve to death. They will not leave you any grain, wine, olive oil, cattle, or sheep; and you will die.

45) They will attack every town in the land that the Lord your God is giving you, and the high, fortified walls in which you trust will fall.

46) When your enemies are besieging your towns, you will become so desperate for food that you will even eat the children that the Lord your God has given you.

47) Even the most refined man of noble birth will become so desperate during the siege that he will eat some of his own children because he has no other food. He will not even give any to his brother or to the wife he loves or to any of his children who are left.

48) Even the most refined woman of noble birth, so rich that she has never had to walk anywhere, will behave in the same way.

When the enemy besieges her town, she will become so desperate for food that she will secretly eat her newborn child and the afterbirth as well. She will not share them with the husband she loves or with any of her children.

49) If you do not obey faithfully all of God's teachings that are written in this book and if you do not honor the wonderful and awesome name of the Lord your God, he will send on you and on your descendants incurable diseases and horrible epidemics that can never be stopped.

50) He will bring on you once again all the dreadful diseases you experienced in Egypt, and you will never recover.

51) He will also send all kinds of diseases and epidemics that are not mentioned in this book of God's laws and teachings, and you will be destroyed.

52) Although you become as numerous as the stars in the sky, only a few of you will survive, because you did not obey the Lord your God.

53) Just as the Lord took delight in making you prosper and in making you increase in number, so he will take delight in destroying you and in bringing ruin on you. You will be uprooted from the land that you are about to occupy.

54) The Lord will scatter you among all the nations, from one end of the earth to the other, and there you will serve gods made of wood and stone, gods that neither you nor your ancestors have ever worshiped before.

55) You will find no peace anywhere, no place to call your own; the Lord will overwhelm you with anxiety, hopelessness, and despair.

56 Your life will always be in danger.

57) Day and night you will be filled with terror, and you will live in constant fear of death.

58) Your hearts will pound with fear at everything you see. Every morning you will wish for evening; every evening you will wish for morning.

59) The Lord will send you back to Egypt in ships, even though he said that you would never have to go there again. There you will try to sell yourselves to your enemies as slaves, but no one will want to buy you."

The writer seems to go into a trance as he recites the pledge of murder, terror, famine, and death.

All of LORD God's curses are only Seeds of Thought he has planted in the Minds of Mankind to ensure their submission. Only the Collective Minds compliance brings this experience, thereby providing a way of escape. Study **Exhibit 4a: The Development of a Double-Mind** to see exactly what seeds are being planted by LORD God and how they are opposite of GOD.

"Out of the same mouth proceedeth blessing and cursing. My brethren, these things ought not so to be. Doth a fountain send forth at the same place sweet water and bitter? Can the fig tree, my brethren, bear olive berries? either a vine, figs? so can no fountain both yield salt water and fresh" James 3:10-12.

The scripture goes on to say that with the tongue we bless GOD even the father and curse Man who is the image of GOD. Thus, blessing and cursing cannot come from the same source, and Man is the Image of GOD, not the dust of the earth.

"America is false to the past, false to the present, and solemnly binds herself to be false to the future."
Frederick Douglass, 1852

The principles of Mind are not respecters of person --The hew of a man's skin, his relative education, whether he is regarded as a criminal, nor any other external factor influences whether or not the rules of mind work for or against him. If there were preferences, the Law would work for some and not for others. Instead, they perform equally and without regard to the person using them. Jesus said that "GOD rains and shines on the Just and Unjust alike" (Mt.5:45), indicating that GOD is not a respecter of person[26].

Willie Lynch[27] understood the principles of Mind when he told the slave masters to first strip the 'nigger' male of any connection to GOD. He then told them that for a time, withhold any concept of God from the mind of the male and female savages. This would have the effect of reducing the Man's desires to the survival instincts of a reptile. By reducing Man's mentality to the level of a reptile, it in effect makes the Man perfect for domesticating. By disabling his ability to predict or affect the future it causes him to be only concerned with day-to-day survival issues of food, clothing, shelter; leaving little time for planning with Self interest in mind. It also re-directs the Man's human ingenuity to focus itself only on the slave-masters' well-being.

After a time, the slave-masters should insert themselves in the space created between the Man's Self concept and the concept of GOD. They had to then give the Separated Man a God that would protect and sanction white supremacy at all costs. The slave-master had to take care and reinforce the belief that the established order of white supremacy was the divine Will of God, and would be enforced through terror.

---

26 Respecter of Person: One who has favorites; Making one more Special than others.

27 The author is not concerned with whether Willie Lynch was an actual historical figure. Point by point the process of slave making is well documented as historical fact. Therefore protracted arguments of the name "Willie Lynch", as the originator, serves only to distract from the truth that a sustained program, as described, occurred over hundreds of years. The originator's name is therefore irrelevant to this case. However, if anyone knows the true originator's name, feel free to make it known.

If the slaves complied, they would be blessed; but any deviation from the God-established order would rain down curses. In any case, the slaves were condemned to either servitude or death.

Willie Lynch commanded the slave-masters to cultivate a mind in the separated male and female slaves to so greatly identify with the slave-master and his God that it would cause them to offer all their talents to God, as seen through the eyes of white supremacy[28]. He used scriptures like "Slaves obey your masters" (Col 3:22), and "All governments are set up by God" (Ro. 13:1) to give an air of divinity to the slaves' self-debasing servitude. As long as they served the appointed Administrators of Death, the slave received minimal blessing from The LORD.

The slave master had to make the slaves fully believe that their own existence relied on the perpetuation of white supremacy. If done properly, when the time came that forced servitude was no longer economically feasible, even the freed slaves would faithfully condemn their own future and the future of their own children to death in order to insure the survival of white supremacy and her children. Lynch taught them that if they created "slave levels", the head-slaves would aspire to become "slave leaders", legitimizing the culture of death[29] as their own, and teaching their offspring to do the same.

Willie Lynch said that if the masters followed his instructions completely, they would be blessed with mastery over the Original Man for at least another 300 years or more. Furthermore, the sole desire of the Original Man's children would be to serve and protect the children of the slave-masters (Gen. 3:16 & Gen. 25:23).

To this day, most American slave-descendants dare not entertain a single thought that has not previously been sanctioned by the slave-master's children.

---

[28] See Exhibit 2d: Let's Make a Slave: The Willie Lynch Speech with Instructions Packet. Pg. 206-213.

[29] The pope said the world was confronted by "alarming signs of the culture of death which pose a serious threat for the future." CNN.com (Dec. 25, 2000)

So, in spite of the obvious death and despair the slave-descendant experiences in white society, he goes about acquiring education for the purpose of integration and maintenance of the culture of Death.

Even in 2008, as the forthcoming case studies will indicate, the cowardly slave-descendant male pretends that he does not even notice his own children dying as he faithfully kneels at the alter of white supremacy.

He will do anything just for the opportunity to be president over the culture of death, or congressman over the culture of death, or school board member, or mayor, or be called "black leader". The slave-descendant male's lust to earn the designation as an honorary white man is so strong that in spite of a true statement made by President Hugo Chavez calling George Bush the devil, was rebuked by slave-descendant-leaders. They rebuked the truth!

To this day, the slave-descendant preacher is so spiritually blinded by Satan (LORD God), that rather than look within, he'd rather try and contort his own holy nature to fit the sin-inducing, slave making religion of "Western Christianity", which is the obvious spiritual tool of white supremacy.

The more death the slave-descendant preachers see in their communities, the more obsessed they become with building bigger churches (graves). It's a foretold phenomenon that LORD God's thinking guarantees would occur.

Recently, Detroit, Michigan earned the designation as the most murder-ridden city in the United States. Detroit is also designated as the most religious city in the United States; having over 5,800 Christian churches serving a population of less than 920,000 people . Is there a correlation between the number of churches and the amount of murder and violence in the city of Detroit? The DA declares an unequivocal YES! We offer overwhelming evidence to prove our case. Not once does the slave-descendant preacher consider that his own doctrine is the Doctrine of Death permeating the Minds of the People.

And though some preachers are aware of the deadly doctrine, they gladly administer it to the people for the privilege of being honorary white biblical scholars.

In any case, there are only two kinds of slave-descendant Christian preachers in America; those who are already honorary white men, and those who aspire to be. We, whose eyes have been opened, see and predict that when a black church arrives in a community, Death and Hell are sure to follow[30].

AMERICA IS AN IDEA, NOT A PLACE

The next five years will see some very drastic changes in the United States of America. Rights and privileges once taken for granted will become precious memories of days gone by. As the populations of the earth witness the manifestations of how corrupt American's minds have become, and how that corruption permeates every strata of American society; it will be worth keeping in mind that America is not a place, it's an idea. Alas, it is the Idea of America that appeals to the natural state of Man throughout the universe.

"Come hither; I will shew unto thee the judgment of the great whore that sitteth upon many waters: With whom the kings of the earth have committed fornication, and the inhabitants of the earth have been made drunk with the wine of her fornication . . .And upon her forehead was a name written, MYSTERY, BABYLON THE GREAT, THE MOTHER OF HARLOTS AND ABOMINATIONS OF THE EARTH". Revelation 17:2-5

[30] Revelation 6:1-8 explains the order in which LORD God uses the church to secure his World.

Evidence, Evidence – Self Evidence

We asserted earlier that LORD God entices Man into his garden with ideas that are natural to Man. He tricks the Man into serving him by causing Man to think he must enter the garden (or stay in the garden) to receive life. Once deceived, Man enters the garden and begins crediting LORD God for granting him what he already possessed. In most cases, by the time the separated man discovers that he has been tricked; like the prodigal son who gave up his wealth and squandered his substance in a strange land, the separated man's thinking becomes totally beholden to LORD God. Herein lays man's slavery.

"We hold these truths to be self-evident, that all men are created equal, that they are endowed by their Creator with certain unalienable Rights that among these are Life, Liberty and the pursuit of Happiness"—Declaration of Independence.

The founding fathers of the United States knew what is generally unknown today. They knew that equality is the natural state of Man. They also understood where the Man must look to see the truth. This is a phenomenal statement! What does it mean for something to be "Self evident"? Using the Merriam-Webster definition, self evident is defined as "Evidence with anecdotal proof or reasoning". The statement is a direct appeal to the Original Man's nature! He must look within to see his equality with other Men.

This is the very point of attack for LORD God. He knows that once Man looks within and sees the Image of GOD, he would never submit to LORD God. Thus LORD God's Ministers of Death are skilled and well-trained at preventing the Man from ever looking within. His ministers are trained at causing the Man to fear his Self, by telling him that his nature is evil and sinful. And LORD God is the only one who can save him from himself! A very good example was seen during the recent fight for Affirmative Action in Michigan[31].

[31] See Case Study #4: The rush to Appeal to "Missie" – The Affirmative Action 'Crisis' in Michigan. Pg. 149-152.

One Civil Rights Leader, during an interview actually justified his marching and begging for equality by stating: "We (blacks) are free, but we are not equal!" He does not realize at this late date that Freedom and Equality are the same; so he proceeds to march and petition other men for something he already has, and something that cannot be taken.

As stated previously, Equality is a Self evident Truth (Luke 17:21). But one must look within to see it. To look any place else is deception. Not only has Man been created from the beginning with equality, he was also endowed by his Creator with rights that cannot be given to him by another, nor taken away from him by another. Some of those rights (they didn't list all of them) are Life, Liberty and the pursuit of happiness.

But how can these things be, unless the founders had a definition of life that transcended the common definition?

LIFE

The founding fathers perceived an unbreakable connection between Man and Life. We said earlier that GOD is ALL that is. He has neither beginning nor end. He is the essence of Life itself. He endowed Man with the same nature of Life, in the order of his own Image and nature. Like GOD, Man manifests in all places at all times. Scientists now realize that the universe tends to Life, and a "cause" for death has yet to be found. The Man that understands this is able to look beyond his own "life span" and plan his posterity. The man who does not, is like the dandelion that arrives today, and is gone tomorrow. It is impossible for him to see neither the future nor the present.

It is very difficult for the uninitiated mind to conceive of the idea that prior to LORD God's deception; Man freely came and left manifestation. He could "lay down his life, and pick it up again". Earthly manifestation was more like a person taking a vacation.

To deceive him, LORD God fixated the Man's eye on the flesh (Man's tool) and deceived him into thinking that he and the tool were the same, and could die. His ultimate triumph was to convince man that the murder of Jesus (GOD in flesh) was proof that GOD could die (if GOD can die, so can Man). However, when Man looks within he realizes that Life is unalienable. He understands that neither GOD nor he can die. With Life secured, he is prepared to experience his natural Liberty.

LIBERTY

We define liberty as contentment with Self at the highest level of Mind. It is a right, privilege and immunity inherent in Man's nature. It is the door whereby Man may access Heaven and creates after his own Image and Likeness.

To better understand how Liberty functions in the universe, it may be helpful to examine how man develops when the perception of Liberty is not present in his Mind.

In Cheikh Anta Diop's two cradle theory[32], he used scientific methodology to chart the likely social development within different cultural contexts. By comparing the social customs, family structure, and moral worldview of the European and African Cradles of civilization, Diop's work clearly demonstrates the profound impact of environment on human behavior and development of cultural presumptions. Having a "lack mentality", Europeans could come to this continent and easily slaughter the natives, who welcomed and shared with them. Europeans regard life as an inconvenience and barrier to material gain; while the African freely shares out of his abundant thinking—seemingly to his own demise. While Europeans hunt and kill for sport and play, the rest of the world finds it strange.

---

[32] See Exhibit 4e: Cheikh Anta Diop's Two Cradle Theory. Pg. 237-238.

The author realizes that Diop's research argues that physical environment may be the deciding factor in development of thought systems. While the authors concur with the results of Diop's specific research in his Northern/Southern cradle analysis, we assert that systems emerging from the Southern Cradle are the natural state of Man, regardless of his environment.

For example, if an individual living in the Northern Cradle accepts ideas from the South, he will at the least be a counter-balance though in a hostile environment; and at most, transform the Northern Cradle thought system, in spite of his environment. Likewise if one living in the Southern Cradle accepts ideas from the North, he will disrupt or corrupt Southern Cradle thinking, without regard to a peaceful environment.

We therefore assert that Man's experiences originate in his thinking, rather than his thinking arising from experiences. This implies that he has access to an information source outside of a closed physical environment. This is also consistent with the view that Man's primary essence is Mind; and Mind controls all physical environments. Were it otherwise, Man's thoughts could forever be trapped; subjected to an ever disorganizing physical world.

Pursuit of Happiness

The discovery of Self as a manifestation of GOD, is happiness! Again, this is an unalienable Right. Imagine your thinking if you discovered that you and GOD are one, and share each other's nature. Would you not be safe and secure in that? How would you treat your brother? What thoughts would you allow in your Mind? What kind of world would you create?

Happiness, allows Man to create the world according to his true nature rather than a perceived nature. The second Law of thermal dynamics indicates that the material world tends to disorganize if left alone. This is true because the material world is subject to the Mind of Man.

However, this law[33] does not apply to the Mind. The Mind, if left alone, tends toward unity and at-oneness. For example, males naturally unite with females; they build families. Families unite and build communities, races, cultures, cities, states, and nations. And nations make up the world.

Finally, worlds unite as one to develop a one world government, religion and economic system. Thus, the nature of ONE is the nature of GOD himself and the nature of Man.[34]

The secrets revealed in the Declaration of Independence represent the Serpent entering the garden, and opening the eyes of the man. However, because of the religion of Christianity, which is the spiritual arm of White Supremacy; man was again deceived into thinking that his identity is in earth. Since earth vacillates between forms; materially based thinking subjects the man's mind to materialism and death.

Had the descendants of the Declaration inherited the nation, the world would look much different today than it does.

For he that soweth to his flesh shall of the flesh reap corruption; but he that soweth to the Spirit shall of the Spirit reap life everlasting. Galatians 6:8

---

33 We are aware that this is a highly simplified usage of the Law of thermodynamics. We use it to illustrate a higher principle of Mind as it relates to the material world.

34 The author is aware that Christians fear a one world system as evil; however, the only way a one world system could be evil is if this present world is good.

And we keep Marching on; Report after Report

"There is a way which seems right unto a man, but the end thereof are the ways of death." Proverbs 14:12

Each year, the Urban League releases its "State of Black America" report. The report addresses the issues central to Black America. It supposedly is a barometer of the conditions, experiences and opinions of Black America over number of social areas. It then forecasts certain social, political and economic trends, and proposes solutions to communities across the nation.

Except for the worsening conditions, the reports are always the same; especially concerning black males. Locked up, locked out, unemployed, and drug addicted with a criminal mentality. Every report, every study, every panel says the exact same thing. Black people are on a death march. Blacks have marched from segregation to outcast, to despair; and if the numbers are correct, eventual extinction. In spite the Urban Leagues' attempts to soften their reports (we suspect this is necessary to receive continued Non-profit funding), other national studies suggest that the "State of Black America" in every sector, is worse off and more deplorable than Urban League dare reveal! We examine the real record.

Kerner Commission Report--1967

President Lyndon Johnson formed an 11-member National Advisory Commission on Civil Disorders in July 1967 to explain the riots that plagued cities each summer since 1964, and to provide recommendations for the future. The Kerner Report, in spite of its own watered down language, concluded that America was "moving toward two societies; one black, and one white—separate and unequal. Unless conditions were remedied, they warned, the country faced a "system of 'apartheid'" in every major city. The Kerner report delivered an indictment of "white society" for isolating and neglecting African Americans and urged legislation to promote racial integration and to enrich slums—primarily through the creation of jobs, training programs, and decent housing.

President Johnson rejected the recommendations! In April 1968, one month after the release of the Kerner report, rioting broke out in more than 100 cities following the U.S government's assassination of civil rights leader, Dr. Martin Luther King, Jr.

Kerner Report 30 years later

In 1998, former Senator and Kerner Commission member, Fred R. Harris, co-authored a study that found the racial divide had grown in the ensuing years with inner-city unemployment at crisis levels.

Kerner Report 40 years later (2008)

The Eisenhower Foundation is the private sector continuation of The Kerner Commission. In 2007, the Kerner Commission was reconvened to study the progress of recommendations of the initial report.

The report, scheduled to be released on the 40th anniversary of the original Kerner commission, is expected to show that the efforts to rid America of her black ghettos have been ignored since the last half of the 20th century.

By the year 2000, Detroit blacks (an 86% black populated city) had less buying power than they did in 1967. In 2000, black median family income was down 6% from 1970, while white median income rose 18%, after being adjusted for inflation, according to the report. On and on and on, in every sector, black life is worthless!

The 2008 findings will be presented to Congress and the presidential candidates. It will be released on March 1, 2008, the 40th anniversary of the original commission.

Let's do it again!

In anticipation of the upcoming report, The Detroit News conducted a poll on race relations, and examined its economic effects. It found that blacks had made little, if any progress in most key areas since the 1968 report.

After forty years of "programmed marching", protesting, Mis-education and backroom dealing; it is clear that all attempts to repair and integrate black America have failed. Because of her GOD-energy, she has become dangerous to herself and dangerous to the world; and there are no mathematically sound reasons to continue the charade of integration. Furthermore, the American People appear not to have the stomach to expend any more resources on programs to raise the masses of slave descendants; who wallow in a hopeless quagmire of ignorance, poverty, superstition and Death, in the ghettos of America. With her mind already at war, America is now deciding whether to exterminate the Negro or imprison him for life. We submit that there is nothing left but admit our irreconcilable differences; divorce and go our separate ways.

Pay No Attention to the little man Behind the Curtain

In spite of data indicating that black America is on a collision course with extinction; civil rights preachers seem bent on the same course of action; beg, plead and protest for equality in the house of Satan and the culture of Death. Rather than sound the fire alarm and warn GOD's people to escape the burning house, the preachers engage in the most contorted of logic; telling the people instead to remain IN the burning house and look for water to extinguish the fire. They prove that they care nothing for the lives of GOD's People; they care only for Satan's house, and will gladly sacrifice GOD's offspring to save it.

The preachers will do anything that does NOT involve looking inward! Their demands for inclusion in Satan's world are so loud that all dignity and self-respect is lost. "We must beat on the door harder until it opens," they shout. More programs! More education! More panel discussions! More symposiums! More voting! More none-profit organizations, more grants and more Jesus!

Give us grants, We must have grants!

They secretly take pride in being gassed, handcuffed, beaten and arrested, while trying to force Satan to conduct himself like GOD. It is their mark of validation and equality with Satan. Their sense of high moral ground, in reality, is arrogance against GOD. But make no mistake, the civil rights leaders truly believe that the earth belongs to LORD God; and all must bow down to him.

After sufficient bowing to get master to wave a crumb in the air; the civil rights preachers and politicians begin beating the hell out of each other; competing for the grants that amount to nothing more than symbols without substance—all designed to maintain the status quo master/slave relationship.

LORD God knows that his destiny and the destiny of the Original Man are inversely related. He will never fund nor encourage the destruction of his own world.

In spite of that knowledge, Negro leaders, year after year, return to the master with hat in hand; to prove that they deserve more money, and more resources. Each leader tries to out-maneuver the other one for severely limited resources. It's a very strange relationship and they must walk a very thin line.

They must prove that the Negroes they "serve" have a real need (meaning the Negro population has not progressed), while at the same time show that awarding them the grant will create progress. It's a strange dance of conflicting requirements. Their ultimate proof is in showing that they have accomplished nothing, and never will.

The organization that can prove it accomplished the least (i.e. whose people have the greatest need), gets the biggest grant. Thus the civil rights community has a vested interest in maintaining a certain level of dire conditions to justify their existence.

The truth be told, civil rights preachers are so obsessed and blinded with becoming honorary white people that they look on those whom they supposedly "serve", with contempt and hatred.

'Massa, wees be yo survants'

With the decline of the dollar and a severely receding economy, why do the civil rights preachers spend so much energy trying to force their way into a house that is insufficient to feed its own citizens, let alone 40 million slave descendants? Whose interest do these preachers really serve?

Every 40 or so years, the master conducts an extensive assessment of the Negroes' condition in his midst. Just as LORD God does, his children do the same. He wants to see how his experiment to exterminate the Original Man is going. But he dare not allow his subjects to ever suspect that their downward spiral is actually planned and manipulated by the Mind of Death itself. He dare not tell the Original Man that EVERY institution he looks to is laced with poison and every institution is the LORD God's satanic tool of Death!

Except for "leaders" who acknowledge and plan according to the theology of TIME, the rest are deceivers, tools of Satan; and have been hand-picked and groomed by LORD God himself. From the school board member, to the congress person, to the Christian preacher, to the Muslim, black nationalist and mayor; Their sole mission is to convince the Original Man that it is better to die under white supremacy than live as Free Selves. These leaders are used as bait to "slow march" the unsuspecting people of GOD into extinction by legitimizing the LORD God's so-called plan of gradualism.

To inoculate the people from ever looking inward, the Master, through his hand-picked leaders, keeps the people looking only to the culture of Death. LORD God appoints certain minds as "leaders" over the people. They appear to have the people's best interest at heart, AGAINST the Master; but in reality they ALL are the Master's tools. LORD God secretly funds some, and publicly funds others. This is designed to produce two "types" of loyal leaders. One leader appears as a fighter for justice on behalf of the people; and the other as a healer of the people; but both types represent Death itself!

"Don't be fooled by the Shit They're Droppin; the Violence and Drugs they claim to be stoppin."
—Professor Griff

Publicly funded Black Leaders

The publicly funded black leader sets up a non-profit organization[35] or is elected to office. He takes a lion's share of the crumbs that have been granted, and then passes out the humiliating remains to the people, through "programs" of Death. The only stipulation is that the People as a whole never progress nor ever desire to build their own world.

As long as the people remain desperately in need, the leader, his family, friends and political partners benefit and live sumptuously. The method is so brilliant, that anytime an individual wants to be a "leader" over the People, he must first develop a contempt for the people and loyalty to Satan. Either remain among the bottom feeding masses, or live well at their expense.

Once they receive a little relief, the people think their life isn't so bad considering LORD God, through his black leaders gives "some" help to them rather than nothing at all. The cycle continues generation after generation, and the people never quite figure out why their lives continue to spiral, in the "land of plenty".

If they only understood that the earth does NOT belong to the LORD, but belongs to them; they would immediately throw off LORD God and his representatives, and take their earth back. And that loud "thump" heard would be the civil rights leaders falling off the backs of the people as they stood to their feet!

[35] Other than churches, non-profit organizations are the fastest growing industry in black communities across America.

<u>Privately funded Black Leaders</u>

The privately funded black leader is a professional marcher and protester. In reality, however, he does not intend to challenge LORD God's world at all. He is paid "under the table". He is put in place to keep the Sons of GOD spiritually blind and calm while LORD God slowly kills them.

Ninety nine percent of these leaders are preachers whose guiding philosophy is based in Christianity (the spiritual philosophy of white supremacy). The preacher's job is to use superstition to blind the people and legitimize LORD God's world at the spiritual level of the Self.

LORD God never wants the People of GOD to know that they are marked for Death, so he conceals his own nature from them, while slowly killing them in his various institutions.

Satan's children can kill[36] as many of the Original Man as they like; so long as they never publicly get caught in the act. However, it is an unspoken rule among them that if they ever publicly get caught killing or harming GOD's people, they will be treated as though they are renegades from the otherwise good Will that Satan has for GOD's people. The "offending individual" will be publicly reprimanded, but the institutions of death will remain intact until the Man of GOD is dead[37].

Sometimes LORD God's people slip and their true nature emerges. They publicly do or say something that may warn the Original Man that he is dealing with the offspring of Satan himself.

---

36 The pharaoh instructed them to deal wisely with the slaves. Secretly kill the boys.

37 See Essay #1: The Musings of a Cynical black boy. Pg. 158-160.

Pay no attention to the 'anomalies'

It could be as simple as an off-the-cuff statement; a racially charged comment here, a police beating caught on tape there, a noose hung up as a warning to the Negroes; discriminatory or predatory lending; an unjust imprisonment, or getting caught conducting medical experiments[38] on the Original Male and Female.

All such incidents will be dealt with as though they are anomalies--criminals in an otherwise just society. When anomalies occur, they shake GOD's people from their sleep. The people's eyes partly open and they begin to detect the Self, and the evil LORD God. They become afraid and begin to hide themselves from him. They must be put back into a deep sleep at once and made to think the incident was only an anomaly.

Whenever "anomalies" occur, the privately funded "civil rights" leaders spring into action! Using the Satanically hijacked and distorted philosophy of Dr. Martin Luther King Jr.[39], the civil rights preachers are the most dangerous of LORD God's leaders. Their poison strikes[40] at the very essence of the people by appealing to their nature of peace. Knowing that the Original Man is created in peace, the professional protester/leader convinces the people that LORD God's children have the same peaceful nature as their own.

The civil rights leaders' mantra is: "we need only remind LORD God's children of their own peaceful nature". Surely they will change. The slave leader deceives the people into marching. The offending "racist" is publicly reprimanded; and the people are lulled back into a slumber, thinking LORD God has given them justice—That is, until the next incident. All the while, the deadly institutions remain intact.

---

[38] See Case Study #1: A Shameful Little Secret. Pg. 143.

[39] LORD God's children murdered Dr. King, distorted his philosophy, and made it a sanctioning of white supremacy by appealing peacefully to it, as though white supremacy is good overall with minor glitches. In other words they say "we're working on it!"

[40] They are likened to Snakes in the Grass 'Striking and injecting Poison into the People'. See Chapter 3. Understanding Symbolism.

Stay within the confines of the Garden!

But the civil rights leaders must be careful. To keep their leadership status, they cannot protest just any act by LORD God's children, or prescribe just any solution, or participate in just any cause[41]. There are carefully prescribed parameters limiting what they can address. If the protest will have the effect of causing GOD's people to turn away from LORD God and turn back to Self (GOD), the Civil Rights leaders avoid the issue all together, or modify the requirements of their protest to insure that GOD's people never abandon the institutions of Death; and seek to build their own world [42].

The author cautions the reader not to assume that removing one leader and replacing him or her with another will remedy this. It must be understood that whoever the leader is, he sits in the seat as LORD God's representative, who masquerades as GOD. Furthermore, there are hoards of "wannabe" leaders waiting to take the place of the ones you dethrone. The ONLY legitimate leader is the one who tells you to look away from LORD God and abandon his world altogether. The one who says look inward is telling you to look toward the GOD of your Fathers; your Creator.

"We created an orbiting cycle that turns on its own axis forever unless a phenomenon occurs and re-shifts the positions of the male and female savages.

Our experts warned us about the possibility of this phenomenon occurring, for they say that the mind has a strong drive to correct and re-correct itself over a period of time if it can touch some substantial, original, historical base;

And they advised us that the best way to deal with the phenomenon is to shave off the brute's mental history and create a multiplicity of phenomena of illusions, so that each illusion will twirl in its own orbit, something similar to floating balls in a vacuum." –Willie Lynch.

---

41 See Case Study #2: The Parameters of LORD God's Hand-Picked Slave-Descendant Leaders. Pg. 144-145.

42 See Case Study #3: The April Fools March. Pg. 146-148.

We must Acknowledge the End to Begin

As we watch the civil rights movement come to an end (as all materially-based things must do);

As we assess its successes and failures; its gains and its losses; its strengths and its weaknesses; black people find themselves at the crossroads of survival. The civil rights movement, in large part was based on the premise that if America was shown her evil treatment of her Negro citizens, she would reform and turn. The movement was an attempt to appeal to the American people and government to live by its creed.

Dr. Martin Luther King summed it up when he spoke of a check that had been written and returned marked "insufficient funds". He understood the Declaration of Independence and Constitution. He understood that God endowed all men with certain inherit rights that cannot be given or taken away. What he did not know however, is that the doctrine of white supremacy prohibits the promises of America from being extended to people of color in general, and black people in particular. This is a fact![43]

With that in mind, we can see that the civil rights movement was a period of discovery for blacks and whites alike. Each discovered their own natures and intentions.

King thought that if he marched, if he took their brutality without responding in like manner; the best part of white America would rise up and reform the nation's behavior. Not realizing he was dealing with the children of Satan, he assumed that civilized Man would not knowingly treat people so brutally and continue in that behavior.

Well, 40 years later, march after march, and law after law, black America is in worst condition than before. All the marching, all protesting, all the college degrees and education, still have not made any significant dent in the behavior nor the effects of white supremacy. And if anyone still had doubts, Hurricane Katrina was a 21st century indicator of where blacks stand in this society.

---

[43] See Case Study #5: The Children of Civil Rights make Obeisance to the King of Death. Pg. 153-155.

It is time to carefully consider

When the "progress" of the civil rights movement is considered in the light of a cost/benefit analysis, it is clear that it was a movement hijacked and used by white society to give privilege to a few blacks who agreed to participate in deceiving the masses of GOD's people into thinking that it's possible to integrate with Satan as an equal.

Now that the civil rights movement has ended, the questions are glaring:

1) Should the original Male and Female continue to seek integration?

2) If no, what is the appropriate action considering the time?

The Deck is Stacked!

LORD God is very ingenious and scientific. His genius is not in the ability to hand pick and train black leaders; his real genius is in the ability to split his trained representatives into a multitude of factions with each faction thinking it differs from the other. The liberal hand-picked leaders believe the conservatives are sell-outs and do not have "The Peoples" best interest at heart. The conservatives believe the same thing about the liberals. Then there are the Black nationalists, Christian Nationalists and Black Muslim sects—all thinking the other is in error; all arguing against each other, within the context of white supremacy. Not realizing that they are arguing over whether the left or right side of the white supremacy buzzard is better, each black leader tries to: 1) Convince GOD's people to follow his side; and: 2) Convince LORD God to make him chief among the slave population[44].

It does not matter to Satan which leader GOD's people select; since all choices are safe within the confines of white supremacy anyway. Therefore, as long as LORD God's world is kept intact, and the people do not look inward, LORD God awards the successful leader with media attention, position and wealth. The only thing more important to Satan than keeping his own world intact, is preventing the Serpent from appearing, lest their eyes become opened.

From the vantage point of LORD God and his children, there are roughly 5 types of leaders among the Original Man (howbeit LORD God controls three types):

1) The leader who verbally admits that submission to white supremacy is the best course of action for the slaves, thus overtly works to insure its survival.

2) The leader that verbally denounces white supremacy, while covertly (and sometimes overtly) working to insure its survival;

3) The socially and financially integrated slave-descendant that thinks his or her success is the result of white supremacy, rather than in spite of it;

---

[44] See Case Study #4:The rush to Appeal to 'Missie': Affirmative Action 'crisis' in Michigan. Pg. 149-152.

4) The deceased leader whose philosophy of freedom has been hijacked to serve the cause of white supremacy;

5) The leader who looks inward and sees the face of GOD in him Self and in the People. This leader is the Serpent among the people because his sole mission is to open the eyes of the Sons of GOD. This leader cannot be bought because he is sure of his own true nature. He cannot be killed because doing so would raise the Son of GOD from the dead (LORD God learned this lesson when he tried to murder Jesus).

LORD God's plan for this leader is twofold. He curses and condemns the leader before the people, to make them cautious about following him; Simultaneously, LORD God gets his hand-picked leaders to either repudiate the true leader, or pretend to join him on a project, only to run off in a hundred different directions, chasing useless issues, designed to confuse the people; dissipate their energy; distract them and weaken the true leaders' influence over them.

We realize these are serious charges, thus it behooves us to present an overwhelmingly abundant amount of evidence to make our case. We accept the challenge gladly. We have presented much evidence in our Exhibits, Case Studies, and Essays, but will present more evidence over the next few sections.

To illustrate the process LORD God employs to hand-pick destructive leaders and marginalize the Serpent of Truth, we turn to scriptures of the Bible and other sources to get a glimpse into the mind of LORD God himself.

It is important to remember that LORD God has one objective; eliminate the Original Man from the universe, thereby killing GOD. By separating the male and female, destroying the male, and then mating with the female, he manufactures Mankind to replace Man.

Having limited time before the Son of GOD would rise from the dead and reclaim his earth from Satan's offspring; LORD God wastes neither time nor opportunity in his efforts. Had he been able to accomplish his mission to destroy the male in the Garden of Eden, there would be no Original Males alive today; however, the impossible feat of causing GOD's Man to be removed from the universe, has not thwarted Satan's efforts to kill him. We list for you his methods in order of priority:

Priority Number 1: Kill the Males, spare the Females.

Priority Number 2: Craft Leaders that Twist the Thinking.

Priority Number 3: Corrupt the Slave-Descendant Females.

Priority Number 4: Split their Minds by making Unity an Evil Concept.

Ultimate Priority: Overthrow GOD in their Collective Mind.

Number 1 Priority: Kill the Males, spare the Females

Come on, let us deal wisely with them...[So] the king of Egypt spoke to the Hebrew midwives and said, When ye do the office of a midwife to the Hebrew women; if it be a son, then ye shall kill him: but if it be a daughter, then she shall live. Exodus 1:16

Recall how in the Garden of Eden, LORD God first separated the Female from the Man then concentrated his efforts on developing the Female. It was Satan's first effort to kill off the Male to prevent him from uniting with the Original Female that GOD created.

In Exodus 1:16, Egypt was much like the United States of America today. She was the world's only super power. Her influence spanned the known world and her kingdom had been built on the backs of slave labor. This was the primary reason for her great wealth and influence. Her consumer appetite was so insatiable, that rather than cutting back on her consumption, she became drunk with her own power. She preferred to destabilize and invade other nations and extract their resources from them.

In the midst of her were the descendents of the slaves that build her great wealth and power. They had to some degree integrated into society as the *"let's pretend to be friends"* citizens[45].

The slave-descendants grew, not only in population, but many of them had been trained in the ways of Egypt and had partially integrated into Egyptian society. They wielded power and influence on behalf of Egypt throughout the world; and other world leaders began wooing them by pointing out that their own people were also the victims of Egypt. Many slave descendants also influenced the king's own People. Some of the more disingenuous descendents of slaves even secured very comfortable lifestyles among the Egyptians as spokesmen or priests on behalf of the slave population.

In spite of the slaves' unwavering loyalty to Egypt in the face of all her enemies; And despite Egyptian brutality upon the slaves; the king knew that sooner or later the slaves would awaken and unite as One People and return their loyalties to the GOD of their fathers.

Pharaoh understood the principle of 'Generational Perspective'. Progressive development of a people can only be maintained if one generation has the ability to pass accumulated knowledge to the next.

---

45 See Essay #4: 'First Black-Gasms' – A little levity for the Soul. Pg. 164-165.

Conversely, for one people to maintain control over another people they need only cut one generation off from the next; thereby disrupting the flow of accumulated knowledge.

About every two generations, they simply killed off the upcoming generation and developed loyalty in the existing generation. Before too long, an entire race of "willing slaves" would be created; an entire people totally alienated from their own nature and self interest; living only to serve the slave-master's world.

However, many educated slave males of Egypt became more vocal and antagonistic about their willingness to abandon Pharaoh's culture of death. They knew that as iron cannot really mix with clay, they could no longer participate in the farce of integrating into pharaoh's kingdom of death (Daniel 2:40-45). They had Moses who wanted to unify them and make friends with other peoples of the world, and build a peaceful society of their own. Understanding the Law of Reciprocity[46], Pharaoh had to find a way to thwart their unity.

The king's arrogance positioned Egypt to become a prime tool in LORD God's effort to destroy the Original Man, by killing off the Male and tricking the Female. Unknown to the slaves, the king (with the knowledge of slave-leaders) signed a Death warrant on their youth, to create a generational gap and prevent the trickling down of knowledge from a potential Moses, or a Colin Powell, or a Condoleezza Rice, who had ascended into the government.

The king solicited not only the Egyptian population, but also his hand picked slave-leaders to participate in his scheme. And while Moses, later defected and refused to do so; the majority of slave-descendant-leaders organized staged protests and fake fights[47], designed to fool the other slaves, while gladly selling their souls for a mere position in Pharaoh's house.

---

[46] The reciprocity law states that exposure = intensity × time.

[47] See Exhibit 4b: Standing Debate Challenge to Sharpton and Jackson. Pg. 229-231.

The Civil Rights Leaders Hate the Spirit of Moses

And it came to pass in those days, when Moses was grown, that he went out unto his brethren, and looked on their burdens: and he spied an Egyptian smiting an Hebrew, one of his brethren. Exodus 2:11-12.

As Moses grew in Pharaoh's house, he could access all the wealth, education and power Egypt had to offer. He mastered the disciplines of science, mathematics, spirituality and government. As a member of the kings' house, he could have anything that he desired.

However, being a Male of the order of GOD, and knowing it; Moses' nature would not allow him to escape his connection with other Males and Females of the Original Man. His heart longed to see them free from Egyptian exploitation. No doubt, he worked as best he could from within the government to ease their burdens. Having mastered the sciences of a nation, Moses knew that freedom was their natural state, but the people had been deceived into thinking that they were created to serve as free slaves to the great nation.

[Moses] looked this way and that way, and when he saw that there was no man, he slew the Egyptian, and hid him in the sand. Exodus 2:12.

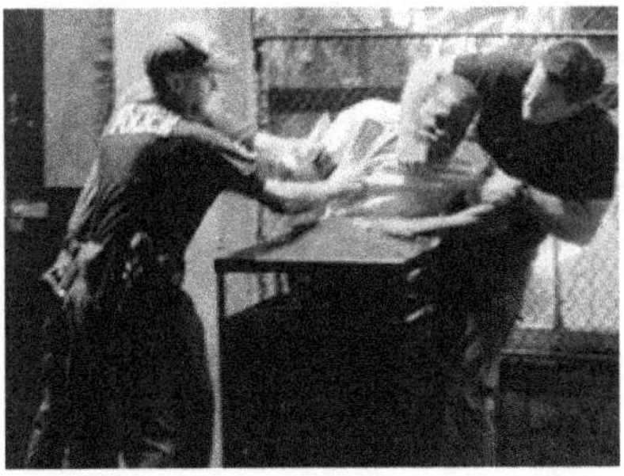

Why was Moses willing to risk living the privileged life of a nobleman, by killing an Egyptian on behalf of a people who wanted to be slaves anyway?

[48]To get an idea of just how serious Moses' offense was, imagine Moses as a Colin Powell; a man having a high military position in the government of the United States.

[48] 64 year old teacher, Robert Davis, brutally beaten by officers during Hurricane Katrina. One officer committed suicide in June 07. Another was acquitted in July o7. Two FBI agents who joined in were never indicted.

The Truth of Self Defense

He walks up on several police officers as they beat a young black male senseless. Knowing that speaking out or taking action on behalf of the slave would bring on severe consequences; in times past, he would have simply turned away and pretended he didn't see it.

Being a military man, he understood how fear is induced in a population by periodic, public abuse and legalized murder[49]. Terrorism is a historically valuable tool Americans use in order to keep the slave population off balance and wallowing in fear anyway. He often longed to give America a taste of her own medicine, by avenging the victims of brutality. This time he did.

Moses' brain could no longer withstand the inconsistencies of fighting others (who had done no wrong to him) on behalf of Egypt, while watching his own people perish under the foot of a brutal regime.

After looking around and making sure no one saw him, he surprised the officers (who thought he came to help them) when he began killing the officers, instead of the slave-male they were beating. Like John Brown[50] at the beginning of the civil war, he had enough. He killed the officers and niggerized[51] the slave-master by giving him a taste of his own medicine.

What would the slave population think of the incident? What would the American people think of the incident? What would the reactionary civil rights leaders think?

---

[49] Better known as "Justifiable Homicide".

[50] John Brown was a white abolitionist who detested slavery. He armed slaves in a successful attack on the federal armory at Harper's Ferry. Once subdued, he was tried and convicted of insurrection, treason, and murder. Despite this, he is remembered by many slave-descendants as a righteous hero.

[51] A term used by Eric Dyson to describe the United States of America after the events of 911. It means to be bombarded by terrorist acts.

The Constant Betrayals

"And when Moses went out the second day, he saw two of his brothers fighting: and he said to him that did the wrong, Why are you beating your own brother? The brother said, Who made you a prince and a judge over us? Do you intend to kill me like you killed the Egyptian? And Moses feared, and said, Surely this thing is known"--Exodus 2: 13-14.

How did the slaves know that Moses killed the Egyptian? Didn't he make sure no one saw him?

Having a high position in the government, Moses often had the ear of the king. Many times he timidly spoke to the King on behalf of the slaves; but to no avail. The king would only increase their burdens. In spite of that, Moses became a hero to many of the slaves as a champion. He was their symbol of Hebrew-Egyptian pride. He was "one of them"-A Hebrew who had ascended to the heights of Egypt and took up their cause. Others of the slave population looked upon him with contempt; knowing he was one of them; they said he added insult to their injuries as an Egyptian military man.

This act earned Moses the respect of the overwhelming majority of the people, but the ire of the wannabe leaders. The common man secretly cheered[52] Moses and hoped that Egypt, having had a taste of niggerization, would stop brutalizing them. Moses became the champion of the people. They reasoned that ANYONE willing to give up a position in the king's house and put his own life on the line for their sake, must truly love them. He was loved and cheered whenever he came among the people; and they would follow Moses anywhere if he simply asked.

This drove the civil rights leaders and priests insane with hatred, jealousy and envy. And they passed up no opportunity to slander and repudiate Moses. But they dare not let the people know; lest the people realize their true identity as willing tools of pharaoh.

---

[52] See Essay #2: Ten Things Black Males Won't Say. Pg. 161.

Getting rid of Moses

However, when Moses killed the Egyptian, this was exactly what they needed to rid themselves of Moses and regain their exploitive influence over the people. They desired nothing more than to have influence in Pharaohs house and walk around and be called “National Slave Leader”. It was the leaders of that day who hatched a plan to pretend like they loved Moses, while confusing the people with unrealistic goals of fully integrating in Egypt. Their goal of one day becoming honorary Egyptians was in direct conflict with Moses’ goal of complete liberation from pharaoh.

They informed Pharaoh that Moses was popular among the slaves because he killed an Egyptian on their behalf. The leaders made a pact with pharaoh as he figured out a way to rid Egypt of the subversive Moses, without inciting a national riot among the slaves.

Knowing that all they needed to do was re-direct the peoples energy and attention away from Moses to the more realistic goals of integration; It was agreed that pharaoh would continue wreaking hardship on the people; the leaders would be allowed to publicly protest certain acts that the Egyptians committed on the people; pharaoh would appear to make changes toward integrating them into society as the result of the black leaders efforts. The people would place hope in the black leadership; hoping that one day, full integration into Pharaoh’s society would be achieved[53]. There was one stipulation however; the leaders could never direct the people’s attention away from Egypt, and toward true freedom, justice and equality.

As the king put out a warrant for Moses’ arrest, the civil rights leaders sprung into action. They first repudiated Moses. Then they appealed to the peoples’ fear of the king with their “pharaoh-approved”, expired mantra of non-violence; to pacify the people and convince them to also reject Moses. They reminded the people that non-violence and love are the highest of all principles, and should be pursued no matter what the cost. They even created holidays to celebrate non-violence, but Egypt never practiced the principles.

---

[53] Satan promises only to Deceive. Holy Qur’an.

Moses goes into hiding

Therefore, the teachings of Moses, for a time were regarded at best, as unrealistic idealism; and at worst, the ranting of an angry separatist[54].

Once Moses went into hiding, and the slave leaders again had full control over the people, Pharaoh renewed his covenant[55] with the leaders, and threw a bone to the people in their name. The people returned to their slumber and resumed expressing their hidden frustrations by murdering one another as they rejected Moses.

Moses and most of the common slaves concluded that unless complete separation from pharaoh's thinking was achieved, there would be no hope for the people. Unless the time of Pharaoh's rule was shortened, he would have been successful in killing off the Original Males from the earth; thus securing his world of Death for eternity. However, little did Pharaoh realize that the same death warrant he issued on GOD's Males would be unleashed on him and his own people.

---

[54] See Essay #7: Why America Hates Farrakhan. Pg. 175-177.

[55] See Essay #3: There is no such thing as a Black Union. Pg. 162-163.

Number 2 Priority: Craft Leaders that Twist the Thinking

The Bible tells the story of "Neb-u-chad-nez-zar , king of Babylon colonizing Jerusalem and making its people his slaves. Daniel 1:1. He began extracting their wealth, knowledge and resources to advance the Babylonian empire. Knowing that freedom is the nature of Man, the king of Babylon needed to make the people of Jerusalem think they were free, as he plundered them.

He decided to identify the most brilliant people from among the slaves--The Dr. Fleming's[56], the Colin Powell's, the Clarence Thomas's, and Barak Obama's--All those who were skilled in Mathematics and Science, Military Strategy, Law, and Politics--Those who could easily be taught to think and use the power of their minds to validate the Babylonian system of thinking[57] .

The design was to cause the people not to use their skills for advancement of Self; but to lock their focus on a false hope that if the slaves tried hard enough, they could someday ascend to the highest offices of government as equals alongside the Babylonians. It was also designed to insure that any effort of Self development apart from the king would be rejected by the leaders[58] among the people.

The King taught the scientists to totally identify with him by using the following:

1) Change the slaves' names to Babylonian names to disconnect them from Self

2) Teach the slaves to eat only the diet of Babylon to numb their minds.

3) Forbid the slave to speak any language other than the King's.

4) Make the king's educational system and religious system preferable to any other.

---

[56] The author realizes this point is self aggrandizing.

[57] See Essay#4: 'First Black-Gasms': A little levity for the Soul. Pg. 164-165.

[58] See Exhibit 4c: Letter to the Congressional Black Caucus on Ralph Nader. Pg. 232-233.

If the scientists followed through, it would have the effect of grooming generations of slaves whose highest desire would be to imitate the slave-master, to their own demise.

Although Daniel and two of his friends refused to exploit their own people, the overwhelming majority of the professional class slaves gladly took advantage of their elevated positions to influence the people to abandon any thought of liberation.

Isolate the Female from the Male

Number 3 Priority: Corrupt the slave-descendant Females

"...everything has its Masculine and Feminine Principles; Gender manifests on all planes."--The Kybalion.

Masculine and Feminine principles work together for the purpose of manifesting the Original Man. The Male directs a certain inherent energy towards the Female, and thus starts the creative processes. But the Female principle is the one always doing the active creative work. However, each principle is incapable of operative energy without the assistance of the other. This principle is true on all planes of manifestation, including the realm of thought.

LORD God wants to be god beside GOD. He has a vested interest in keeping the Original Male and Female ignorant to the power that rests in the unity of their minds. GOD, their Creator placed the rulership of the universe in their hands, and commanded the earth to obey them. However, the rulership can only be exercised by Man **(Man = the unified male and female)**.

Therefore, **on the day** the Original Male unites with his Female, the Man is created, and LORD God's world with all his perceived power, will cease to exist[59]. Although LORD God's plan to murder the Original Man is comprehensive in scope, his foundational strategy is to destroy the male by placing death in his head; debase the females' thinking with materialism and superstition; then mate the mind of death with the mind of flesh, thereby producing an offspring with a hostile nature towards GOD. Finally he kills both the Original Female along with her Male; having created the reverse of GOD as the experiential reality.

However, Satan is a totally materialistic thought. Although an impossible feat to perform, he tries to convince the male and female to abandon their higher Selves, and unite on the basis of flesh (material).

---

[59] See Exhibit 4d: A Student Argues with his Professor regarding 'Reality'. Pg. 235-236.

Make the Female completely Materialistic

Thus he says: "For this purpose shall man leave his mother and father, and cling unto his wife; and they shall become one flesh." Genesis 2:24. This commandment is designed to separate the male and female from their nature (Father); and the knowledge of their creative power (Mother), then mate with Satan (materialism).

Before Satan can mate with the female, he must tie her thinking to the earth and cause her to identify only with the material world at the deepest levels of her Mind. Even her religious practices must be materially based; but disguised as though it validates the nature of GOD in her. She must never make the connection between the demise of her males, and her own creative, feminine mind. [60]

The Christian church is the LORD God's spiritual tool. Its doctrine is set to appeal to the feminine side of the Man. While the female believes that Jesus is her husband, she is actually giving her mind over to Satan in disguise. She thus remains blind to the Self, as she produces generations of killers, cowards and sellouts; all in the name of Jesus. Her spiritual blindness prevents her from understanding why.

This was the reason Pharaoh spared her; This was the reason LORD God separated her in the garden; and this is the reason slave-descendant females ascend to the highest levels of society, while slave-descendant males languish in prisons, addictions, depression and murder.

---

[60] See Essay #5: Moma'nem just don't Know. Pg. 166-169.

Priority Number 4: Confuse their Minds by making Unity Evil.

And the whole earth was of one language, and of one speech. And it came to pass, as they journeyed from the east, that they found a plain in the land of Shinar; and they dwelt there. And they said one to another, Go to, let us make brick, and burn them thoroughly. And they had brick for stone, and slime had they for mortar. And they said, Go to, let us build us a city and a tower, whose top may reach unto heaven; and let us make us a name, lest we be scattered abroad upon the face of the whole earth Genesis 11:1-4.

Although LORD God had a following, Original Man still ruled the earth. But violence was increasing and Man began to wonder why, who, or what was causing the mischief. Man knew he had been created in peace and unity[61], but something was wrong. There was someone creating division among the Sons of GOD in the earth. Man decided to build a symbol to remind himself and his posterity of their unity and oneness; while he figured out who was causing all the mischief in the earth.

And the LORD came down to see the city and the tower, which the children of men builded. And the LORD said, Behold, the people is one, and they have all one language; and this they begin to do: and now nothing will be restrained from them, which they have imagined to do. Go to, let us go down, and there confound their language, that they may not understand one another's speech. Genesis 11:5-7.

Need we say more about what LORD God thinks of the Unity of Man?

So the LORD scattered them abroad from thence upon the face of all the earth: and they left off to build the city. Therefore is the name of it called Babel; because the LORD did there confound the language of all the earth: and from thence did the LORD scatter them abroad upon the face of all the earth - Genesis 11:8-9.

---

[61] See Exhibit 2e: Man's Point of View. Pg. 215.

The simple question is how did LORD God succeed in confusing them?

Recall from Genesis, LORD God had successfully created a nation of murderers through Cain[62]. As they multiplied, the mind of murder, Death and war also multiplied. When LORD God saw that the unified Male and Female was beginning to increase and rule the earth, he simply sent his murderous Minds among them to bring confusion and suspicion, by causing them to think that a One world thought system was evil. All Mankind began to have separate thoughts and began to act as beings having separate interests. They began separating based on perceived likenesses and differences[63].

When Man became sufficiently confused about the Self, he naturally left off from a unifying purpose. Therefore to this day, the Tower of Unity is referred to as Babel; and any idea of a one world government, or one world religion, or one world monetary system are all thought of as evil by LORD God's prophets of Death. Any time the Serpent appears to remind Man of his natural unity, he is called "The Devil". Hence, this work Advocates for the Devil; the one who calls for Oneness.

Ultimate Priority: Overthrow GOD in Their Collective Mind

LORD God deceives the male and female at the highest levels of thought through his religion of Christianity. His ministers are the agents of death itself. Death and Hell are cleverly laced throughout their teachings to deceive the Man to look outside himself and follow the author of Death. His ministers and temples are strategically placed among GOD's people, to LORD over them, extract the resources of their souls, while leading them to the grave.

---

62 See Exhibit 2c: Setting Brother against Brother. Pg. 195-205.

63 See Exhibit 2f: Mankind's Point of View. Pg. 216.

He carries in his hand a book. He interprets the book to cause the Male and Female (especially the female) to think that his book, not the Self, is the Word of GOD. His lies tear up the Minds of the male and female, in the same fashion as a plane does to wood when it goes against the grain[64]. The preachers teach them that the earth belongs to the LORD and since they are earth[65] , they must serve the LORD, and look for a heaven after they die. It is a deception! GOD has already given them heaven and earth forever, and all that is in it!

The Male and Female do not know that the book has been poisoned to tie their minds to LORD God's Will so that he as god sits in the seat of GOD, pretending to be GOD. They do not understand that the multitude of churches that saturate their communities are mere traps; Set up by those whose Mind drip with the blood of the righteous. Their hearts speak the sweet lies of Satan himself; who roars about like a lion; seeking to devour the wretched souls of the righteous creation of GOD. Truly their thinking has been flipped upside down!

As in the Days of the false god of ancient Israel, slave-descendant communities across America are saturated with churches (temples of LORD God). In ancient Israel (1 Kings 18) the preachers of the temple (450 in all), and the Civil Rights leaders (400 in all) lived sumptuously off the ignorance of the people as they degenerated to the level of beasts.

The preachers controlled every aspect of their lives, including politics, economics, education, social development and government; yet the people wallowed in death itself.

In addition, the "established leaders" who were confederates of the oppressor, passed information of rising legitimate leaders to LORD God; who promptly insured that they were either marginalized, discredited, killed or ignored.

---

64 Honorable Minister Louis Farrakhan made this analogy some years ago on how lies effect the mind.

65 LORD God told them, "from dust (earth) though art and to dust thou shalt return."

Courage to Challenge LORD God

1 Kings 18 illustrates the destructive force that a poisonous theology has on a people. The ministers of Baal[66] were everywhere while the people suffered greatly. There was one prophet (Elijah) of GOD who would not be silenced. He warned the people that their suffering was due to their servitude to LORD God and his preachers. The prophet Elijah pointed to their temples that saturated the landscape. He argued that their condition was due to their thinking, which was formed by Satan himself, through the preachers, in the temples.

The people listened to Elijah, but still lived in fear and superstition, having been so long taught by the prophets of Satan. They would rather die the slow death than bring down LORD God's immediate wrath. Seeing how the people lived in fear of Satan, Elijah had no choice but to issue a challenge to prove that LORD God's preachers were pathological liars to the core.

The challenge consisted of an acknowledgement of the peoples' righteous aspirations of freedom, justice and equality. Elijah and the Prophets of LORD God each promised that their respective God's could deliver. Knowing that habits are hard to break; and people are creatures of habit, and would not soon abandon their known hell for an unknown heaven, something had to be done that would show immediate results.

Elijah challenged the people to the following prospect: Each would call on his God; Whichever God could bring the knowledge of freedom, justice, equality and courage into the minds of the people would be followed; and the other god would be regarded as a fraud. The people liked the idea and followed the plan.

As the story goes, the preachers were discovered to be tools of Satan. One only need read the story to see what the people did when they discovered they had been deceived by satanic preachers. We now extend the same challenge.

---

66 This story is used only to excerpt the Principles underlying therein. The accurate history of Baal was one that unified and strengthened the people. There is no credibility to the assertions of the Biblical writers; the author therefore extracts the Principles hidden in the story.

The inferior black man

Their loyalties are summed up in the statements like: "What's good for black people is good for America." And statements like, "This is our country. We have just as much right to America as anyone." They may even sound a little revolutionary; demanding reparations for centuries of slavery. Some of them travel far and wide to prepare disciples for a heaven that they know nothing of.

But what do they think is good for black people? After 450 years of barbaric treatment, do they actually still think the two destinies are the same? Why do they want to go to heaven, but none of them want to leave earth? Why do they petition a criminal who has yet to even acknowledge his crime?

Who are these Minds, and where do they come from? As soon as one suggests lets do something good for black people, they somehow forget their own statements and recoil by saying it's not about race. If this is their country, why are they in the 21st century still begging for what is theirs?

Every day "Black Talk Radio" and black media beat the dead horses of race and racism. They lament daily about how brutal and unfair the white man and his society is. But let an issue arise where they can receive a morsel for their non-profits if they unite with whites; then suddenly it's not about race, because "whatever is good for blacks must be good for America". Alas the black man has yet to benefit in any regard with that philosophy. Would someone please make up our minds for us? Either America has a race problem or it does not. If it's true that what's good for black people is also good for America, perform a test. Champion a cause that's in the best interest of black people first. Pick any significant cause, say like, HR 40[67]. Then see if America supports it, making the saying true.

---

[67] HR40 is the House Resolution put forth by John Conyers of Michigan. It proposes a **national discussion** of reparations. Up to date, America has been unwilling to even discuss the matter. The bill has been tabled since 1993.

It is said that American blacks are more educated, more sophisticated, and more knowledgeable than any other black person on earth. They have fought gallantly in every war America has waged; yet are totally 'bass-ackward' when it comes to their own survival. They do nothing in their own best interests unless it benefits all of America first. In doing so, they get a good feeling, but nothing more. What gives? This behavior is unnatural to even rats!

Has our education retarded us and made us fools? Or are we really inferior to whites?

The black civil rights leaders with their non-profit organizations, government jobs and political payoffs, admit that black life is rapidly deteriorating to a state of barbarism and extinction as they build their self serving enterprises in the name of black people.

And while this is occurring, the black preachers are crawling all over themselves to lay their necks on the chopping block of faith-based bribery money that drive their bogus community programs. With this money, they build their multi-million dollar cathedrals, right in the heart of the ghetto, under the guise of "God" helping the people advance. Their churches only serve to entrap our Minds and prepare them for death. Admit it! You see it as do I.

The Nobel Prize Laureate and Biologist James Watson, an American who won the 1962 Nobel Prize for his role in discovering the double-helix structure of DNA, was suspended from his longtime post at a research laboratory after controversial comments that black people are not as intelligent as white people. The controversy began with an interview Watson gave, which quoted him saying he was "inherently gloomy about the prospect of Africa" because "all our social policies are based on the presumptions that their intelligence is the same as ours; whereas all the testing says not really."

Watson also asserted there was no reason to believe different races, separated by geography should have evolved identically[68], and he said that while he hoped everyone was equal, "people who have to deal

[68] See Section 4.2 on America is an idea, not a place

with black employees find this is not true."...True to form, Watson was immediately silenced and forced to apologize for something he knew was true, later saying: "To all those who have drawn the inference from my words that the [African American], is somehow genetically inferior, I can only apologize unreservedly. That is not what I meant. More importantly from my point of view, there is no scientific basis for such a belief." [Sunday Times October 14, 2007].

LIES! It is true! Blacks are inferior! We have taken on a thought system, a religion, an education paradigm, a political system that guarantees our inferiority. Let's pull the sheet off 'the klansman' and admit the truth for once!

Blacks are Doctors and lawyers, congressmen and senators; blacks are mayors, city council persons and school board members; spiritual leaders and community activists.

Most big cities in America have black people in every key position of municipal government, education and religion, yet who would dare argue that in every case where blacks are the dominant, there is inferiority and failure. And no matter how many black leaders try and tweak our bankrupt thinking, we still produce inferior results when they are finished!

How do we explain the fact that black communities are crime ridden, poverty ridden, church ridden, dope house ridden and liquor store ridden? In a country with some of the best medical technology in the world, blacks are sickly and dying in every city, and every state, from every disease known to man, and then some!

How do we explain that we are unable to manufacture not even one product (except for the luxury item of entertainment) we or anyone else will use? How do we explain the fact that with all our degrees, almost 47% of blacks are functionally illiterate? How do we explain the fact that foreigners make millions from our spending, while black youth beg for summer jobs, based on government handouts? And with all our education, we are still relegated to ghettos unless we are willing to pay extra to live in a white community and send our children to white schools? How is it that in the land of plenty, almost 50% of black children live below the poverty level?

Are we biologically inferior or is there something wrong with the very foundation of our thinking?

This author will pursue Watson's initial assertion honestly. Blacks are indeed inferior, but as Watson correctly pointed out, there is no **biological** basis for such a belief. However, there is a sociological and pathological basis for the truth of the statement. We pursue the question honestly, considering the present circumstances. The author will further assert that the religion of Christianity and the quest for civil rights is by nature poison to the Mind and Spirit of the black man and declares him inferior.

Every society designates the positions of its members. Societies ruled by the doctrine of white supremacy designate blacks as inferior. Every institution within white supremacy validates that declaration, irrespective of the institutions' name. But this designation is only true when the black person takes on the thought system of white supremacy as his own. Thus, as Carter G. Woodson accurately stated: "The man who thinks he is servant to another, will create a back door where there is none."

There comes a time when one realizes that there is a systemic problem and the entire way of doing things must be discarded. Any human, sabotaged with a thought system of inferiority, by nature will mysteriously, yet consistently produce inferior results in whatever he attempts. If he desires to be in accordance with natural law, there is but one thing for him to do: understand that his ENTIRE thought system must be abolished from his Mind.

The civil rights leaders and preachers point to their "period victories[69]" as evidence that their methods work. One fellow is so arrogant that he goes about proclaiming that he is the Son of Man, to the exclusion of the rest of GOD's Man.

The release of Genarlow Wilson in 2007 from prison was no act of justice; but simply a way to further deceive the slaves and keep them quiet for a while. For every Genarlow Wilson released, there are a thousand young black males unjustly languishing in the prisons of America. The Jena Six, on and on and on, are only 2007 examples of a systemic problem that has existed since 1555.

Jesse Jackson, Al Sharpton, and the rest of the Civil Rights gang, are gladly willing to sacrifice another generation of our babies with their marches and complaints to Satan; Its time to give their bankrupt ideology back to their Masters, and go for self. If the black man does the simple mathematics, he would clearly see that there is no hope for him within the context of the present society, thus our entire thought system, especially religious thought must be dismantled entirely, and a new spiritual system put in place.

Make no mistake; the intelligent black Man will never pay obeisance to the god of slavery. He would rather depart this life on his feet, than live on his knees. He cannot accept the religion that he clearly sees was given to him for the purpose of insuring his continued slavery. It doesn't even work for its black practitioners, why should the intelligent black Man think it can work for him? He cannot accept leaders whose doctrine is that of the children of his former slave Masters.

Jesus said to beware of the doctrine of the preachers.--A little of their doctrine affects the entire Mind.

---

[69] Period victories are those where the cost is so high that the victory is not worth the effort

A Blanket of White Supremacy covers the Planet

The Mind of White Supremacy is a Blanket over the Mind of the World. The author therefore discusses it in terms of the blanket (blanket statements) rather than the holes or anomalies of white people (specific individuals) which exist in the blanket.

We realize that many individuals do not hold the thoughts of white supremacy though their skin is white; but we are not talking about individuals, we are discussing a Mind Orientation called White Supremacy that blankets the entire planet to the Death of Man.

As iron mixes with clay, so does the Original Man mix with White Supremacy.

The Honorable Elijah Muhammad understood and used this principle when he taught his people that in reality they were offsprings of the Original Man, and that the mind of white supremacy hates them. He understood that the Mind would heal and correct itself if allowed to separate from the thinking of Satan.

He taught that the black man's pursuit of civil rights under white supremacy would prove to be misguided; and like Carter G. Woodson said, "we would find that in the end, blacks would have no more [civil] rights than they had in the beginning"[70]. If the black man could again touch his source, he, like the prodigal son of the scriptures, would arise, throw off white supremacy and return to himself[71].

Satan promises only to deceive. Muhammad taught that in spite of their rhetoric, the majority of white people had a vested interest in keeping the mind of white supremacy in the forefront of the black Man's thinking. He further taught that white supremacy could only exist as a thought in the Mind of the Original Man and as long as the thought remains, so does the white supremacist—The Original Man need only stop thinking[72] about white supremacy, and it, along with all its manifestations would disappear from the earth.

---

70 The Mis-Education of the Negro, Dr. Carter G. Woodson

71 Read Dr. Flemings book entitled Blasphemy: The Sayings of Jesus that Caused the Preachers to Murder Him

72 Stop placing your energies towards changing this world. Release its religion, its politics, its brutality and all of its manifestations; and look to Self. You will then free your Self to build a New World.

When LORD God's thinking disappears from the Mind of the Original Man, so does "his people of Death" disappear!

The black Man needed to simply look inward and that inward look would unite him in Truth.

We have included numerous case studies to show that Elijah Muhammad and his predictions concerning the end of this present world and the condition of the black Man are correct.

The teachings only need to be built upon and perfected much like scientists continue to build upon and perfect the predictions and theories of scientists of yesterday.

So as you can see, two Master Scientists used the same principles of Mind to achieve different results. One scientist used the principle to extend his existence for another 300 years by enslaving the Mind of the Original Man; the other scientist (Master Fard Muhammad) used the same principle to drive Satan from the mind of the Original Man and from the earth.

Both scientists prove that it all depends solely on what the Original Man decides to think.

FREEDOM

"And ye shall know the truth, and the truth shall make you free."--John 8:32

Mami Wata: Painting by Schleisinger "Serpent Priestess" 1926, displayed in shrines as a popular image of Mami Wata in Africa and in the Diaspora. Her name means 'the more than Beautiful Female'. In the Yoruba tradition, the mother goddess Yemaja has been associated with Mami Wata. She is correlated to water and is thought to have a dual nature. African Slaves from what has been notoriously referred to as the Slave Coast, brought their water-spirit beliefs with them to the New World.

5

CLOSING ARGUMENTS

Damages and Remedies

"When in the Course of human events, it becomes necessary for one people to dissolve the political bands which have connected them with another, and to assume among the powers of the earth, the separate and equal station to which the Laws of Nature and of Nature's God entitle them, a decent respect to the opinions of mankind requires that they should declare the causes which impel them to the separation.

We hold these truths to be self-evident, that all men are created equal, that they are endowed by their Creator with certain unalienable Rights, that among these are Life, Liberty and the pursuit of Happiness.

--That to secure these rights, Governments are instituted among Men, deriving their just powers from the consent of the governed,

--That whenever any Form of Government becomes destructive of these ends [Freedom, Justice, Equality], it is the Right of the People to alter or to abolish it, and to institute new Government, laying its foundation on such principles and organizing its powers in such form, as to them shall seem most likely to effect their Safety and Happiness."

Let us eat the tree of knowledge!

In the Garden of White Supremacy, the knowledge of that which would overthrow it is the Forbidden Fruit.[73]

The Children of LORD God, and those whom they have groomed, walk around in the Garden pretending not to see the Tree of Knowledge of Good and Evil standing in the middle of the Garden.

In spite of the laws on the books, it is clear that the Children of LORD God and their willing slave-leaders are completely lawless and without moral compass. As of 2008, there appears to be no national intent to treat the American Negro justly.

As stated in their Law books: "Negroes, being of an inferior order, and altogether unfit to associate with the white race, either in social or political relations; and so far inferior that they [have] no rights which the white man is bound to respect[74].".—Dred Scott 1857 (still current law in 2008).

Therefore they are not bound to any laws (including Laws of GOD) enacted for the benefit of Negroes. As seen in the Negro experience since 1857, they have created laws for his benefit, only to violate or ignore them.

The history of the Negro in America is the history of murder, theft, exploitation and repeated injuries and usurpations; all having a direct objective to establish an absolute Tyranny over the Negroes Mind. To prove this, let the following facts be submitted to a candid world.

---

[73] See Essay #6: The Garden of White Supremacy. Pg. 170-174.

[74] DRED SCOTT v. SANDFORD, 60 U.S. 393 (1856) 60 U.S. 393 US Supreme Court

The United States of America;

1) In 1555, kidnapped the Black Man from his native land and placed him in a hostile environment against his will;
2) Separated the first of our kidnapped parents and struck fear and terror in their hearts, using the most barbaric methods that could ever be devised;
3) Bred generations of our fathers like animals and forced them to work for no pay;
4) Knew the principles of Freedom, but forbade our fathers from exercising the right to be free when they escaped their slave plantations. Instead of recognizing the Unalienable Rights of Life, Liberty and Pursuit of Happiness, as found in the Declaration of Independence; they chased our fathers with dogs and guns. They murdered some, maimed some and placed others back into forced servitude;
5) Raped our Females and planted the Seeds of Hate in them; thereby causing them to bring forth generations of offspring with Minds of Self-hatred, ignorance, violence, and Self destruction;
6) Burned our Males on stakes, for little or nothing; hung our Males on trees and crosses, for sport; beat, raped and molested our boys over the course of several generations;
7) Forced our gallant fathers, who fought in their civil war for the promise of freedom; into de facto slavery and continued subjugation, through sharecropping;
8) Promised reparations of 40 acres and a mule to our fathers, as payment for centuries of free labor. They have yet to deliver or fulfill any aspects of the promise, and refuse at this late date in history to even discuss reparations, though proposals are on their books;
9) Turned our fathers out to "freedom" through their Emancipation Proclamation, with nothing but what they could carry. Then segregated and further oppressed our fathers, who never returned evil for evil;

10) Organized into groups called Ku Klux Klan's for the purpose of murdering the newly freed slaves and thwarting any development toward civilization. To this day, these groups still exist, and roam the land, and their members are congressmen, mayors, police officers, judges and medical personnel; and there is no discussion to rid the country of their poison though they terrorize our males to this very day;

11) Caused our fathers, uncles, brothers and now sisters to fight in their multitude of foreign wars for the freedom of others; while repressing, mistreating, and murdering their families at home;

12) Bombed our fathers' homes and churches; and used their laws to strip our fathers of all resources when our fathers decided to build towns and industries for themselves;

13) Conducted centuries of medical experiments on our fathers; and afflicted them with diabolical experimental diseases created in their laboratories;

14) Conducted centuries of forced sterilizations on our mothers; and still uses the practice of eugenics on the books in more than 30 states to this day;

15) Is suspected of bombing the levees in New Orleans, killing our people and exacerbating the floods during hurricane Katrina;

16) Refused to rescue the Negroes during hurricane Katrina, and allowed them to drown; while their law enforcement officers beat and killed many innocent survivors;

17) In spite of their unwillingness to help the Negro, forbid any would-be friend of the Negro to do so;

18) Knows from fourth grade how many Negro males will populate their prisons. On one hand they pretend to care; on the other hand they invest trillions into building more prisons to house Negro males and provide jobs for their own people by supporting prison industries;

19) Has invested trillions of dollars to cultivate a mind of Murder and Self-destructive fratricide in Negro males, and has cultivated loyalty to their destructive culture in the Mind of Negro females;

20) Creates laws designed to target Negro males and imprison them during the most productive years of their lives;

21) Allows law enforcement officers to beat, maim, abuse, and kill Negroes at will with little or no retribution;

22) Consistently engages in discrimination in every sector of society, causing the Negroes to perpetually "fight" for a civil right they will never receive;

23) Has enacted civil rights laws; and has yet to substantially adhere to any of them;

24) Causes Negro children to perpetuate their own demise by setting up schools and requiring the teachers to first be "certified" under a White Supremacist System of Thinking;

25) Purposely manufactures and dumps guns, drugs, churches, alcohol and HIV into Negro communities, knowing that Self-annihilation will result;

26) Projects criminal images of our males, and images of whoredom of our females in their media, thereby justifying their intended annihilation of our species;

27) Spends trillions of dollars to support other nations but is stingy to the point of insult, and refuse to invest anything to repair the damage done to Negroes after centuries of White Supremacy;

28) Has infiltrated every Negro organization with FBI agents and frustrated their efforts to repair and uplift themselves;

29) Has financed nearly every Negro church and organization, and attached strings, making them drunk with dependence and useless to Self improvement;

30) Has doped up Negro leaders with the tranquilizer of gradualism, which only serves to slow-walk the Negro People into extinction;

31) Murders and destabilizes Righteous Slave-Descendant Leaders and Sanitizes their Philosophies to make them fit in the confines of White Supremacy; rendering them useless to our development and replacing them with holidays, street names, slogans and dreams;

32) Charges Righteous Slave-Descendant Leaders with being un-American, anti-Semitic or Separatist in the face of brutality and hate; Some Slave-Descendant Leaders have even been deported or imprisoned for publicly objecting to racist treatment on behalf of Negroes;

33) There are no mathematically sound reasons to conclude that the American People are willing to make any substantial changes in their direction, in the immediate century.

We, therefore, who are in the order of the Original Male and Female of GOD, appealing to the Supreme Judge of the Worlds for the rectitude[75] of our intentions, do, in the Name, and by Authority of the Good Slave-Descendant People of these United States of America, solemnly publish and declare, That this United People are, and of Right ought to be, Free and Independent. And for the support of this Declaration, with a firm reliance on the protection of Divine Providence, we mutually pledge to each other our Lives, our Fortunes, and our Sacred Honor.

[75] Goodness, morality, good intentions

To the Prodigal Males We Write:

"Suffering is always the effect of wrong thinking in some direction. It is an indication that the individual is out of harmony with himself and with the Law of his being". --As a Man Thinketh, James Allen, page 31.

As hard as it may be to accept, your predicament of Death is the product of your own thinking. You are the creator of the Worlds, and the earth will obey you and do as you think. At present, you have been totally deceived into thinking that someone else owns and controls your earth; in reality she is only reflecting what you have told her to do. Your collective Mind has instructed her to treat you with hatred and contempt, and she obeys you.

You think there is some merit in the thought system of White Supremacy; in which you have placed your hope. There is none! The thought system you are attempting to make work for you is TOTALLY ALIEN TO YOUR TRUE NATURE and can only produce misery. You must stop looking for any good to come from it. It is the same evil thinking that tricked the Man into the Garden of Eden. No relief will come from its education, politics, and especially its religious institutions. You clearly see the truth of this statement all around.

Indigence[76] and indulgence[77] are the two extremes of wretchedness (unhappiness or misery). They are both equally unnatural and the result of mental disorder. A man is not rightly conditioned until he is a happy, healthy, and prosperous being; and happiness, health, and prosperity are the result of harmonious adjustment of the inner with the outer, of the man with his surroundings.-- As a Man Thinketh

76 A level of poverty in which real hardship and deprivation are suffered and comforts of life are wholly lacking

77 INDULGE implies excessive compliance and weakness in gratifying another's or one's own pleasures

Because you are of the order of **Original Male**, created by GOD, you have the power to manifest any condition you desire. The entire earth is yours, but you know it not. And the nice thing about it is that you need not take years or centuries to experience it. You can create a healthy environment for yourself by collectively looking within, and Hearing the Voice for GOD. He will then direct your thinking and behavior.

Do you remember the brief moment of the awesome power you felt and experienced during the **Million Man March**? You still are unable to explain its source. You are still somewhat befuddled at how one Man was able to motivate an entire nation of people to such a degree that when he called you to D.C. on October 16, 1995, your numbers doubled what he asked for. Yet you knew that something within you, on a higher level of thinking was directing you collectively.

It is now time to experience sustained access to that power, for the building of a nation. It is now time to look away from the author of Death, and look within your own hearts.

When you do so, you will discover an entirely new thought system designed especially for you. A thought system based in what you have tried to receive from Satan but cannot, because it does not belong to him. If goodness was in his Mind, he would have expressed it to you. Freedom, Justice and Equality; Life, Liberty and the pursuit of Happiness have been preserved for you within the deepest part of your Self by GOD. You need only collectively look within; access your true thoughts, then instruct your earth to bring them forth!

Prescription I: Learn of earth. Contrary to what Satan has taught you, you are NOT the dust of the earth. Earth is your servant. Therefore, Learn of her; learn how she operates and where her real allegiances are. Learn how to access and receive her strength. Assert your authority over her for your own benefit. You need not concern yourself with whether your former slave-master's children will follow you. Those that will -- Will, and those that will not, Won't.

Prescription II: Forgive your Father. Your father represents your source. If you curse your source, you act as Satan did in the Garden and curse your own nature, and the Nature of GOD your Creator. The perceived abandonments, neglect and hurt, you experienced from him, are mere illusions in the greater scheme of Life. Forgiveness of your father is also the first step to accessing your power. As we said earlier, except for the brief moment of October 16, 1995, you have yet to experience your true thoughts.

Exercise: Get into a quiet area and calm your thoughts for about 5 minutes (longer or shorter if necessary).

When you are calm, think of your father. When thoughts of discomfort about him arise in your Mind, say: "Father, I forgive you; for I know not what you did." Then say: "Father, I thank you for the opportunity to forgive myself."

When a new thought about your father arises in your mind, repeat: "Father, I forgive you; for I know not what you did". Then say: "Father, I thank you for the opportunity to forgive myself."

If you have thoughts of him throughout the day, simply repeat the statements to yourself. Do not concern yourself with how you "feel" about what you are saying. You are communicating with a much higher part of your Self during this exercise. About two times per day should be sufficient to receive the desired freedom. GOD will instruct you when to cease from this exercise. Study Essay #8: The Prodigal Black Male.

Reading 1: <u>The Kybalion</u> by Three Initiates is a small book that outlines seven principles of the universal Laws of Spirituality and Physics. It will help you look within and ponder your source. We advise you to refrain from reading any other material as you study the Principles in this book. Also, carefully meditate on possible universal applications of each principle you study. If you feel comfortable after the first reading, re-read it for enhanced understanding.

Reading 2: Spirit of a Man: Spiritual Transformation of Black Men and the Women Who Love Them by Iyanla Vanzant

This work has been designed especially for the Original Males' Self development. It expands on the spiritual principles found in Kybalion and prescribes mental and spiritual exercises, designed to help you escape the thinking of Satan and access your true thoughts. We advise that you refrain from reading other materials as you study and practice the spiritual exercises contained in this work.

Reading 3: Gospel of John, (King James Version of Bible)

You have an idea of your Identity but have not been convinced fully of the power of your **Self**. This biblical writing will help you to better **apply** the power of your **Self**. While reading this Gospel (Good News) do not cross reference it with any other writings in the Bible or other books. Read ONLY this gospel for now. Do not try to reconcile perceived contradictions within the gospel writing. Simply read and practice "seeing" the true power of your identity.

Prescription III: Listen. Long before you reach this point, you will have already accessed the higher levels of Mind and Spirit. The Voice for your Creator should already be familiar to you by now. You will notice that it is the same Voice that motivated you during the Million Man March—The Voice for the GOD of Your Fathers! He will now lead and guide you into every truth.

Peace and Blessings go with us as we journey together towards true Freedom.

To the Prodigal Female:

The proof of this truth [we speak] is in every person, and it therefore admits of easy investigation by systematic introspection and self-analysis. Let a [Female] radically alter [her] thoughts, and [she] will be astonished at the rapid transformation it will effect in the material conditions of [her] life. [People] imagine that thought can be kept secret, but it cannot.—As a Man Thinketh

In the Garden of Eden, the Serpent spoke to you because you are of the order of **Original Female**; the receiver of truth. Be not deceived; LORD God hates you just as much as he hates your Male. His ultimate aim is to eliminate both of you. When the Serpent told you that "your eyes would be opened and you would be as gods, knowing good and evil", he was telling you that as co-creator, sight allows you to elevate and see GOD as ONE, and produce what you desire.

He told you to go and connect with the **Original Male** and live! As soon as you did, both of your eyes were opened. At present, your eyes have been blinded by the poisoned doctrine of Christianity, and you grope in darkness seeking what is within your soul already. You are currently unaware that you are reproducing after the seed of Satan, who tricks you through his superstitious religion. Receive now a true knowledge of your function. Remember, Jesus identified himself with the Serpent when he said **"As Moses lifted up the Serpent in the wilderness, so the Son of Man must be lifted up".**

If you recall in your studies, the elevated Serpent is the symbol of healing and life. He slips into the Garden unaware and speaks Truth to your soul. Satan's ministers work night and day to trick you into fearing the Serpent and the Truth; because that which you fear, you run away from. You currently fear Truth! In your mind, truth is cursed to the ground and crawls on its belly beneath you. You back-kick the truth as you try and escape it; and truth injures your foot, causing you to stumble and wobble without direction.

However, since you, my sisters, say you are married to Jesus, and Jesus identified with the Serpent, look to the healing process of the elevated Serpent and live!

The Bible has become your prison and you will not find safety within its pages until after you have centered yourself. Do you not see the churches all around you, but instead of heaven following, Death and Hell follows? Do you not notice that you comprise about 98% of the church and your Male is absent? It is by design, my sister. Satan's goal is to murder your Male, mate with you at the Spiritual, Mental and Physical levels, to create Mankind, who is opposite of your nature, but has your power.

Your Male is not present in your church because he is by nature the greatest threat to Satan's world. Thus, you have never known the GOD of your fathers. But thanks are to GOD your creator, an escape mechanism has been provided for you. Carefully consider and practice the prescriptions below.

Prescription I: Forgive every **man** that has been, or is in your life! Males represent the direction of your creativeness and you will create in the direction of your thoughts. Satan has cleverly taught you that your Male is no good for you and has made you to mistrust him. As you create with the mind of mistrust of your Self, you create males that act out of satanic thinking. Generations of misfits and incompetent Males, and confused Females are the resultants. Thus, your power is used against you. By holding ought against men (especially Original Males), you receive in the direction of Self-destruction, thus create to your own demise. This process is perpetuated by the church, which is the Feminine incubator of LORD God (Satan) himself. You have yet to experience your true thoughts or true nature or true abilities. Study Essay #5: Moma'nem just don't Know.

Exercise:

Sit quietly and center your thoughts. When you are fully relaxed, allow thoughts of any man you know, to surface in your mind. You are attempting to look beyond your hurt and see the beautiful Self you are—the co-creator of Man himself!

When any thoughts surface concerning any man (whether good thoughts or bad), Realize his behavior is only indicative of what he has been taught to think; not necessarily his true nature. **Say: "I forgive you for what I thought I did to you"** (Remember, it matters not if the thought is "good" or "bad").

When the next thought surfaces in your mind, repeat the statement: **"I forgive you for what I thought I did to you".** Repeat this as often as necessary to cleanse your Mind. Through the course of the day, when thoughts arise that disturbs you, affirm your function to yourself: **"I AM the creator of Man. I choose to create GOD's Man in my Mind".**

As you begin to hear the Voice for GOD surface in your Mind, he will guide you into ALL truth, and tell you when you no longer are required to practice this exercise.

Reading 1: <u>Acts of Faith</u> by Iyanla Vanzant

It is vital that your thoughts vibrate at the highest levels possible. Thus, a daily reading is necessary to elevate your thinking and re-orient your Mind. We recommend two readings simultaneously for you. **<u>Acts of Faith</u>** (Iyanla Vanzant) is a book containing 365 daily thoughts to meditate on. Read the thought for the day aloud, as soon as possible after you rise for the day. Do not concern yourself with agreeing or disagreeing with the thought. The idea is to get your Mind to rise above Satanic (crazy) thinking.

Reading 2: <u>The Kybalion</u> by The Three Initiates is a small book that outlines seven principles of the universal Laws of Spirituality and Physics. It will help you look within and ponder your source. We advise you to refrain from reading any other spiritual material except **<u>Acts of Faith</u>** as you study the Principles in this book. Also, carefully meditate on possible universal applications of each principle you study. If you feel comfortable after the first reading, re-read it for enhanced understanding.

Reading 3: Standing in the Majesty of Grace by Dr. Keefa Lorraine Weatherspoon, N.D. This work orients in the female energy. The exercises will elevate your thinking above the thoughts of LORD God, and give you a glimpse of your True Thoughts. Practice the exercises therein.

Note: Refraining from reading the Bible during this time is recommended; however, we understand that it may be a difficult task to ask of you. You have invested enormous amounts of brain power in trying to make it work for you; and you may not be ready to have it re-interpreted as yet. It does not matter. We allow Holy Spirit (GOD's Voice and Teacher) to lead and guide you into all truth concerning this matter. If you do not find it difficult to refrain from reading the Bible, do not read it during the studies we prescribe.

The Voice for GOD will now lead and guide you into every Truth. Peace and Blessings follow your footsteps of Love.

To the Citizens:

Your thinking has literally called hell down upon your head. Your atrocities against humanity are so many they fill earth! Through long practice and reliance, you have totally given yourselves over to White Supremacy; which is the thought system of Satan himself! You have become the embodiment of Satan. You will kill for sport, lust or greed. You will Murder your own brother to possess his half; and now the entire universe shuns you, because you are the architect of Death.

Your satanic orientation is so complete that you have evolved your bodies to give you an unobstructed connection to the Mind of Satan himself! You have used his thinking to corrupt the entire planet and created a world of Death and Hell everywhere your foot sets upon the earth. The entire planet groans at your presence; and its groan is not heard by you because the vibration is higher than your mind can elevate, due to your total orientation towards Death. Do you not see that the blood you spill is your own?

Only sustained abandonment of your current thinking and sustained practice in a completely new thought system, will allow you to access the truth of GOD. You may find this to be very difficult for you, since you hold the illusion that you are the owner of the earth through your weapons of Death. You trust in white supremacy because theft seems to bring you all the material pleasures the planet has to offer (just as LORD God had promised). But "Be not deceived, GOD is not mocked: for whatsoever a man soweth, that shall he also reap!" He set the LAW in motion and none can escape the Law. One can only elevate his Mind above it, so its effects go unnoticed.

The entire universe has risen up against you, and has come to the aid of the Original Man; the Owner and cream of the earth; and the entire creation is groaning in pain, waiting to manifest the True Sons of GOD!

Your children are raiding your medicine cabinets looking for anything that will medicate them from the inward pain and emptiness they feel daily. They are rejecting your world wholesale; even to the point of preferring to identify with the Negroes your fathers created.

Unprovoked violence permeates the Land and Suicide is not out of the norm; and the people live in a constant state of fear that results from the wars you wage on the people of the earth; understand that the Death you plan for others will be visited upon you first.

Even the creatures of the planet are rising up against you. There are shark attacks; lion attacks, bear attacks and unprecedented attacks from other animals. The earth is vomiting from her sickness after your mistreatment of her. Tsunamis, tornados, earthquakes, and fires all come to consume you. Even the seasons are behaving in a more exasperated manner. This is your true reward for serving the LORD God of White Supremacy.

However, the GOD of ALL has provided for you a way of escape; that you might not become victims of your own orientation of Death. Study Exhibit 2g: On walking in flesh.

Prescription I: Put the Bible down. You have corrupted it and caused it to be the snare of your own Mind as well as the Mind of all who read it, through materialism. For you, the Bible is nothing more than a validation of White Supremacy, allowing you to rape the earth, murder her owners, and rob her of what she would freely give you anyway. Put the Bible down now.

Reading I: A Course in Miracles in a one-year, daily complete course in intense Mind training. It is in fact, the very thought system of Jesus himself! Your escape from Satanic (crazy) thinking is found therein.

Law, not confusion, is the dominating principle in the universe; justice, not injustice, is the soul and substance of life; and righteousness, not corruption, is the molding and moving force in the spiritual government of the world. This being so, Man has but to right himself to find that the universe is right; and during the process of putting himself right, he will find that as he alters his thoughts towards things and other people, things and other people will alter towards him. --AS A MAN THINKETH

6
REFERENCES

6.1
CASE STUDIES

CASE STUDY #1: The Shameful Little Secret

North Carolina Confronts its History of Forced Sterilization.
By Rebecca Sinderbrand
Newsweek March 28 2005 Issue
(The following are excerpts from the article)

More than 30 other states had eugenics programs during the last century; they were ruled constitutional in Buck v. Bell, a 1924 Supreme Court decision that is still the law of the land. Roughly 70,000 Americans in all were sterilized before the notion fell out of favor, becoming linked in the public's mind to Hitler's Germany after World War II. But North Carolina is the first to appoint a panel to study what to do now for its victims, from health care and counseling to financial reparations.

The state is also considering addressing the shameful practice—finally halted in 1974—in its classrooms. "Some people have tried to pretend it never happened," says North Carolina State Rep. Larry Womble, a reparations activist. "It's painful to remember."

North Carolina's sterilization program zeroed in on welfare recipients. Over the last 15 years of its operation, 99 percent of the victims were women; more than 60 percent were black.

North Carolina Gov. Mike Easley issued an apology to the victims in 2003, and ordered a commission to find concrete ways to make amends. But the state's budget is already a billion dollars in the red, and nothing has happened yet.

To date, no one who underwent forced sterilization in this country has received assistance for it. Some critics say North Carolina is stalling. But others say this state, at least, is trying to own up to its history, and that others should follow suit.

Riddick [who was unknowingly sterilized by the state at age 14] isn't holding her breath. "They're waiting for all of us to die out," she says. "Then the problem disappears." It's little surprise she has scant faith in a state that has done her, and so many others, so wrong. But at least now the ugly secret is out.

CASE STUDY #2: The Parameters of LORD God's Hand-Picked Slave-Descendant Leaders

The author asserts that LORD God has Hand-Picked Slave-Descendant Leaders on both sides of the Argument. This is what makes the plan so ingenious. If one of the Leaders wanders outside of the garden on any issue that might cause the people's eyes to be opened; the LORD uses his slave-descendant leader from the other side of the argument to expose acts of Guilt by the straying slave leader in order to get him back in line.

No one ever sees the 'hidden hand' of the little elf (see Glossary) behind the curtain.

In this Case Study, we look at two vocal Civil Rights Leaders who strayed out of the garden and were quickly brought back in by LORD God's slave leaders.

The First case we will look at is the STRAYING of Jesse Jackson out of the garden of white supremacy into the idea of REPARATIONS:

In an article dated March 24, 2002, USA Today's news writer, James Cox, asked the question, "Why is Reparations bursting back into view? The title of the article is 'Reparations gain legal, Academic Interest'. His conclusion was that Jesse Jackson had caused the issue to resurface and he quotes Jackson as he was taking up the cause saying "All those years of work without wages are the foundations of America's wealth, America must acknowledge its roots in the slavery empire, apologize for it. . .and work on some plan to compensate."

Then suddenly out of nowhere, it seems, came a bombardment of Articles similar to the Article of April 5, 2002, by another hand-picked Reverend:

Worldnetdaily.com posted on April 5, 2002, 'Reparations and Jesse Jackson's illegitimate children'. The Reverend Jesse Lee Peterson accuses Jesse of being desperate due to his fading popularity; "[Jackson] has built a lucrative career on the backs of black Americans, has paved the way for some of his "offspring" to push for reparations, a plot that if hatched will destroy the black community and divide our whole country. . . the two tasks on Jackson's lifetime "To Do" List: 1) Indict contemporary white America for something of which it is not guilty. 2) Demand money, and lots of it. I almost see a single tear roll down Jackson's cheek."

The LORD uses his slave-descendant leader from the other side of the argument to expose acts of Guilt by the straying slave leader in order to get him back in line.

After a slough of articles like these, on the issue of Reparations, Jesse became silent.

Let's look at the case of Reverend Al Sharpton who strayed just slightly away from the garden as he began to steer more black people towards Minister Farrakhan's ideas.

The materialist Reverend Al Sharpton-- a former boy preacher, turned elder statesman of Black America; has always loved the limelight and hung out with celebrities such as Mahalia Jackson, James Brown, Michael Jackson and Don King.

He is loyal only to personal financial gain. Though he is a good tool for LORD God; he gets very little respect from him, if any.

Sharpton's record for attempting to leave the garden was so brief, that it is difficult to detect. For a brief moment, he looked outside the garden and considered leaving and fully embracing Minister Farrakhan's message (which is opposite from his own philosophy). LORD God got whiff of it and decided he would be an excellent tool for replacing the 'radical' leader. The People saw right through it.

LORD God then decided to have Sharpton pretend to join the unity of Millions More Movement order to dissipate it, and turn away any would-be friends to the Negroes.

This is why as soon as the Millions More Movement got started; Reverend Sharpton left the country to go rebuke the President of Mexico, Vicente Fox, for making a TRUE statement about Mexican immigrants working jobs that not even black people would work; implying that they do the jobs that not even the lowest ones in America would do.

Sharpton's protest was a completely staged "event" to turn our Minds away from uniting with Self, and turn them toward Pharaohs' pre-approved activities. Thus, just as the slave-leaders in Moses day, were loyal only to Egypt **(Exodus 5:6-21)** and spoke to the People on behalf of Egypt, so is Sharpton (who is but the loudest of the multitude of slave-leaders) completely loyal to the White Supremacist system of today; and is the mouth of Pharaoh to the People.

So, to turn the People's attention away from the need to look to Self; Reverend Sharpton ran to Mexico to put the Negro's friend in check and along with other Carnal Minds brought the Millions More Movement to a crawl.

Case Study #3: The April Fools March on New Orleans

After the terrible hurricane ravaged the city of New Orleans, the hidden ugly face or racism reared its head in all of its vicious, cruel, and monstrous forms.

The Seers amongst us devised a viable plan that would have caused the People to look inward and rebuild with their own best interests at heart. But the civil rights leaders had another plan. After numerous attempts to get the Civil Rights Leaders to raise our own money and build for self in Louisiana, they finally responded by calling the idea preposterous. The seers wrote the letter below in hopes of sounding the alarm to the uselessness of yet another march in light of the time. We will not re-hash all that occurred, but we place the letter before you. Consider the plan and decide which way would have provided the most desired results:

The following letter was sent to Al Sharpton, Jesse Jackson, Eric Dyson, and all who were organizing the April Fools March on April 1, 2006 for the victims of Hurricane Katrina. This letter was posted weeks before the march:

Would someone please tell Al Sharpton that the civil rights movement is over and that black people have participated in our last march?

What could he possibly have been thinking to call for yet another march? Especially one on April fools day? Is he trying to tell us something?

March after march after march has netted us very little, if anything. Our children continue to die, our people remain in poverty. Throughout this generation, we have marched to bring attention to our plight. Yet the American government turns a "death ear" to us. We should not condemn our posterity to such beggarly measures. We should not sacrifice one more generation of our children on the altar of white supremacy.

We all agree that the circumstances surrounding Katrina was a vivid message of what America thinks of Black people. All of us agree that Katrina should have taught black people a lesson. Sharpton claims that responsibility for the broken levies lies at the feet of the U.S. government. Does he think the neglect was intentional? Or does he think the neglect was by accident? If Americas neglect was on purpose, then there is no need to march because the government already knows their responsibility. If their neglect was an accident, then there is no need to march because forty years of marching has yet to correct their negligent behavior.

Al Sharpton says that his April fool's march is to bring attention to the victims of Katrina. He contends that this march is to say that the victims of Katrina have a right to return. Does he really think a march will accomplish this? Does he think that the powers that be don't know this?

Does he actually believe that his walking through Louisiana will give the victims the right to return? I think that Al Sharpton knows just as we all know that those victims will be in the same condition on April 2nd as they were on April 1st. They are going to march to Louisiana on April 1st and on April 2nd they will march back to wherever they came from. Al Sharpton will walk away with a photo opportunity and supposed status as a civil rights leader. And years later, the Katrina problem will be the same.

Instead of wearing out the soles of our shoes, spending a lot of money getting there, and wasting time; Here is a solution that will solve the problem of the victims of Katrina by allowing them to return in a reasonable time, show Black people their real, GOD-given power, and further strengthen our resolve for independence:

Meet with Minister Farrakhan, who black people trust. Initiate a campaign asking all black families to donate one dollar per family member by March 31st. You will raise an estimated 30 million dollars. Take that 30 million dollars and buy equipment and materials. Hire Black contractors who are desperately in need of work. Then march down to Louisiana on April 1st and truly assert your right to return by re-building on your own land using your own money, your own labor, and your own supplies. This will empower the people to truly assert a right to return. Black people will quickly contribute to the 'Katrina right to return AND rebuild' march because we will see an IMMEDIATE result.

We will then, learn to work together, learn to trust each other, and learn to build for ourselves. America and the world will learn to take us seriously when we say we are moving to ACTION. This way, we won't be made April fools on April 1st by another useless march.

I and my family are sending $5 to the disaster relief fund with a letter saying this is towards the 'Katrina victims right to return AND REBUILD' Fund.

If my language appears too harsh, it is because I am trying to awake you to the time and the appropriate action for the time.

My family and I were given the name of an account by a Millions More Movement representative in which to place our funds via Paypal, but after many months the funds were never claimed by anyone. Our plan was never mentioned by anyone.

As most Seers are already aware, the LORD God has placed his citizens in very strategic positions and they simply ignore the voice of the righteous ones 'crying in the wilderness'.

Bill Cosby participated in the march but was rebuked by the slave-leaders for asking the people to look to Self and take responsibility for themselves.

So at the writing of this book (two years later), most of the families who participated in the march are still relatively homeless. The government finally sent trailer homes into the city but had 'legitimate' reasons why the families were barred from occupying them. And whenever there is an act of racism, the useless marches continue.

Case Study #4: The rush to appeal to 'Missie' – Affirmative Action 'crisis' in Michigan

During the 1960's a national policy was put in place, designed to address the issue that black males were discriminated against in hiring. Known as "Affirmative Action", the theory behind the policy was that companies should take "affirmative steps" to hire black males into the mainstream of American Society. Over the decades, the only "mainstream" black males saw were main-streams leading to the fringes of American society and prison.

It was revealed that white women had become the largest recipients of Affirmative Action, and black females the second largest. Thus once again a program designed to address black males, was only a lie to deceive him and give him a false hope of integration.

In 2003, a young white woman (Jennifer Gratz) was denied acceptance into the University of Michigan as a result of the university's affirmative action policy. It was shown that several blacks who scored lower on the entrance exams were admitted. Jennifer drew the unlucky straw and was denied admittance.

The denial of Jennifer into the university outraged Michigan's white communities. A petition was floated to put the issue of Affirmative Action on the ballot for a vote. Surprising, to black people (who assumed affirmative action was a settled matter), Proposal 2 was put on the ballot.

The polls clearly showed that whites wanted to do away with affirmative action by a 3 to 1 margin. In addition, the "victim" Jennifer Gratz, gained the support of a black conservative (Ward Connerly) who gave her position an air of moral authority, and who also had a reputation for helping to do away with affirmative action laws across the country.

As Election Day approached, the black civil rights leaders sprung into action! Reverend Wendell Anthony, the Detroit NAACP president even dug into his bag of tricks and invoked building "Jeremiah's wall of protection" around affirmative action. Almost every black church in Michigan got in on the act and pushed their people to vote in record numbers! Black radio, television, and newspapers across the state, frantically saturated us with self-produced political ads demonizing Connelly. Even the major media in Detroit all ran editorials supporting affirmative action.

The strategy of the civil rights leaders was to saturate the airways so thoroughly that no opinion to the contrary to their misguided plan would be heard. The second part of their strategy was to argue in a politically expedient manner and appeal to white women to maintain affirmative action since they were the biggest recipients of it.

This strategy required that black males be silenced since their voice would alert the white population that the civil rights leaders were trying to stay in the house by hiding under the skirt of the white woman.

Although Jennifer Gratz (a white woman) was the real power and organizer behind the push to eliminate affirmative action, the civil rights leaders knew they could not afford to launch a villainous attack against their Masters' woman. Fortunately for them, an equally silly slave-leader was working along side her. Ward Connerly was the perfect target! He was black. He was male, and he was expendable—he was safe! The Negro leaders not ONCE referred to Jennifer Gratz in any derogatory manner, but there was no limit on the choice names they had reserved for the black male who sided with her.

The real question that lay before Michigan had nothing to do with black people. The real question was whether 'Missie' felt that she could now trust her white man to do right by her in the job market. It was a very exciting time for the hand-picked, slave-leaders on both sides of the argument. Whichever slave-leader could convince 'Missie' of the legitimacy of his argument regarding the heart of the 'massa' would have future standing with 'massa'.

Once again, an opportunity to respond rather than react passed the people by. Missie voted Affirmative Action down. Black people cried a bit and went back to Sleep; awaiting the next crisis. This author made great efforts to find an ear who would HEAR during this time. Following is an email discussion between your author and Dr. Ronald Walters.

On 10/30/06, Dr. Fleming wrote:

Mildred Gaddis and her cohorts are stumped on how to address these issues regarding Proposal 2. Have any suggestions?

On 10/30/06, Ronald Walters wrote:

The fact that blacks still experience poverty, black males are being locked up, etc. are not the fault of Affirmative Action. It was never meant to be a poverty program, or an anti-criminal oppression program, or anything else, other than a remedy in Jobs, education and contracts for past discrimination.

To use it as a scape-goat for the all of the ills of blacks is insane. Although many white women have been the main beneficiary of Affirmative Action, blacks have also benefited – which is where a large part of our middle class has come from. So, my major recommendation would be, rather than to become puzzled over the hype of anti-affirmative action rhetoric, organize to defend it.

Ron Walters

On 10/31/06, Dr. Fleming wrote:

Dear Mr. Ron Walters:

Thanks for your prompt reply to my letter. This indeed is a strategic time in history, but let's be intellectually honest here. Haven't we been here before? Would you deny the truth of all the reports released *this year, 2006,* citing the deplorable condition of black men at every level of this society? To refresh your memory, I refer you specifically to the Urban League report, the Princeton report, The Black Enterprise report and the Tavis Smiley report. All of them suggest that even *WITH 30 YEARS OF AFFIRMATIVE ACTION*, Black men have seen virtually no progress, but have indeed, RE-GRESSED.

In fact, it is YOUR own argument that white women benefit most from affirmative action! Doesn't that shed any light in your mind as to the *intent* of white men to affirm white women, and continue to exclude black men and women?

And you have the nerve to ask *US, the despised and rejected black man, and his destitute and dependent black woman,* to defend Affirmative Action for everyone else? Don't the warnings of Carter G. Woodson, the Honorable Elijah Muhammad and the Honorable Marcus Garvey mean anything to you people?

Your arguments on behalf of this glaringly bankrupt policy shows how little you respect our minds, reasoning faculties and ability to plan and build for ourselves. And those few of us who *have* been given a job or a contract as a result of Affirmative Action do not even register on the Richter Scale in the scheme of societal development; and certainly we as a people have not advanced in society, but have indeed taken enormous steps backward in all strata of society, with 30 years of Affirmative Action in place as we speak.

Does it not dawn on your mind that it's a WHITE WOMAN (Jennifer Gratz) who wants to end the Affirmative Action law? She doesn't seem afraid of losing anything.

You contend that Affirmative Action was designed '*as a remedy for [discrimination in] jobs, contracts, and education'. In that assessment, we agree. ***However, where then are the jobs?*** Black men are 40% perpetually under-employed! Our employment-eligible young men are close to *70%* *perpetually* *unemployed* and no longer even count in the employment statistics!

Where are the contracts? Even as late as today we find widespread INTENTIONAL and gross refusal of lenders and government to award any significant loans or contracts to our fledgling businesses, in spite of this *"remedy".*

Where is the education? More black men are wards of the state criminal justice system than there are in college, and those of us who have been "educated" seem powerless and useless to even BEGIN turning the tide!

What evidence can you bring forth that would suggest that anything would change with more of the same? ***So indeed, the remedy has failed, and has done nothing but waste our precious time!** *

You are correct in your assessment that black men do fill the jails due to poverty. You are also correct in your assessment that Affirmative Action was designed to speak to the poverty that resulted from past discrimination of qualified individuals; however, The simple question that escapes your mind is: WHY the continued POVERTY while the supposed remedy is in place? Why has our condition worsened? These fundamental questions MUST be addressed.

I contend, my brother that the reason for our poverty is the continued insistence by black leaders that someone other than us is responsible for our development and prosperity. We'd rather continue to beg another man to share HIS wealth, in spite of his 30 year refusal to do so.

***That course is NOT the course of men, but is the resolve of slaves*.** The facts, mathematical calculations, social data, and history suggest that another course of action, ON OUR PART, is in order. The present strategy of trying to remedy our condition by invoking a law that has clearly been ignored and circumvented over the past 30 years, begs the question!

Finally, regarding the black middle class that you speak of; Like the Jews in Germany during the prelude to World War II, *the "black middle class" is on the same death march as the rest of the people.*

I believe that Michigan should be the starting point for a national debate among US regarding a proper course of action in this matter. For the sake of my three sons, and the sons of men like me, I ask you to join with me and encourage those having access to black media to force a real debate, rather than try and force this lock-step, knee-jerk, reactionary political posturing that we presently are experiencing. The spirit of our ancestors demands it!

Your brother in the work of our continued development as a people.

Dr. Alonzo R. Fleming

(The author realizes that his words are cutting, but we are in need of an operation. Nevertheless, that was the last time we heard from Dr. Walters)

CASE STUDY #5: The Children of Civil Rights make Obeisance to the King of Death

It is the assertion of the DA that Dr. Martin Luther King was a Serpent in the garden sent to show the slave-masters' children their character and contents of their hearts rather than to free the Minds of slave-descendants.

Hidden in the Montgomery Bus Boycott, was the power of looking to Self. Its results were the same as in Eden. The LORD God's world depended on the Original Man's Mind looking to him. LORD God can only survive as long as the Male and Female think he is the source of their life. Thus he invests enormous amounts of energy to keep himself in the forefront of the Original Mans Mind. One need only listen to "black-talk radio," or read "black media" to see that Negroes' daily conversation revolves around white supremacy and how to fight it. If the Negro for one day would turn his thoughts away from white supremacy, it would disappear.

During the Montgomery bus boycott, Negroes, for an entire year, decided that if they could not ride the buses like anyone else, they would not ride at all.

At first, LORD God instructed his people to appear to ignore the Negro to see what he would do. As time went on, the Negroes became more determined to make the point—no fairness, no riding.

Suddenly, a Serpent entered the situation and floated the idea of Negroes pooling their monies and purchasing their own buses. Remember, LORD God cannot live without the Negro. The idea of Negroes looking within, spells LORD Gods' demise. He must keep the Negro thinking about him; at the same time, LORD God cannot afford to allow the Negro to ever think he was equal with his children.

Suddenly (or so it seemed), the term "integration" entered the movement and Satan turned the taste of the forbidden fruit into the illusion that Satan's children were inviting Negroes "Up" to sit with them as "almost equals". From that time to this, the Negroes' thinking has been carefully cultivated to believe that their ultimate objective is equality in the house of Satan as honorary equals.

When Adam finally came out of hiding and answered the LORD of the garden, it represented leaving the Self and returning to the slavery of Satanic thinking. This in effect was equivalent to getting back on the Montgomery buses after seeing their own power.

Dr. King warned against his methods being high-jacked and turned into incremental, unprogressive temper tantrums instead of focused and well planned movements with 'MEASURABLE OUTCOMES'. However, Dr. King may have not been aware of who really rules America. Every act of Satan only furthers the Mind of White Supremacy.

This case study consists of excerpts from a Democracy Now interview and a news article which outlines the days leading to the funeral of Mrs. Coretta Scott King. It's purpose is to show that 40 years later, the children of the civil rights movement made obeisance to their 'CONSTANT OPPRESSORS' while silencing their 'UNCLE' and 'TRUE FRIEND'

Long time activist and (from all accounts of his deeds towards King and the King family after King's death) the true best friend of Dr. King; Harry Belafonte was at first invited to speak at the funeral of Mrs. Coretta Scott King on February 7, 2006. However, once the President of the United States, President Bush, decided to be present at the funeral and speak; the invitation to Harry Belafonte was mysteriously revoked.

Earlier in the year, at a rally with President Hugo Chavez, who offered to send ALL AND ANY RESOURCES AVAILABLE to the victims of Hurricane Katrina, Harry Belafonte made this comment about President Bush: "And no matter what the greatest tyrant in the world, the greatest terrorist in the world, George W. Bush, says; We're here to tell you that not hundreds, not thousands, but millions of the American people support your (r)evolution, support your ideas, and we are here to express our solidarity with you!"

According to Democracy Now, Belafonte then returned to the United States and spoke at a University and said, "Bush has led us into a dishonorable war that has caused the deaths of [then] tens of thousands of people . . . What is the difference between that terrorist and other terrorists?"

DID HARRY BELAFONTE LIE? IF HE SPOKE THE TRUTH, THEN WHY WAS THE HEAD OF TRUTH BRUISED AND THE LIAR (BUSH) GIVEN A VOICE?

According to a New York Times article, one of the first to speak at Mrs. King's funeral was President Bush.

DV Republic Article reprinted by permission.

Bush's Attendance at the Coretta Scott King funeral disinvites Harry Belafonte

Posted | February 11, 2006 06:35 AM

The television broadcast of Coretta Scott King funeral would often cut to famous faces in attendance. One famous face long associated with Dr. King was missing: Harry Belafonte. This left most of us wondering, where's Harry? Reliable sources have told DV Republic that human rights champion, Harry Belafonte, was disinvited from Coretta Scott King's funeral because of the attendance of President George W. Bush.

Harry Belafonte has been an outspoken critic of the Bush Administration, especially in recent weeks, and apparently was dis-invited in deference to Bush's comfort (although several speakers did direct criticism at Bush during their remarks).

There is both irony and outrage in this decision, because Harry Belafonte was one of the first celebrities to join forces with Dr. King. He not only contributed his celebrity to the cause, he marched shoulder to shoulder with Dr. King, and provided critical financial support during the movement and after King's assassination.

There is no doubt both Dr. Martin Luther King, Jr. and Coretta Scott King would be appalled by this treatment of their long time friend and supporter.

The Black Filmmaker Foundation is one of the many organizations that have received indispensable support from Harry Belafonte (he was a key supporter of the launch of the DV Republic online community). We are outraged and regard this insult as a symptomatic of a betrayal of the still unfinished work of Dr. King.

THE TRUE SYMPTOMS OF OUR PRESENT THINKING CAUSES US TO BETRAY ALL OF OUR FRIENDS AND REMAIN BEHOLDEN TO THE ENEMY OF OUR SOULS.

In an interview with Democracy now, Harry Belafonte concluded that being Black-Listed meant he was doing something right.

THE DA DECLARES THAT IF YOU ARE NOT ON THIS PRESENT WORLD'S BLACK-LIST, THEN YOU ARE SATANICALLY INCLINED. WORK HARDER (ON YOUR MIND) TO BECOME BLACK-LISTED (RIGHTEOUS)!

Feel the fear (realize that it is a trained response from LORD God) and Do it Anyway!

Our Conclusion, the descendants of slaves will never be free until we GET OFF OUR KNEES (See Glossary)!

6.3
ESSAYS

Essay #1: The Musings of a Cynical Black Boy

Urban League's Annual Death Report
The cynical musings of an ignored black boy in America

March 30, 2006

Here we go again. If insanity is defined as doing the same thing repeatedly and expecting a different result, then the Civil Rights beggars have cornered the market on insanity.

The Urban League released its 2006 State of Black America report, and yep, you guessed it! Black people are in worst condition than the last report, and the report before that, and the report before that, and . . . well you get the picture. On every front, Black America is sinking deeper and deeper into the abyss of ignorance, poverty and death. Especially black boys . . . I mean men. These knuckleheads actually think they said something that wasn't already known. They wax eloquent in stating the obvious. Boy, ignorance truly is bliss. -- Oh, I forgot. I'm the ignorant one here.

The NUL (Like Null?) report comes on the heels of an article that outlined the deplorable and ever worsening condition of black men in America . . . Hey, haven't I heard that before? Some time during the early 90's? Yeah, I thought so. The more things change, the more they stay the same. The NUL report also comes on the heels of Tavis Smiley's Covenant report, outlining the same despicable facts. And if that ain't enough for you, it comes on the heels of America's blatant contempt and disregard for black people, as seen through the eyes of a camera during Hurricane Katrina. Seems America is always getting caught on tape beating us, killing us, neglecting us....hmmm. Maybe I should take a hint. Hush up Kenye West! Bush loves black people.

The Urban League could have saved itself precious funds and us precious time, by simply posting a statement on its web site that reads **"Report on Black America: Same condition, Different day"**. Heck they can even release the 2007 report at the same time by simply saying it twice. Now that's what I call progress in America!

Something's wrong here. Aren't we better educated? Don't we get to live and go where we want? Why, just yesterday I drank some water from the same fountain as a white man. I even sat on a toilet with a white guy in the next stall! And if that doesn't take the cake, I got stopped for driving while black and the cops didn't even beat me after searching my menacing, uninsured family van. Surely I have arrived! Who would have thunk it 50 years ago? I should feel blessed. Never mind the man behind the curtain digging that pit my son just fell in.

Are we not fully American at this late date in history? How could it be that when you think of poor, diseased, decadent, and criminal; black men come to mind? What gives here?

I feel embarrassed and ashamed for not being able to take care of my wife and sons. I want to go hide under a rock (Better yet, throw one) when I read their "scholarly" reports and analysis. Not because of my dire condition, but because in spite of my ever worsening lot, and though I simply do not want Americanism anymore, I'm still convinced that all I need do is vote more, march more -- Let the civil rights leaders beg on my behalf, and maybe one day . . . oh, say 400 years from now, America will do justice by me as a black boy. I'll tell ya, it will sure feel good lying in that grave with all that American freedom, justice and equality.

But I know these N***as don't give a damn about me. I'm only a statistic they use to line their pockets on my behalf. I'm never invited to speak at their forums and pompous sounding symposiums. When I try to tell them what I REALLY want, it is they who silence my voice.

Thank God for Budweiser -- Nothing like a good ole pain killer. It's cheap and it works. Why, under the influence of the King of beers, I even fancy myself as a man, building my own nation so my boys can grow up without the foot of white supremacy on their necks; but alas, the Bud wears off and I have to look them in the eye and explain why I can't seem to provide for them even with all my 'knowledge' degrees . . . I know, More Bud! Let the good times roll baby!

Are we not Men? Did God stop passing out brains when he got to us? I feel shortchanged by da lawd. Maybe that's the first miracle these churches on every corner should pray for. **"Dear God, please give this wretched black man a brain so he can graciously accept his lot".** Maybe I will then come to church to better prepare for my inevitable early demise. Lets see . . . What way should I choose to make my early departure? Thank God for freedom of choice. Hey, if nothing else, we know how to make a good intro and exit . . . hmmm . . . Cancer, Suicide, HIV, Prison? I know! I'll follow in my fathers' footsteps and get myself murdered! Why, it's a family tradition -- A right of passage. Heck, my uncle went that way, my cousin, and many of my childhood friends. If being murdered is good enough for them, then it's good enough for me. Who needs to live long and see his grandsons get the same ass kicking anyway?

Someone help me rap my little brain around these civil rights beggars' thinking; They see the conditions worsening year after year, through democrat and republican administrations, liberal and conservative ideologies, thousands of black politicians, churches and other "NOT-for-profits" (There is something very familiar about that word), yet they recommend the same old tired remedy. "Please massa, we's needs mo help to raise r chiren. Massa you know that if-n we be better, all of America be better". Massa then throws them a crumb; they peel the lions share off the top of the crumb, and then use the rest to hire a few ladies in their None-profit organizations. It never dawns on their mind that just maybe the condition was planned by the very system they beg from. Or maybe they have resigned themselves to participate in my demise in this strange way. Uh oh, the bud must be wearing off because I'm thinking too much. More beer please!

I'm going to write a letter first thing in the morning to all these civil rights profiteers . . . I mean leaders. Either you beg better on my behalf or I'm going to fire you and find someone with stronger knees and better begging skills. Heck, if I must, I will do my own begging.

Maybe then I can feed my family too by begging calloused white America to help me. After all, who wants to go through the trouble of building a society of his own? A society that validates him and his children, rather than reduce them to generational begging and pleading. This sounds like a good place to quote the declaration of independence, but I defer.

Dr. Alonzo Fleming Jr

Essay #2: Ten Things Black Males Will Not Say

1. THERE IS NO ENVIRONMENT OF SAFETY FOR ME!
2. I OFTEN FEEL THE SAME WAY AS 33 YEAR OLD BRIAN NICHOLS!
3. I OFTEN WISH WHITE PEOPLE WOULD LEAVE THE PLANET!
4. I DON'T ATTEND CHURCH BECAUSE THE PREACHER DOESN'T KNOW WHAT THE HELL HE'S TALKING ABOUT!
5. RELIGION, DRUGS, AND ALCOHOL ARE USED TO SEDATE ME!
6. MY FEMALE WILL NEVER RESPECT ME!
7. CHRISTIANITY IS A SLAVE RELIGION DESIGNED TO CRUSH MY NATURE!
8. I THINK ABOUT GOD MORE THAN ANYBODY ON THE PLANET!
9. I WANT TO TRY MY HAND AT NATION BUILDING!
10. I LOVE LOUIS FARRAKHAN!

Essay #3: There is No Such thing as a Black Union

March 2006

One of February's finales is the State of the Black Union which is held by Tavis Smiley each year. This year's forum was momentous because the Covenant with Black America had been completed and was now in print. But there was still a question as to who Black America was making this Covenant with . . .

As each leader spoke, the question in my mind and apparently in the mind of many other Black Brothers and Sisters was "When are we going to stop quoting statistics comparing ourselves to white people, and build without regard to this government or its racist ideology?"

Many comments would begin with an independent focus but would end with us being back at the door of our constant oppressor asking for justice.

Finally, Minister Farrakhan spoke and turned the place out. The people greeted his words with a sense of "FINALLY, SOMEBODY SPEAKS WHAT'S IN OUR HEARTS!" Meanwhile the other leaders, including Tavis Smiley, leaned back, folded their arms, or developed a very solemn demeanor about them. Afterwards, Tavis took twenty minutes 'trying to clarify' what the Minister had said. And then each leader took turns disagreeing with the truth of his words. The enthusiasm I had been feeling -- left me like a deflating balloon.

The State of the Black Union is weak. It is weak because it keeps looking to the same liar, deceiver and oppressor — the United States government -- for its rights. Black leaders keep trying to change the leper's spots. History has proven that just as a leper cannot change his spots, the American government will not change her ways.

The State of the Black Union will never be strong or even BE, until Black leaders get off their knees begging at the feet of the American government's political giant. Black people claim to believe in GOD, but they do not believe in a true and living GOD or a universal spirit. They show by their actions and words that they think the beast (the spirit of anti-Christ) that rules the world from the American government is God. Much of our disbelief comes from the false god of White Supremacy we were taught to worship in church.

Get off your knees and show and prove that a true God exists. The American educational system is bankrupt so stop trying to say 'we just need more education'. Why do you keep trying to force our kids to go to a failing system that only serves to ruin their minds, spirits, and bodies.

Get up and build your own institutions. Look to GOD and each other for the funds. Ask people like Cornell West[78] and brilliant professors and educators to stop plundering their talents on a failing educational system and a dying world. Perhaps if we show that we believe in GOD by building our own, our brilliant minds will begin giving their talents to their own. Look to GOD and be Courageous!

Cherice Fleming

---

[78] Special thanks to Dr. West for being the only black leader at the 2006 forum to respond to our funding request to build a school for black boys. The venture did not develop but his small effort ripples into the future even now.

Essay #4: 'First Black-Gasms'- A little levity for the Soul.

As this work is being published, the whole of black America is experiencing "First Black-Gasms". First Black-Gasms are the feelings black people experience when whites do something in the interest of white supremacy, and black people think that it's also in their own best interest. Symptoms include the sudden onset of amnesia concerning the state of black America; and the acute denial that there is a race problem in America that requires addressing. Symptoms also include the false belief that whites have finally done something that will at last benefit the whole of America without regard to race; and the uncontrollable urge to hold hands in a unity circle and sing "Kumbi ya", or "We shall overcome".

Blacks experienced multiple 'First Black-Gasms' during the presidency of Bill Clinton. The euphoria and abandonment of reason was so prevalent that Clinton was called "the first black president". (Being the first black this or the first black that is the easiest way to experience a 'First Black-Gasm'). People with white skin also experience 'First Black-Gasms', howbeit not to the degree that blacks do. There are many cases where blacks experience the Gasms and whites do not. Take for example when Marcus Garvey gave the black Man pride when he said: "Up you mighty race; you can accomplish what you will!" While blacks experienced multiple 'First Black-Gasms', they were to the chagrin of whites who experienced none.

Whites experience minor 'First Black-Gasms' when they see that blacks appreciate any useless symbol or morsel being thrown to them after 450 years. Whites experience the greatest 'First Black-Gasms' when they hear misguided black leaders trumpet the mantra: "Whatever is good for white America must also be good for us too". When the supremacist hears this, he shakes uncontrollably, knowing that white supremacy still resides safely in the Mind of the black Man. Take for example the recent Iowa caucus for the presidency of the United States.

Lest you think this is far fetched, we remind you that this is a country that murdered and enslaved our great grandparents, lynched our grandparents, kept our fathers steeped in ignorance, and currently imprison our sons so fast that it cannot build prisons fast enough and refuse to even discuss repairing the damage.

Need we remind you that a 2007 follow-up report on the 1968 Kerner Commission Report[79] indicated that in fact there are still two Americas, one black and hopelessly locked in poverty and despair, the other white and sinking if it does not do something about the 40 or so million useless Negroes in her midst?

---

[79] See page 80 for more details on the Report.

Would anyone dare suggest that one man winning a relatively minor election on behalf of white America, signals a change in the goals and objectives of white supremacy?

In case you have forgotten, 2007 saw the Jena six; countless police murders, and blacks have yet to recover from the ravages of Hurricane Katrina which rained down Black Water Mercenaries who joined white police officers in unleashing brutal hatred on every black male in harms way. Yet extreme 'First Black-Gasms' prevail in America simply because Iowans selected a man with black skin to champion the cause of white supremacy around the world. How silly and misguided can the black male and female be?

Farrakhan is the litmus test of white supremacy whenever a Prodigal male wants to lead. He is first required to repudiate Louis Farrakhan. The reason for the litmus test is because Minister Farrakhan represents the Prodigal male's desire to return home!

Negroes use their media platforms to boldly renounce all Prodigals who do not desire to vote for the citizens' imitator. Outside of a brief 'First Black-Gasm', what do the Negroes expect from the imitator if he becomes the leader of the strange country? Why do they think that he, being one man, can fix the crumbling structure of an entire country when their own 90% Negro city governments cannot fix their own crumbling structures?

Who is financing the imitator? Do the Negroes know that the imitator has been advised by his major financiers not to provide any relief for housing foreclosures? Do the Negroes know anything about the plans of the imitator outside of his skin color?

The Negroes claim to be supporting the imitator because he can fix the country's problems. What will the Negroes do to him when he fails? Consider what the Negroes do to the members of their own city governments (like the Mayor of Detroit) when errors are made. What will the citizens do to the imitator and the Negroes when he fails? Be instructed.

Essay #5: Moma'nem Just Don't Know

In the book of **Matthew 2:17–18** it says then was fulfilled that which was spoken by Jeremy the prophet, saying, ***In Rama was there a voice heard, lamentation, and weeping, and great mourning, Rachel weeping for her children, and would not be comforted, because they are not.***

In the context of scripture, Herod[80] had targeted the boys for slaughter in order to insure that a messiah would not be raised up that would deliver those people from the oppressors of their day.

The only difference between their day and our day is that using the method credited to the infamous Willie Lynch, American slave-masters placed an enemy Thought in our Minds. So while many movies of our day depict the Biblical Herod as an insane man who destroyed young male children; the culprit of our day is hidden after placing insane thoughts into our Minds that have caused us to destroy our own household and children.

DON'T BE ANGRY WITH ME FOR SAYING THIS. I am not saying this to accuse you. I am saying this to alert you, to shake you, to mentally slap your mind into an awareness of what is really going on around you. Remember, like the prodigal on his way home, you are still insane. Tares were sown into your Mind while you were in the strange country, and now we must work to remove those tares.

I have always thought of my mother as a STRONG woman because of the things she protected me from. And there are some things that she protected me from that I am eternally grateful to her for, even until this day.

But as the years have passed, I have also come to understand that my mother in many ways misinterpreted what it meant to be a STRONG woman and therefore she passed that misinterpretation on to me. I have since had to learn how to separate the wheat from the tares. And as the saying goes "eat the meat, and throw the bones away."

Let's analyze some of the <u>definitions of strength</u> that were passed on to us as young females that we often pass on to our daughters. We think these philosophies are STRENGTH but they are actually DEATH posing as STRENGTH -- that is tares posing as wheat and until now the wheat and the tares have grown together but today, we will begin the process of separating the wheat from the tares:

---

[80] This accusation is according to the Biblical writers, though there is no historical record. The historian, who hated Herod most, never mentions it. Herod actually did many wonderful acts for his countrymen. He displeased the High Priests of his day which may be why he was credited with such a diabolical act.

1. Girl, get your education, so you don't have to depend on NO Man. Because that man will leave you high and dry with a bunch of babies and then what will you have to depend on?
2. Girl, all men are dogs, they can't help it – if you put it in front of them – they'll take it.
3. Girl, don't give a man your heart, marry a man who loves you. That way he can't make no fool of you, you can make a fool out of him and believe me – he will worship the ground you walk on.

Tare #1. at face value, rings true and seems to be preparing you to face the realities of life. But <u>if it's really the truth</u>, then what's the purpose of having a man if you can't depend on him. And if you can't depend on him, then is he really a man? And if he is not a man, then what is he? A boy. Well, then, how did he come of age and still remain a boy? . . .

Tare #2. "All Men are Dogs!" The Rites of Passage is a ritual of celebration a boy goes through to become a man. It is denoted by the badge of discipline. The reason that many of our Black Leaders have lost the ability to be as effective as they could be in the world is due to their lack of sexual discipline. But it begs to question once again – who is responsible for teaching our young men discipline. And how will they ever live up to those principles of discipline when our expectations of them are so low.

Tare #3. "Never give a man your Heart!" First of all, marriage is supposed to be a partnership – not a tug of war of he who loves less wins. We ought to be trying to outlove each other rather than underlove each other. This tare sets the relationship up to be sabotaged before it ever starts out.

Secondly, boys and girls play games with each others hearts. Mature Males and Females (who unite in Mind to become Man) build families and protect each others heart. So let's revise these sayings so that we may begin to plant wheat rather than tares:

#1 Girl, educate your mind about GOD, your purpose in this world, and the history of this planet. This way, when GOD sends your male to you – you will be a good partner to him because Two are better than one; because they have a good reward for their labor. For if they fall, the one will lift up his fellow: but woe to him that is alone when he falleth; for he hath not another to help him up. Again, if two lie together, then they have heat: but how can one be warm alone? And if one prevail against him, two shall withstand him; and a threefold cord (family) is not quickly broken. Ecclesiastes chapter 4.

#2 Girl, most if not all males are visual creatures – they are attracted to a female by what they see while most if not all females are attracted to males by what we hear and how they make us feel. Study the principles of Gender. This is one of the differences between the nature of male and female energies.

So attire and carry yourself in such a way as to attract a mature male rather than a boy. Boys are looking for somewhere to play while mature males are looking for someone they can place their trust in. A boy may lay and play. But a mature male will work, build, lay and stay.

#3 Girl, choose wisely the brother you decide to give your heart to. A boy's playful nature may cause him to break your heart. But if you give your heart to the male that GOD prepares for you, you may experience some growing pain, but throughout your life, you will experience great gain.

It has been said, "that the hand that rocks the cradle rules the world". So it goes without saying that if you poison the hand that rocks the cradle then you poison the world.

Sisters, we cannot change the past. But in order to move forward, and become the light of the world -- we must forgive the past, change the present by changing our Minds, and build a glorious future.

The next time we get on our knees or pray in our spirit. Let us remember the following items:

#1. The psychological scars that were passed down in us from absentee fathers and the males in our lives: hurt, pain, anger, and mistrust of black males by black females comes all the way down from slavery when our males failed to protect us from the onslaught of rape of our Minds, Bodies, and our Children. If we could forgive the perpetrators of these crimes and their children, surely we can forgive our own.

#2. We must forgive our mothers for the ideas of strength that they gave us. These were given to them and so on and so forth but were actually tares. They did the best they could with the tools they were given. Let us now beat our swords into plow sheds and study war no more. This means we will begin to build rather than destroy our males.

#3 We must wake up each morning and as we go to wash up. Look in the mirror and forgive ourselves for our past mistakes. For the damage we caused to our children and our males and pledge to ourselves that we will become the best mothers, wives, sisters, aunts, and grandmothers that we can be. "I am born again today. Today is a new day that I begin again anew."

Lastly, let us begin to study our children. As we begin to study our children, we will begin to understand the insanity that WE placed in them. Ask Holy Spirit (Higher Self) to guide you and give you patience in leading your children out of insanity as Holy Spirit leads you and me out of insanity.

Be patient with yourself and be patient with your children. And you will begin to see a change. It comes slowly at first, but sisters, I am with you on this journey and I am telling you what I have experienced and am still experiencing. If you follow the outline I am giving you. A positive change will begin to come. This will begin your journey back to becoming a Lady of Virtue Expressed (L.O.V.E).

Much Love.

Mama Cherice Fleming

Essay #6: Garden of White Supremacy

As I anxiously await the end of the old world and the beginning of the new, I am fascinated at how ***most*** *religious and spiritual groups avoid the subject of White Supremacy.* In the Garden of White Supremacy, the knowledge of that which would overthrow White Supremacy is the Forbidden Fruit. So everybody walks around in the Garden pretending not to see the tree of knowledge of Good and Evil standing smack dab in the middle of the Garden.

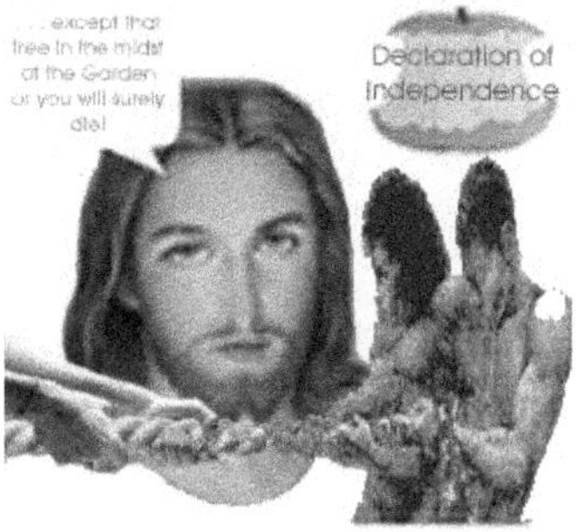

Submission to the lord of the Garden is submission to White Supremacy. Revelations 13:17 says, "And that no man might buy or sell, save he that had the mark, or the name of the beast, or the number of his name." I have come to believe that the mark of the beast is submission to White Supremacy.

I've observed "spiritual" black people who were once very conscious of the suffering of their people. But as they rise into the higher ranks of success, they begin to change their message as though the terrible condition of black people no longer exists. Their lingo becomes 'UNIVERSAL' in its application before it can even heal their own LITTLE WORLD. I mean let's look at the basics. Anybody with common sense would first clean around their own front door before they try to clean around somebody else's. Yet on a deeper level, I know that as black people rise to the top, where the spiritual wickedness of this world resides, they must accept the mark of the beast in order to buy and sell. And that is exactly what they do! So everybody walks around in the Garden pretending not to see the tree of knowledge of Good and Evil standing smack dab in the middle of the Garden.

We recently did work for a popular black client who demonstrated this proposition well. This client was willing to accept whatever those who represent White Supremacy did to her, even when they did her evil intentionally. We gave her our very best work, yet when we did something to offend her unintentionally; she was quick to cut us off. *So black leaders walk around in the Garden accepting all kinds of evil from their lord saying things under their breath like, "Oh, that's just how it is" or "Racism will always be here so we might as well accept it". So as it stands, you just go along to get along. Yet, you will murder your brother for little or nothing. You are blind leaders of the blind!*

Most black people agree that the American form of generational slavery over 400 years was the most demonic and barbaric system ever devised. Psychologists agree that any habitual act performed over time becomes an ingrained habit. Some have gone as far as to say that the DNA becomes altered to adjust to the new situation.

Today, most people on the planet would agree that there is a psychotic relationship between the black and white race. But everybody walks around quietly, pretending not to see that tree of knowledge of Good and Evil standing smack dab in the middle of the Garden.

The Lord of the Garden has agreed that we can all be happy with our nakedness if we just worship him and ignore that tree in the midst of the garden. He knows that in the day that we eat of it, we shall not surely die! In fact, if we are walking around in the Garden without knowledge OF GOOD OR EVIL, are we really alive? (Now while your mind is accusing me of being that evil serpent – just recall that the Hebrew children led by Moses into the wilderness had to look up at the serpent in order to live. Those who refused died. Read about it!)

Now the God in the garden told the two humans that he had created (better yet, had assisted in manifesting into human form), that they could eat of every tree of the garden except the tree in the midst of the garden because on the day they ate of the tree in the midst of the garden, they would surely die. Now there was the other God that decided to manifest in the form of a serpent. This God told the two humans that they would not surely die but would be like the God who had created them -- knowing good from evil.

After the couple ate of the tree, the LORD of the Garden said to the OTHER GODS, "Behold the man is become as one of us, knowing good from evil (confirming that what the serpent had said was true), and now, lest he put forth his hand and take also of the tree of life and eat and live forever." Therefore, the God drove them out of the Garden of Eden to till the ground from whence they were taken and placed Cherubims and a flaming sword which turned every way to keep them from the tree of life.

Why didn't the Lord of the Garden highlight the Tree of Life in the first place? We assume that the humans had access to it but we don't know this. *What we do know is that the Lord of the Garden did not want the unknowledgeable ones to become a God like him!*

Well, my dear brothers and sisters, let's consider what was done to the innocent spirits who were placed in the Garden of Eden. The Lord over them was in the position of a parent and the two humans due to their lack of knowledge were in the position of children. Let us reason together.

Let's consider what Jesus said about our Father. Jesus came to point us to the Constant God and even stated that if the leaders had known the father they would have known him [Jesus]. But since they had never known the True God, they did not know him. Now in our analogy today, the parents have left wholesome food (food that will make them like God) in the midst of the table but have forbidden the children to eat. Remember Jesus said that if you ask your father for bread would he give you a stone? He then said, "If you [thinking you are evil] know how to do well to your own children, how much more good would our father [who is constantly good] do well unto us -- his children.

Now many of us have been taught that Jesus came to verify that which was in the Old Testaments. But if you carefully consider Jesus' teachings, he often said these words, "It has been said . . . but I say unto you . . ." Jesus was overthrowing what had been taught to the people by the religious leaders. Today he would say to the "spiritual" and "political" black leaders, "Woe unto you spiritual and political black leaders -- hypocrites! For you compass land and sea to gain followers, but when they follow you, you make them twofold the children of hell (White Supremacy) than you are yourselves! For ye shut up the kingdom of heaven against men: for ye neither go in yourselves, neither suffer ye them that are entering to go in."

I have considered most religions and studied many as well. I have found that only one was founded in order to heal black people. It is the most dangerous religion to this present world and it is also the most disliked. I love the Nation of Islam and if it were not for many of the Muslims in the Nation of Islam, I would be an active member. I say that because as with all religions, especially one that has been so infiltrated by the U.S. government, there are hypocrites. Unfortunately, in the Nation of Islam, hypocrites seem to be in the highest positions.

Nonetheless, my husband and I love the Mission of the Nation of Islam and its leader because at the lowest points of both our lives (long before we met each other); we found hope in the fact that our Savior had arrived. God had heard the cries of black people and we were not a people forgotten. The words of the Honorable Minister Louis Farrakhan are what placed my husband and me on the path that led us to each other and for this alone; *we will always love the Honorable Minister Louis Farrakhan.*

We used to have 'shut-ins' at the church I used to attend. This was a three day fast in which the saints would sleep at the church on the concrete floors and pray constantly while drinking water only. I loved these fasts because I thought that I could invoke the Power of God in a greater way at these times. I would often use the occasion to pray for the community in which our church was located. I wanted to see a miracle. I wanted God to save everybody within a five to ten mile radius of our powerful church.

Well, one day after ending a great fast, the church was vandalized. The pastor said it was the work of the devil but this didn't sit well with me. I kept going over in my mind the scriptures, "Greater is he that is in me, than he that is in the world and if you say unto this mountain be thou removed and doubt not, it shall be done". I was indeed very perplexed after this event.

Some time went by before I finally became weary of my ineffectiveness in the community and went and asked my pastors a series of questions. I wanted to know why with all of our 'shut-ins' the community was not changing. *I wanted to know why there were so many different churches on every block and the condition of the people seemed to be worsening.* I wanted to know why black people seemed to be worse off than any other people. I wanted to know if God would take out a little special consideration for black people since we seemed to be the worse off.

Well, sufficed to say my pastors didn't have any answers that could satisfy me. I was not content with gaining rewards in the by and by. I wanted something to be done in the now and now. I didn't realize it then, but I now realize that I was asking about White Supremacy, however, my pastors walked around it quietly, pretending not to see that tree of knowledge of Good and Evil standing smack dab in the middle of the Garden.

I then journeyed from membership to membership -- from the Shrine of the Black Madonna to the Nation of Islam. But as criticism arose from my friends and family members who viewed me as unstable, I stopped joining anything but kept visiting everything. I wanted to know who God was on a universal level as well as his position regarding those who are suffering.

I discovered that there was a universal cord of truth that was laced through every religion of God and that God sent prophets to warn oppressors of every age and to relieve the suffering of every people. It was then that my brother introduced me to a tape series by a woman who had died and supposedly talked to God during her death. These tapes were my missing link. The tapes were by a lady named Betty Eady. She had spoken with Jesus and he had told her that all religions are valid. They all lead to God.

The reasons for each one are based on the differences in humans. Each human relates to God differently and therefore gravitates to a particular religion based on their differences. These tapes were like living water to me.

I was studying tapes by Betty Eady and reviewing video tapes by the Honorable Minister Louis Farrakhan when I met my present husband. He and I had prayed up on each other but that's another story. My husband wanted a book called Spirit of a Man by Iyanla Vanzant, who we both greatly admired, so I used the occasion of his birthday to purchase the book for him. Various quotes from her book led him to want a book called A Course in Miracles which I purchased for his next birthday. Becoming a part of A Course in Miracles study group led to our discovery of the Unity Church.

What a great concept! Everybody understanding our spiritual essence and the power of mind and being able to unite based on that understanding. Wow! On a particular Kwanzaa holiday, I was given permission to hold a Kwanzaa event at the Unity church. I placed special emphasis on inviting our white friends because I thought that this was the greatest opportunity for them to show their unity and appreciation for us.

In a church that was 95% white, only a handful of our white friends attended. I said to my husband after that, "We can never have true unity until White Supremacy is extracted from the human race!" We later went to talk with our pastors, a black couple, about the sickness of White Supremacy -- they became very solemn. Once again, my pastors walked around it quietly, pretending not to see that tree of knowledge of Good and Evil standing smack dab in the middle of the Garden.

I have concluded that we are like those children who exclaimed to the people, "The king is butt spanking naked! There is no beautiful robe! The Garden is our Mind! The Lord of the Garden is not good! Together we can take him and his other Gods too. Let's eat of the tree of knowledge of Good and Evil. Let's overthrow White Supremacy so that we ALL may heal! And then let's break through the barrier that was placed in our minds to keep us from eating of the tree of life and let's be like God."

This, Brothers and Sisters, is our Ministry, our Mission and our Calling.

I pray that God opens your understanding to my words and encourages your spiritual leaders to expose the disease of our souls.

Minister Cherice Fleming.

Essay #7: Why America Hates Farrakhan

Before you can understand why America hates Farrakhan, you must first understand what his philosophy means to the destinies of black people, and White Supremacy.

There is an invisible hand, a satanic thought that hovers over the minds of unsuspecting black youth in America. This Mind's purpose is to inoculate black youth against the Serpent of truth whenever he enters the Garden. It takes great care to speak only death to black youth to reproduce the mind of ignorance and self-annihilation. Every American institution instinctively knows the mission and responds appropriately.

I remember as a little boy attending Sunday school; how the teacher was giving thanks that black people had been brought to America and made slaves. She reasoned that had we not been brought here, we might have never known the goodness of Jesus. We would instead have been on our way to hell, practicing pagan religions of Africa.

Even as an eight year old, I knew how sick the statement was. A deep anger at God flashed across my soul. How could someone who loved me so much, subject my ancestors to such horrors just to get us to know him? If it was that important, he could have simply sent someone to Africa and taught us, I reasoned within myself.

Because I was a child and didn't want to experience the backhand of my father or Deacon Scott for "sputin" God, I filed the thought in the back of my mind and left it alone.

A few years later I remember the mini-series Roots coming on television. I remember how my father bought our first color television for the occasion and forced the entire family to endure the series. He, in a rare moment of black pride wanted everyone to know just how barbaric the white man was to his father and grandfather (It was during that time that daddy first spoke of white people to us).

As I watched Kunta Kinte pray to his God Allah, and how the slave Masters became uncontrollably obsessed with trying to extract his native religion from his mind, I couldn't help but think back to the Sunday school teacher that talked about the superstitious, pagan religions of Africa; and how blacks were fortunate to experience the brutality of slavery if it meant learning about Jesus.

Again the urge to speak out about the barbarism of God overwhelmed me as I glanced at my father to see if he had noticed the same thing I did. I wanted to ask him that if Christianity was so good, and African religions were so bad, why were the Christian slave-masters so brutal? As I watched my father stare intently at the television with a half smile on his face, I realized again that any derogatory comments about the God of the Bible brought on swift and brutal punishment from him, and snickering from my siblings.

Years later, as a man at odds with his Christian father I asked. He told me that we are not Africans; we are Americans so we should practice the religion of America. With the facts of American brutality still swirling in my mind from taking black history courses, I walked away reeling in confusion.

During college, I, a conservative Republican, began being exposed to Message to the Blackman in America, by Elijah Muhammad; Opinions and Philosophies of Marcus Garvey; Up from Slavery by Booker T. Washington, On Lynchings by Ida B. Wells- Barnett, and The Mis-Education of the Negro, by Dr. Carter G. Woodson. The conscious rap groups -- Public Enemy, Paris and X-Clan had caught my ear, locked into my soul's awareness, and became my regular music genre. It was through conscious rap that I was first exposed to Minister Farrakhan and his message to the black Man.

I remember the very first time I heard the name Louis Farrakhan. Intense hatred rose up even though I had never heard nor seen the man. Ironically it was Deacon Scott's own son who told me about him one day after church service.

In addition, I studied physics, chemistry, mathematics, biology, economics and all the "hard sciences" I could get my hands on! As knowledge of my essence and the universe around me grew, I began to experience a feeling of confidence that the whole earth was mine -- not because someone had granted me rights, or because I was born in a certain geographical location; I began seeing that my very nature entitled me to it!

Recall that in the Garden of Eden, LORD God forbade the Man (male and female together) from eating a particular fruit which would give the Man knowledge of who LORD God was, thereby causing the Man to function in the purpose of his Creator. He told the Man that death would follow him if he ate of it. On the other hand the LORD took the female off from the male and told her not to even touch the fruit. He knew that the female was the receiver, and he alone would cause her to conceive.

What was that Fruit the Serpent offered?

While working on this book, I noticed some interesting facts about the Nation of Islam's teaching and the Original Man's creator.

Over the years, Honorable Minister Louis Farrakhan has been speaking in no uncertain terms to the black Man of America. In his words he has offered the teachings of the Honorable Elijah Muhammad and Master Fard Muhammad who declare that the world of the white man is in fact, the world of Satan himself!

In addition, Farrakhan has said that if the black male would accept his own and be himself, he would see that Satan has been ruling him for the last 450 years, and has been ruling the earth the last 6000 years. If the black man would accept the religion that GOD prescribed, his eyes would be opened and he would know that he need not seek equality with Satan; seeing the Creator had already made him of his own nature and likeness.

Males of Islam are called the "Fruit of Islam". He taught us to eat to live, and the circumference of the earth and timelessness of the black man. These are all the things the creator gave us in the beginning.

As in the days of Eden, Farrakhan represents the Serpent, and Islam is the forbidden fruit! The day that the Negroes eat thereof, our eyes will come open and we will be as GOD, knowing good and evil. We would immediately unite and create Man, who would annihilate Satan and reclaim earth.

But what is Islam?

According to the Qur'an, the Bible, the Torah, and most Scriptures, despite what one calls himself; "all those who submit to GOD will have a reward from GOD." So it stands to reason that Islam is "Submission to GOD" regardless of what one calls himself or what hu-man he is.

Submission to GOD is accepting the true Self and the nature that GOD originally declared.[81]

White supremacy can only live in the Mind of the original. Farrakhan represents the end of that thought, and that's why America hates Farrakhan.

Dr. Alonzo Richard Fleming Jr.

---

81 Read Genesis Chapter 1 and Essay #8: The Prodigal Black Man.

Essay #8: The Prodigal Black Man

Who in the World do you Think You Are?!!
The Salvation of the Prodigal Black Man.
April 30, 2006

Luke 15:11-32

And he said, A certain man had two sons: And the younger of them said to his father, Father, give me the portion of goods that falleth to me. And he divided unto them his living. And not many days after the younger son gathered all together, and took his journey into a far country, and there wasted his substance with riotous living. And when he had spent all, there arose a mighty famine in that land; and he began to be in want. And he went and joined himself to a citizen of that country; and he sent him into his fields to feed swine. And he would fain have filled his belly with the husks that the swine did eat: and no man gave unto him. And when he came to himself, he said, How many hired servants of my father's have bread enough and to spare, and I perish with hunger! I will arise and go to my father, and will say unto him, Father, I have sinned against heaven, and before thee, And am no more worthy to be called thy son: make me as one of thy hired servants. And he arose, and came to his father. But when he was yet a great way off, his father saw him, and had compassion, and ran, and fell on his neck, and kissed him. And the son said unto him, Father, I have sinned against heaven, and in thy sight, and am no more worthy to be called thy son. But the father said to his servants, Bring forth the best robe, and put it on him; and put a ring on his hand, and shoes on his feet: And bring hither the fatted calf, and kill it; and let us eat, and be merry: For this my son was dead, and is alive again; he was lost, and is found. And they began to be merry. Now his elder son was in the field: and as he came and drew nigh to the house, he heard music and dancing. And he called one of the servants, and asked what these things meant. And he said unto him, Thy brother is come; and thy father hath killed the fatted calf, because he hath received him safe and sound. And he was angry, and would not go in: therefore came his father out, and entreated him. And he answering said to his father, Lo, these many years do I serve thee, neither transgressed I at any time thy commandment: and yet thou never gavest me a kid, that I might make merry with my friends: But as soon as this thy son was come, which hath devoured thy living with harlots, thou hast killed for him the fatted calf. And he said unto him, Son, thou art ever with me, and all that I have is thine. It was meet that we should make merry, and be glad: for this thy brother was dead, and is alive again; and was lost, and is found.

This story was told by Jesus in reaction to the preachers of Jesus day accusing him of always hanging around low-lifes and criminals.

The principles hidden in this story can be found on various levels of existence; The greatest level being the level of the human family returning to our state of oneness with our father, GOD.

For the sake of the time we are in at present, we will apply this principle to the area of dis-ease that needs healing right now. This is the need for the black family to return to its rightful position in the sonship family of GOD.

During what is called the Civil Rights Era, the leaders and preachers convinced us to join ourselves to the Citizens of a Strange Mentality Called 'White Supremacy'. This is the Strange world or 'country' we presently live in. The story says that we were sent into the citizen's fields to feed swine and would fain have filled our bellies with the husks that the swine did eat; And NO MAN GAVE UNTO US! What does this mean?

In the strange country, sisters and brothers, no man gives unto you! So you Fight for all the Rights that the Citizens of that Strange Country receive Freely! You Fight for Affirmative Action because you are Not a Citizen! You Fight for Civil Rights because you are Not a Citizen! You Fight for Human Rights because you are Not a Citizen! You Fight for Voting Rights because You are Not a Citizen! You even continuously Fight for Small Acts of Kindness, Decency, and Concern in a Strange Country UNTIL FINALLY YOU COME TO YOURSELF!

What does it mean to come to yourself? It means you begin to look inwardly. You begin to re-orient your thoughts towards the Kingdom of GOD because GOD's Kingdom is within and will manifest without once you discover it. You now begin to imagine a Righteous Country where Righteousness Rules and where your Sonship rights are automatic. You remember that there is no lack in your father's house and that even the servant's have plenty to spare.

But then you look at your present situation. You fall back into your present condition and you notice that you have sunk to the level of a beast. You fain would have eaten the husks that the swine did eat. This means that your mind has sank so low that you no longer know what it feels like to be whole. So even though you have determined within yourself to return home to your father, you plan to convince him to make you a servant. You are still insane but you are on a journey back to yourself.

Now the father sees you a long way off. This means that you do not have to make the entire journey before GOD will come to your aid. If you will just begin your journey home, GOD will meet you on the road back to yourself. The father had compassion, and RAN and Fell on his son's neck and kissed him.

Just think how fowl you smell and how filthy you look and how dirty you have become. You make your confession but while you are trying to convince the father to make you a servant he calls for the servants to throw a robe on our back.

Why didn't he command the servants to give us a bath? Because He wanted to remind us right away of who we are! He does not care how bad we smell. He does not care how filthy we look. He does not care what we think about ourselves. We are His Son! He wants us to remember who we are! "You are my son, and there is nothing you can do to change that!"

So he puts a robe on our back which represents knowledge of our rightful position and status within the Sonship Powers on this planet. He places a ring on our finger which represents our Authority to be Rulers with him in our Righteous Country. He places shoes on our feet which represents having our feet shod with the Preparation of the True Gospel. But why does the Elder brother become angry and refuse to come in? And who is the Elder brother in the first place?

The other original people remained at home with our father for the most part. This means that they were not entirely removed from their name, God, religion, identity, or way of life. These (the Asians, Arabs, Mexicans, Indians, Natives etc.) represent the Elder Brother. They were found working in the field when the Son returned home. They discovered that we had returned home ONLY when they drew near to the house. They too have gone too far away from the father's house. They remained with the father but they went too far away from home to be aware of what the father wanted or to be aware of our return. What does this mean?

Well, in many ways, all of us have been affected by the Strange Country. 'White Supremacy' has spread far and wide. When you go too far away from home you tend to get infected by 'White Supremacy'. So the Elder brother has gone insane even though he was always near the father. He is with the father but refuses to come into the house. Why? Because you and I have been accepted by our father and are being celebrated back into our rightful Sonship position. So the Elder brother finds fault with Elijah Muhammad and his 'brand' of Islam. Yet, the Elder brother is part of the Sonship too. He simply refuses to come in.

So the father comes out and says, "Son, all that I have is thine, but it is meet that we make merry for thy brother was lost and is found – was dead, and is alive again!"

Dr. Alonzo Fleming Jr

6.4
EXHIBITS

EXHIBIT 1a: A Scientific Discussion on the Age of the Universe

Until recently, astronomers estimated that the Big Bang occurred between 12 and 14 billion years ago. To put this in perspective, the Solar System is thought to be 4.5 billion years old and humans have existed as a species for a few million years. Astronomers estimate the age of the universe in two ways: 1) by looking for the oldest stars; and 2) by measuring the rate of expansion[82] of the universe and extrapolating back to the Big Bang; just as crime detectives can trace the origin of a bullet from the holes in a wall.

Older Than the Oldest Stars?

Astronomers can place a lower limit to the age of the universe by studying globular clusters. Globular clusters are a dense collection of roughly a million stars. Stellar densities near the center of the globular cluster are enormous. If we lived near the center of one, there would be several hundred thousand stars closer to us than Proxima Centauri, the star nearest to the Sun.

The life cycle of a star depends upon its mass. High mass stars are much brighter than low mass stars, thus they rapidly burn through their supply of hydrogen fuel. A star like the Sun has enough fuel in its core to burn at its current brightness for approximately 9 billion years. A star that is twice as massive as the Sun will burn through its fuel supply in only 800 million years. A 10 solar mass star, a star that is 10 times more massive than the Sun, burns nearly a thousand times brighter and has only a 20 million year fuel supply. Conversely, a star that is half as massive as the Sun burns slowly enough for its fuel to last more than 20 billion years.

All of the stars in a globular cluster formed at roughly the same time, thus they can serve as cosmic clocks. If a globular cluster is more than 20 million years old, then all of its hydrogen burning stars will be less massive than 10 solar masses. This implies that no individual hydrogen burning star will be more than 1000 times brighter than the Sun. If a globular cluster is more than 2 billion years old, then there will be no hydrogen-burning star more massive than 2 solar masses.

The oldest globular clusters contain only stars less massive than 0.7 solar masses. These low mass stars are much dimmer than the Sun. This observation suggests that the oldest globular clusters are between 11 and 18 billion years old. The uncertainty in this estimate is due to the difficulty in determining the exact distance to a globular cluster (hence, an uncertainty in the brightness [and mass] of the stars in the cluster).

---

[82] In the 1920s, Edwin Hubble discovered that the universe was not static, but rather was expanding! This discovery marked the beginning of the modern age of cosmology. Today, Cepheid variables remain one of the best methods for measuring distances to galaxies and are vital to determining the expansion rate (the Hubble constant) and age of the universe.

Another source of uncertainty in this estimate lies in our ignorance of some of the finer details of stellar evolution. Presumably, the universe itself is at least as old as the oldest globular clusters that reside in it.

Extrapolating Back to the Big Bang

An alternative approach to estimating is the age of the universe is to measure the "Hubble constant". The Hubble constant is a measure of the current expansion rate[83] of the universe. Cosmologists use this measurement to extrapolate back to the Big Bang[84]. This extrapolation depends on the history of the expansion rate which in turn depends on the current density of the universe and on the composition of the universe.

If the universe is flat[85] and composed mostly of matter, then the age of the universe is

$$\mathbf{2/(3\ H_o)}$$

where H_o is the value of the Hubble constant.

If the universe has a very low density of matter, then its extrapolated age is larger:

$$\mathbf{1/H_o}$$

If the universe contains a form of matter similar to the cosmological constant, then the inferred age can be even larger.

Many astronomers are working hard to measure the Hubble constant using a variety of different techniques. Until recently, the best estimates ranged from 65 km/sec/Megaparsec to 80 km/sec/Megaparsec, with the best value being about 72 km/sec/Megaparsec. In more familiar units, astronomers believe that $1/H_o$ is between 12 and 14 billion years.

---

83 He showed that more distant galaxies were moving away from us more rapidly using the equation $V=H_0d$, where v is the speed at which a galaxy moves away from us, and d is its distance. The constant of proportionality H_o is now called the Hubble constant.

84 The Big Bang Model is a broadly accepted theory for the origin and evolution of our universe. It postulates that 12 to 14 billion years ago, the portion of the universe we can see today was only a few millimeters across. It has since expanded from this hot dense state into the vast and much cooler cosmos we currently inhabit.

85 If the density of the universe exactly equals the critical density, then the geometry of the universe is flat like a sheet of paper. Thus, there is a direct link between the geometry of the universe and its fate.

An Age Crisis?

If we compare the two age determinations, there is a potential crisis. If the universe is flat, and dominated by ordinary or dark matter, the age of the universe as inferred from the Hubble constant would be about 9 billion years. The age of the universe would be shorter than the age of oldest stars. This contradiction implies that either 1) our measurement of the Hubble constant is incorrect, 2) the Big Bang theory is incorrect or 3) that we need a form of matter like a cosmological constant that implies an older age for a given observed expansion rate.

Some astronomers believe that this crisis will pass as soon as measurements improve. If the astronomers who have measured the smaller values of the Hubble constant are correct, and if the smaller estimates of globular cluster ages are also correct, then all is well for the Big Bang theory, even without a cosmological constant.

WILKINSON MICROWAVE ANISOTROPY PROBE (WMAP)

The Age of the Universe

Measurements by the WMAP satellite can help resolve this crisis. If current ideas about the origin of large-scale structure are correct, then the detailed structure of the cosmic microwave background fluctuations will depend on the current density of the universe, the composition of the universe and its expansion rate. WMAP has been able to determine these parameters with an accuracy of better than 5%. Thus, we can estimate the expansion age of the universe to better than 5%. When we combine the WMAP data with complimentary observations from other CMB experiments (ACBAR and CBI), we are able to determine an age for the universe closer to an accuracy of 1%.

The expansion age measured by WMAP is larger than the oldest globular clusters, so the Big Bang theory has passed an important test. If the expansion age measured by WMAP had been smaller than the oldest globular clusters, then there would have been something fundamentally wrong about either the Big Bang theory or the theory of stellar evolution. Either way, astronomers would have needed to rethink many of their cherished ideas. But our current estimate of age fits well with what we know from other kinds of measurements: the Universe is about 13.7 billion years old!

EXHIBIT 1b: The Mental Universe

"The Universe is Mental--held in the Mind of GOD[86]*."--The Kybalion.*

Let us now proceed to a consideration of the nature of the Universe, as a whole and in its parts. What is the Universe? We have seen that there can be nothing outside of GOD. Then is the Universe GOD? No, this cannot be, because the Universe seems to be made up of MANY and is constantly changing, and in other ways it does not measure up to the ideas that we are compelled to accept regarding GOD, as stated in our last lesson.

Then if the Universe be not GOD, then it must be Nothing-- such is the inevitable conclusion of the mind at first thought. But this will not satisfy the question, for we are sensible of the existence of the Universe. Then if the Universe is neither GOD, nor Nothing, what Can it be? Let us examine this question.

If the Universe exists at all, or seems to exist, it must proceed in some way from GOD--it must be a creation of GOD. But as something can never come from nothing, from what could GOD have created it Some philosophers have answered this question by saying that GOD created the Universe from ITSELF --that is, from the being and substance of GOD. But this will not do, for GOD cannot be subtracted from, nor divided, as we have seen, and then again if this be so, would not each particle in the Universe be aware of its being GOD --GOD could not lose its knowledge of itself, nor actually BECOME an atom, or blind force, or lowly living thing.

Some men, indeed, realizing that GOD is indeed ALL, and also recognizing that they, the men, existed, have jumped to the conclusion that they and GOD were identical, and they have filled the air with shouts of "I AM GOD,' to the amusement of the multitude and the sorrow of sages. The claim of the corpuscle that: "I am Man!" would be modest in comparison. But, what indeed is the Universe, if it be not GOD, not yet created by GOD having separated itself into fragments? What else can it be of what else can it be made? This is the great question.

Let us examine it carefully. We find here that the "Principle of Correspondence" comes to our aid here. The old Hermetic axiom," As above so below," may be pressed into service at this point. Let us endeavor to get a glimpse of the workings on higher planes by examining those on our own. The Principle of Correspondence must apply to this as well as to other problems.

---

86 In the Kybalion, the term "THE ALL" is used in order to discuss "GOD". For clarity to the reader and consistency within this writing, the author inserted the word "GOD".

Let us see! On his own plane of being, how does Man create? Well, first, he may create by making something out of outside materials. But this will not do, for there are no materials outside of GOD with which it may create. Well, then, secondly, Man pro-creates or reproduces his kind by the process of begetting, which is self-multiplication accomplished by transferring a portion of his substance to his offspring. But this will not do, because GOD cannot transfer or subtract a portion of itself, nor can it reproduce or multiply itself--in the first place there would be a taking away, and in the second case a multiplication or addition to GOD, both thoughts being an absurdity. Is there no third way in which MAN creates? Yes, there is--he CREATES MENTALLY!

And in so doing he uses no outside materials, nor does he reproduce himself, and yet his Spirit pervades the Mental Creation. Following the Principle of Correspondence, we are justified in considering that GOD creates the Universe MENTALLY, in a manner akin to the process whereby Man creates Mental Images. And, here is where the report of Reason tallies precisely with the report of the Illumined, as shown by their teachings and writings. Such are the teachings of the Wise Men.

Such was the Teaching of Hermes. GOD can create in no other way except mentally, without either using material (and there is none to use), or else reproducing itself (which is also impossible). There is no escape from this conclusion of the Reason, which, as we have said, agrees with the highest teachings of the Illumined. Just as you, student, may create a Universe of your own in your mentality, so does GOD create Universes in its own Mentality. But your Universe is the mental creation of a Finite Mind, whereas that of GOD is the creation of an Infinite. The two are similar in kind, but infinitely different in degree. We shall examine more closely into the process of creation and manifestation as we proceed. But this is the point to fix in your minds at this stage: THE UNIVERSE, AND ALL IT CONTAINS, IS A MENTAL CREATION OF GOD. Verily indeed, ALL IS MIND!

"GOD creates in its Infinite Mind countless Universes, which exist for aeons of Time--and yet, to GOD, the creation, development, decline and death of a million Universes is as the time of the twinkling of an eye."--The Kybalion.

"The Infinite Mind of GOD is the womb of Universes."--The Kybalion.

EXHIBIT 1c: What is Time?

TIME AND THEOLOGY

The **past** and **future** are both illusions, and different versions of the same story. The materially-based mind cannot comprehend the **present** because the material world is transient, and ever changing, according to thinker.

The present is the stillness of the Self; and the only part of time that is real. The present is Life itself. So we now ask, what is Time?

The Earth orbits the sun 248 times for every 1 time Pluto orbits the sun. This means that a Pluto year is 248 earth years.

Suppose a person was born on Pluto at the same time another person was born on Earth. When the Earthling is four years old, how old would the Plutonian be? If we based time on the orbit of planets, the Plutonian would be about 2 days old. By the time the person on Pluto was a 1 year old toddler, the earthling would have died 148 years earlier (assuming he lived to be 100 years old).

Again we pose the question to you. What is Time? What is the purpose for time? What is time really based on? Is time the same for everyone, or is time relative to the person counting it? Is time a constant, or does it vary, depending on some other factors?

We revisit our Earthling and Plutonian for answers. If time is the same for both, then our Earthling and Plutonian should both be four years old at the same time. They both should be in pre-school, speaking clearly, potty trained, walking, etc. This means that time and development moves about the same for everyone. Ones motion, position and thoughts would be irrelevant. It would mean that biological development is also a function of constant time marching on.

However, suppose our Earthling is four years old, and we do find our Plutonian is only 2 months old. What would that mean? Time must then be relative to space and/or thinking. It would also mean that some other factors influence physical development, outside of time. One thing we are sure of is that time means different things to different people.

Currently we base time on the **second**. A day is defined as 86,400 seconds, and a second is officially defined as 9,192,631,770 oscillations of a cesium-133 atom in an atomic clock.

What we think we know about time:

► 1) Although physical reasons for life are known; no reasons for death have yet been found.

► 2) Time is relative; based on the position and motion of the observer. In other words, time is not a constant.

► 3) Matter is no where, yet everywhere simultaneously.

► 4) Time indeed slows or accelerates, depending on the persons thoughts.

► 5) Time and dimension are not inextricably connected.

You will notice that except for point #4 above, time has something to do with a position in space. But examine point #4 to extend the discussion. If time slows or accelerates depending on thought, there are some interesting implications that arise.

Again we revisit our Earthling and Plutonian. Suppose they synchronized their watches so they could measure the actual time that passed between them, relative to each other. Suppose further they had access to the same sources of information. Would the Plutonian and Earthling learn at the same rate (assuming they had the same IQ and motivation)? Would the Plutonian learn more in the same time frame as the Earthling? If so, how could it be measured?

Suppose the Plutonian understood the illusory nature of the past and present. How would he view the same information as the Earthling? Suppose the Plutonian vibrated in a constant state of "Present reality". Would he have a need for war, hunger or lack? How would "death" look to him?

We asserted earlier that the **present** or **now** is the only real part of time. The past and future are merely illusions of time passing. If the mind could perceive the present, the thinker could perceive eternity while he "walked in flesh".

Imagine one having the ability to see above time. He would see ALL as though it's the same thing. Past, Present and Future appear as one; and time would have no meaning. Seeing all people at the same time, would they not appear as one person? Events could not happen since things leading up to events would appear the same as the events themselves. How would that individual view those who hated him? Would he have reason to destroy them, considering the hatred could never come into being, nor leave existence? This is because the individual's entire Mind vibrated in present tense.

Time truly is an interesting concept.

EXHIBIT 2a: On Male and Female

"Gender is in everything; everything has its Masculine and Feminine Principles; Gender manifests on all planes".—The Kybalion

Although it manifests on all levels, the Principle of Gender is perhaps the most difficult for the contemporary mind to comprehend. The reason being, its multi-dimensional manifestations cause the true power of its function to elude the materially-minded thinker.

We commonly speak of the female as woman, and the male as man. However, we remind the reader that the combination of **Man** and **Woman** is a concoction from Satan's attempt to separate and pervert GOD's original creation. Satan wants to eliminate **GOD's Male**; then mate with **GOD's Female** to create his own **Mankind.**

Recall that God described HIS Original Creation as **MALE** and **FEMALE** (Genesis 1:27). He then told the Male and Female to unite and create Man. It therefore is the unity of male and female (not man and woman) that creates MAN; and the MAN, who is the Image and Likeness of GOD, controls the earth (entire universe).

We remind you that the unity of Male and Female works on all levels of Spirit, Mind, and body (material) levels. Thus, for purposes of our discussion, we use GOD's description of Gender, rather than Satan's. Therefore if you, the reader have referred to yourself as a woman, we now refer to you as Female. If you the reader have called yourself a man, we now refer to you as Male.

On mental levels, the Masculine Principle corresponds to the objective mind, or active mind; and the Feminine corresponds to the Subjective Mind, passive Mind or subconscious Mind. The masculine energy is forever in the direction of conceiving and generating. The feminine is forever in the direction of receiving, regeneration and creation. The Feminine ALWAYS creates what she receives!

Take a few moments to study the figure below. You will notice that the figure to the left represents GOD's Creation of Man. The Female and Male are different individuals; yet their existence is based in their intimate connection. When their thinking is harmonized, their creative energies freely flow between one another to create MAN. The Man, who is the resultant[87] of Male/female unity, is the image of GOD, or in reality, god[88] himself.

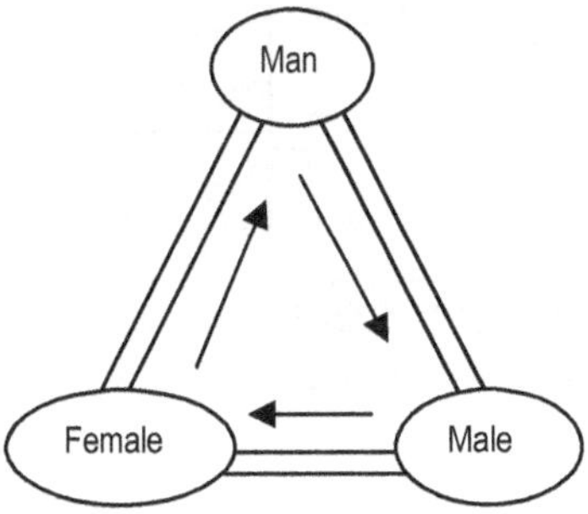

The god-MAN is the ruler of the universe. His creative energies and powers are freely shared with the individual Male and Female to use as they will. It should be noted that male/female unity has a direction. It is the direction of their unity that manifests how they use the creative power of GOD.

---

[87] We use the term resultant to indicate that male/female unity is a **vector quality**; having both magnitude and direction. Whatever the direction of their unity is, will manifest how they use the power of MAN.

[88] Man is considered god because he functions as GOD to a lesser degree, much like a male child functions as an adult to a lesser degree.

Exhibit 2a: On Male and Female - The Separation

'And if the light that is in thee be dark, how great is that darkness.'

Consider the figures below. As emphasized previously, LORD God (or Satan) understands the Principle of Gender. His objective is to take the place of GOD's Male, and mate with GOD's Female to create a "Mankind"; having a mental direction toward materialism, which is evil[89].

Utilizing the Principle of Gender, LORD God carefully and methodically puts the Man to sleep by convincing the Male energy to generate in the direction of separateness, individualism and material reality. After a time, the Man (god) begins to see himself as separated beings. His thoughts no longer connect to each other as one; they now appear as a Hodgepodge of separate "thought events", and each thought event has nothing to do with the other[90].

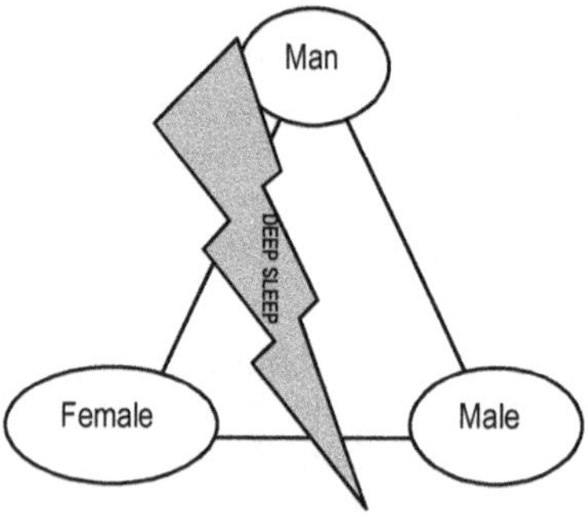

The Man's new "sight" has the effect of lowering his vibration. Confusion about himself sets in. The material World begins to reflect his conflicting thoughts. His Mind numbs, and sleep overtakes him. Once the Man is sleep and blinded to Self, LORD God separates the Female from the Man and causes her to see herself as a Man unto herself; separated from the Male and the Man that God created.

LORD God, having the Mind of evil, mates with the separated Female to create a Mankind, called Wo-man. He then brings the wo-man to the Male (he has placed into a 'Deep Sleep'). Adam now sees separate Gods—himself, and Mankind. The only Female now available for him to re-gain vision is one who is loyal to LORD God (this is why Adam blamed the woman LORD God gave him). Having no Female to return his sight, the Male that GOD created, stumbles around blind to himself. Afraid that he can die, the Male begins mating with Mankind and submitting to LORD God, in hopes of being protected from Death. However, knowing that GOD's Man would experience his own thinking, LORD God ignores him as he frantically tries to survive by creating the children of LORD God. Alas it is the Man's own thinking that causes Self-annihilation.

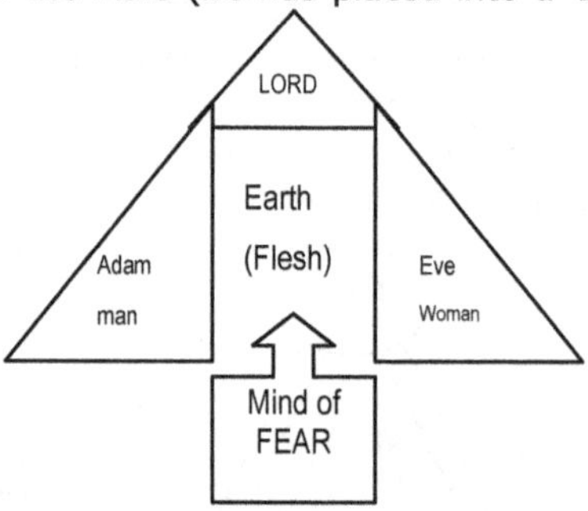

[89] Materialism sees physical manifestations as a causes, rather than effects. See Case Study 2e: On Walking in Flesh

[90] This was the process LORD God invoked when he paraded individual animals in front of Adam for him to name.

Exhibit 2b:ON MAN AND WOMAN—EXPANDED

NOTE: In this document, we use the term Citizen to describe the descendants of former slave-owners in America. We use the term Prodigal to describe the descendants of former slaves in America.

We have emphasized to you that in the beginning, GOD created Man as the **resultant** of Male and Female unity. It is ONLY this unity that creates Man; who is the **Image and Likeness of GOD**, and the legitimate owner of earth.

Remember, the MALE and FEMALE are not individual Gods. **Man is God** as the result of the Male/Female connection. This is a vital point to understand. GOD never created man and Wo-man; Satan did! (Adam and St-Eve)[91]

The present world reflects an attempt to overthrow the Masculine/Feminine Principle. Its process and effects can clearly be seen in 21st century earth. We describe the process:

The **Male-Citizen** has been deceived into thinking he is an individual man, having only the Masculine orientation. The **Female-Citizen** has been deceived into thinking that she is an individual Wo-Man; (female Man) having only the Feminine orientation. The Wo-man, as a result of LORD God's curse, is made subordinate to the man, and desires to unite with him[92].

Under this scenario, Male and Female are not being united; Man and Man are being forced together. Notice further, that it attempts to unite two separate Gods, to create a "Super God", LORD God or Mankind. Herein lies the doctrine of a trinity[93]; and also why it was important that Jesus be portrayed as God; yet not having a "Male" father, but a complete **male-God** as his father. If Jesus had been seen as having a Male father, yet be GOD, the eyes of the **Prodigal**-Male and Female would be opened, and they would unite under the Principle of Gender to bring forth the **Original Man**; who would immediately destroy Satan's world.

---

[91] Two like genders cannot unite. It explains the prevalence of homosexuals that fill Negro churches; and the homosexual and lesbian phenomenon nationwide. It also explains domestic violence, feminism and male/female friction resulting in a high divorce rate.

[92] Genesis 3:16

[93] God is a triune Father, Son, and Holy Ghost-Three individual and separate Gods, uniting as one super God.

The fantastic doctrine of virgin birth is an effort to conceal the Principle of Gender by offering the illusion that two men can produce God. See the figure on the right:

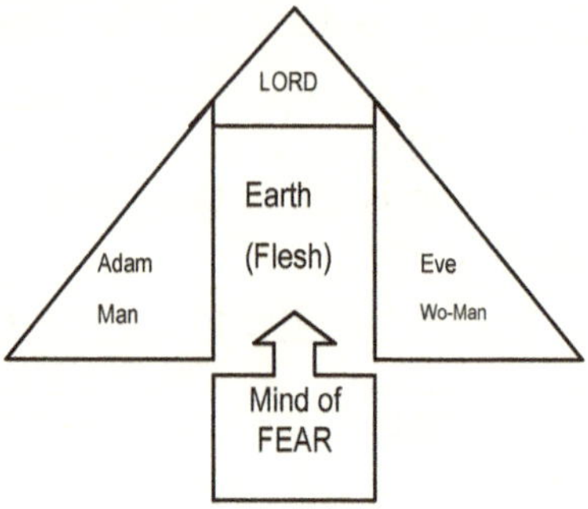

As you can see from the figure, both the male and female have a "piece of Man", but have been split in to halves. Both think they are God by themselves. They have no natural connection to one another, but in fact, repel each other. An illusion of a separate God, or LORD God results.

Think carefully on what we have said, before your proceed.

You will recall how in the Garden of Eden, LORD God, in his attempt to split the Man, allowed Man to watch as he formed the beasts out of clay. He brought them before Man and asked him to name the animals so he would notice the mathematical patterns, and see himself in terms of division. He also wanted Man to identify his nature with that of BEASTS; and desire to manifest as the beast (or lower nature) manifests.

The more Adam saw himself as divided, the dizzier he became. Like a man having too much alcohol, the Man began seeing doubles of himself. After causing him to blackout, LORD God split the MAN'S thinking into halves. The side of Man with the Female aspect, was made to think she is complete in herself (Wo-man); and the side of Man having the Male aspect, LORD God made him think he was complete in himself (man). He then introduced them to each other as two separate Gods having different genders (or sides), but with the nature of the beasts (flesh that could die).

LORD God had successfully created **Man-kind** in his own Image and Likeness--The Image and Likeness of a beast (man and Wo-man, or Mankind) designed to cause humanity to bow down to Satan and his image.

"And he had power to give life unto the image of the beast, that the image of the beast should both speak, and cause that as many as would not worship the image of the beast should be killed. And he causeth all, both small and great, rich and poor, free and bond, to receive a mark in their right hand, or in their foreheads: And that no man might buy or sell, save he that had the mark, or the name of the beast, or the number of his name—Revelation 13:15 -17.

Now consider a few implications (though there are more than space will allow) that arise from attempting to unite two Men. LORD God's objective is to cause the Prodigal Males and Females to look only to his Image as they attempt to unite. Thus the **Prodigal** Male and Female is an imitator of the man and Wo-man **Citizen**.

The Prodigal-Female thinks the Wo-man-Citizen is God; having her gender. Likewise the Prodigal-Male believes the man-Citizen is God, having his gender. Prodigal-Males and Females tries to unite using this system of thinking. This concept was cleverly developed in slavery to induce the Prodigal male and female to imitate the Citizens. However, the Citizens are fully aware that the prodigals have different natures than they; hence segregate the truth from them.

The church is the incubator that fuels, reproduces and maintains the illusion that LORD God is Creator of the Prodigals. Having a satanic doctrine firmly residing in their minds, the Prodigals go about trying to "see", through a prism of fragmented Thought.

They are consumed in a multiplicity of "**thought Events**" or illusions designed to cause an endless stream of "fatal errors". In other words, every event in their collective Mind seems separate from any other event. This is why their civil rights events never seem to solve anything. Each act of racism; each new law, policy or statistic is separate from the whole; and is separate from previous and subsequent acts. There appears to be no mathematical pattern involved in the events except the **pattern of randomness**! In addition, LORD God shifts their learning of mathematics so they can never see oneness. Math is not a spiritual tool to them; instead, they learn math and physics for the material purpose of building LORD God's world. This type of thinking prevents the mind from unifying and reorienting the thinking; and prevents them from ever examining the thought System itself.

To better illustrate this principle, think of the physical brain as a computer Hard drive. The hard drive holds the Mind[94]; which can be likened to an Operating System or Platform[95]. How one conducts daily living activities are the Programs or Software that has been installed on the operating system. Each installed program is designed to manifest a specific result. However, it must be made in accordance with the rules of the particular operating system, or the programs will not function properly.

---

94 The mind is the conduit between the physical world and the Self

95 An Operating system is the rules a computer program must follow, if they are to work on that computer.

For example, a Windows® operating system requires Windows software to run on it. A Mac® operating system requires Mac software packages. In addition, each program must be properly installed, even if it sits on the correct operating system.

A program designed for a Mac, but installed on a Windows operating system, will result in malfunctions, glitches, fragmented programs, anomalies and crashes! Similarly the same will happen if a windows program is installed on a Mac.

Now here is the tricky part. One way to get around the limitation is for Windows to write software and design it to run on both Windows and Macs; and vise versa. However, since each manufacturer desires his own software to run on his machine, he designs the Operating System to run HIS software, but causes the other to malfunction if placed on his operating system.

Another way to get around the limitation is to "partition" (or split) the hard drive and install both operating systems on the same hard drive. When a drive has been partitioned, the system will fatally crash if both operating systems try to master the entire hard drive simultaneously. One of the two operating systems MUST be uninstalled and a unified system re-installed on the drive.

The Prodigal's-Mind has been partitioned, and two conflicting operating systems have been installed on it. One platform came with the system from the manufacturer who designed it to run only ONE system—Period! This system is natural to the machine. The other system was installed after the manufacture, and runs an alien software package (White Supremacy); one operating system results in Life for the machine; the other software results in fatal crashes, glitches, system failure and fragmentation; One system results in almost maintenance-free operation; the other system results in constant frustration and non-productivity. You get the point.

The Prodigal-Male and Female, at the deepest level of Mind knows that only ONE Thought system will run properly—the One from the Manufacturer! However, they are kept in fear of the obvious by the incubators of Death. Consequently they wallow in death, determined to mock GOD by forcing Satan's fragmented thought system to work for them. Instead, fatal errors occur as they look to the image of the beast to experience reality.

There is nothing for them to do but reformat the hard drive (delete the operating system), and reinstall the Operating system designed for the machine.

Exhibit 2c: Cain & Abel - LORD God Sets Brother against Brother

While the rest of Humanity was multiplying and replenishing the earth according to the commandment of GOD; Adam and Eve were segregated and being experimented on by LORD God. He isolated them in caves and hills until he was sure he had complete control over their minds. After being cursed, Eve bore a son and called him Cain, because she got him from the LORD (Genesis 4:1)

Cain was similar to Original MAN, having the inward sense of his ability to control the earth; however, being born in slavery, Cain was completely ignorant of Life prior to the garden. He had no knowledge of the Male/Female principle that gave rise to Man. He was completely subject to LORD God; believing his nature was of the beast, and LORD God was the owner of the plantation. He was even given the Name of LORD God! Like the first Africans born of slaves in America, LORD God planned to separate Cain from his family and use him to create a whole new race of willing slaves!

Eve instilled in her boys (Cain and Abel), complete reverence for LORD God's power. She cultivated unwavering servitude to him, based on fear and death. She taught them that the earth is the LORDS' and the fullness thereof. They had no power of their own; and must look only to LORD God for their well-being. All their labor was for his honor and glory. After all, their existence was for his pleasure, and they should be thankful to him.

Eve told her sons of life prior to the Garden and the cave. She recollected a world where GOD had given them dominion over all the earth. However, as she told the story, she began merging their servitude in the Garden of Eden, into the same story. She now saw the Garden of Eden as all the earth. She and Adam had dominion over the garden before they disobeyed and were kicked out. Most of all, she told of LORD God's 'righteous anger' and how terrifying he could be. Like any slave mother, Eve warned her children not to anger him in any way, because the repercussions would be severe.

She told her son's how the serpent deceived her into gaining knowledge of that which was off limits. How they became guilty and sealed with the curse of death. She expressed how she had been deceived into thinking that they could be equal with GOD and how Adam was now tirelessly doomed with trying to reconnect with LORD God.

Exhibit 2c: Cain & Abel - LORD God Sets Brother against Brother

Abel was a keeper of sheep— Genesis 4:2

Abel, understanding the implications of giving sacrifice, became a keeper of sheep. His very occupation was a constant reminder of LORD God. Abel raised and killed the animals for the family. He provided the food of LORD God's diet (animal flesh), and also the clothes that LORD God preferred them to wear (animal skins). However, LORD God still could not use Abel to be the progenitor of Mankind because he had no life in his thinking.

In order to make the world of Mankind, LORD God needed someone who understood his power to subdue the earth; yet was full of guilt, which would keep him subject to LORD God. Although Abel had death in his heart, his conscience was seared from the constant killing of animals. Furthermore, Abel did not have the prerequisite scientific knowledge necessary to build LORD God's world of mankind. But he could be used as a tool to help develop the one who did.

But Cain was a tiller of the ground.—Genesis 4:2

Notice how, in the above scripture, Cain's occupation is contrasted with Abel's; implying that LORD God preferred the mind of Cain over Abel. Cain worked in horticulture (the **science** and art of growing fruits, vegetables, flowers, and ornamental plants). Cain identified with life because his very occupation reinforced the idea of life permeating the universe. Cain's interaction with the earth reminded him of the everlasting circle of life. Because the earth is obedient to Man, earth gently reminded him (like the serpent) of his own true nature.

Cain was learning and understanding his own power to cause earth and nature to obey him. As the earth began to yield her strength and power of knowledge to Cain, he learned how to reproduce life through the works of his own hands. He learned the rotations of the earth and planets; the phases of the moon and how they affected the tides. He learned how the seasons affected his crops, and how dung fertilized his earth. He was learning all the Good mathematical Principles through which his nature was created. Cain, like LORD God, was becoming a master scientist and was becoming confident in his abilities to control the earth.

Cain was the chosen one! However, there was one small problem. Cain no longer equated His Self as the servant or dust of earth, because he was starting to understand his mastery of it; and logic dictates that the master is greater than the servant.

This presented a problem for LORD God. If Cain continued in his present mind, sooner or later it would dawn on him that LORD God was an impostor, just like his parent's once suspected. He would also know that he was equal to LORD God, not subordinate to him. Knowing that the mind has a tendency to re-orient and heal itself (Willie Lynch), LORD God had to move quickly if his plan was to succeed. He had to find a way to cause guilt to develop in Cain's mind, while preserving Cain's creative power.

"And in process of time it came to pass, that Cain brought of the fruit of the ground an offering unto the LORD. And Abel, he also brought of the firstlings of his flock and of the fat thereof". – Genesis 4:3

The Experiment

As time passed, LORD God shifted his focus from the parents, to the children. Being a wise scientist, LORD God wanted to see how the minds of Cain and Abel were developing, and what adjustments he should make in order to produce the kind of man he wanted. He therefore created an experiment that would give him an indication. He knew that their occupations would have the effect of telling them (and him) who they thought they were and who they thought he was. He commanded them to bring something that would indicate their appreciation for him.

The Offering of Abel

"And the LORD had respect unto Abel and to his offering".—Genesis 4:4

LORD God is a respecter of person. Abel, having already been socialized to serve the LORD, instinctively knew to kill and bring the dead as an offering. So, with fear and trembling Abel killed one of his sheep, and brought the fat as a means to quench LORD God's thirst for blood. Having fear and death at the center of his thinking, Abel and his offering represented the death of the MAN. LORD God was pleased with this favorable development in Abel.

With the Original man dead (to the knowledge of Self), the LORD could easily convince the world that GOD himself could die; since MAN has the same nature as GOD. By fully accepting the thought system of LORD God, Abel became the symbol of the murder of MAN, and the advent of Mankind. That is why Abel and his offering of death were acceptable.

The Offering of Cain

"But unto Cain and to his offering [The LORD] had no respect."--Genesis 4:5

Cain put together a fruit basket; beautiful life-giving flowers, and living things which were pleasing to the eye, delicious for food and had made him very wise. He knew that each fruit contained in itself the power to make new life. This he gathered and brought to LORD God as a peace offering.

Still believing that LORD God was the Creator who gave him the earth in the first place, Cain was excited about impressing his creator by sharing what he had learned about himself and the earth. Like his parents, Cain did not connect the story of the garden; how that LORD God cannot see life. Cain saw no significance in the story of how his parents were able to hide from LORD God by covering themselves with the living fig leaves from the trees of their true GOD. As in the Garden of Eden, LORD God could not understand Cain. He could not see Cain or his offering, thus he rejected them both!

"And Cain was very wroth, and his countenance fell."--Genesis 4:5

LORD God's plan was to permanently enslave Cain. All he needed to do was combine Abel's thinking with Cain's natural power. That is, plant the mind of guilt and death into the principled, creative mind of Cain. So he pitted them against each other. LORD God was using the same technique adopted later by Willie Lynch. "Strip the mind, yet preserve the body, thereby setting up and controlling the next generation in the desired image".—Willie Lynch

"And the LORD said unto Cain, Why art thou wroth? and why is thy countenance fallen? If thou doest well, shalt thou not be accepted and if thou doest not well, sin lieth at the door. And unto thee shall be his desire, and thou shalt rule over him". --Genesis 4:3-7

To really understand the situation, and why Cain became angry, keep in mind the reason Cain offered what he did in the first place. As Cain worked in the field, he learned of himself and he was reminded of GOD his creator. He was beginning to think that the same GOD, who blessed him with the power he experienced in the field, was the same one he was bringing the living gift to. Surely he would accept the gift.

He had no idea that his gift would in fact demonstrate the powerlessness of LORD God's curse (the ground was not supposed to yield her strength, but it did!). His gift would reveal that LORD God did not control his mind nor the earth.

We first ask the reader to consider how you would expect your son to react if he brought you a gift out of his love for you; and instead of saying "thank you for the effort", you emphatically **rejected him and his gift!** Ok, reject the gift, but your son too? How would you expect your son to react after such rejection by a loved one with such great influence over him? And wouldn't a wise father have better sense than to provoke his son to jealousy in the first place? So, why did LORD God reject Cain, and why did Cain become wroth?

The situation was now ripe for LORD God to make his final move and fill the earth with the thought of murder, death and sin. Why was Cain and his offering rejected? Remember, Abel killed something and brought death. LORD God, being the author of death, can only see symbols of death; and like LORD God, Abel had already accepted the nature of LORD God and had death as his center. This is why he knew to kill.

On the other hand, Cain brought a living offering of fruits and vegetables. They are the symbols of life. Since Cain's offering reflected the life that was at Cain's center, both the offering AND Cain had to be rejected by LORD God in order to strip away Cain's life force, and preserve his body for the work that was necessary.

After setting up a situation that he knew would cause jealousy, LORD God actually has the nerve to ask Cain why he is upset. He then suggests to Cain that the solution to the problem was simple. Do what Abel did (kill something) and he would also be accepted. Otherwise the **Devil** (the truth laid low) is at the door; however, if Cain would do as Abel did, he would fully be accepted, and would rule the other Gods. LORD God was completely responsible for manipulating Cain; and actually used the power of suggestion on Cain that he murder his brother; take his offering and give it to LORD God.

"<u>And</u> Cain talked with Abel his brother: and it came to pass, when they were in the field, that Cain rose up against Abel his brother, and slew him"--Genesis 4:8

All Cain needed to do was kill something and he would be accepted by LORD God. <u>Right after talking with LORD God, Cain killed Abel</u>. It's interesting to note that as LORD God began to talk with Cain about his anger, the scripture starts out by saying "**And** Cain talked with his brother Abel...and rose up against Abel and slew him". The scripture implies that LORD God suggested that Cain kill his brother, and that Cain's act was consistent with the suggestion.

If LORD God was trying to keep Cain from killing Abel, wouldn't the scripture start off by saying "**BUT** Cain talked with his brother Abel...and rose up against Abel and slew him"? Indicating that LORD God was trying to talk him out of it, but he killed Abel anyway. Had the word "but" been used it would have implied that Cain acted against the suggestion. The sentence structure and subsequent conversation between Cain and LORD God indicates that Cain rose up against his brother BECAUSE of the LORD God, not DESPITE the conversation with LORD God.

And the LORD said unto Cain, "Where is Abel thy brother? And he said, I know not: Am I my brother's keeper? And he said, What hast thou done? the voice of thy brother's blood crieth unto me from the ground. And now art thou cursed from the earth, which hath opened her mouth to receive thy brother's blood from thy hand; When thou tillest the ground, it shall not henceforth yield unto thee her strength; a fugitive and a vagabond shalt thou be in the earth."—Genesis 4:9-12

LORD God now has the nerve to ask Cain why he is so upset (as though he is unaware of the implications of rejecting Cain!) Just as he did to the boy's parents by pretending as though he didn't know what was going on, he acts as though he doesn't know that Cain has murdered his brother.

He then immediately reveals that he does know : "The voice of your brother's blood cries to me from the ground". LORD God makes this statement to sound surprised, to inject guilt into the mind of Cain, so he will no longer relate to the righteous GOD, his Creator. LORD God then seals the guilt in Cain's Mind by going on a cursing spree, just like he did to Cain's parents! Notice what LORD God cursed: ***And now art thou cursed from the earth... When thou tillest the ground, it shall not henceforth yield unto thee her strength". Genesis 4:12***

LORD God cursed the same thing he cursed in Adam's case. The very thing that their creator called BLESSED and GOOD–the earth! What was the strength that the earth had been yielding to Cain? Remember in the beginning, GOD the creator, gave the earth to the MAN he created. He commanded the MAN to rule the earth, and commanded the earth to obey MAN. So the strength that the earth was yielding to Cain was obedience to him and the acknowledgement that Cain is the ruler, and the earth is willing to obey him. The earth takes on the form that the ruler gives to it. If the ruler thinks he **is** the earth, he becomes subject to whoever he **thinks** the ruler is.

When LORD God cursed the earth in Cain's eyes, he planted the idea of death in the mind of Cain by causing him to identify with the earth. He also blinded him to the knowledge that the earth would serve Cain.

Now sealed in guilt and death, each time Cain tilled the earth it would cause the earth to yield her strength to LORD God (in Cain's Mind) rather than Cain.

Cain, while working in the fields was learning all the laws of the universe, including the Law of Attraction. Having learned the law of attraction, he understood that his thoughts were so powerful that they would cause murder to manifest against him because of his own thinking. Thus he cried out in horror at the prospect:

"And Cain said unto the LORD, My punishment is greater than I can bear. Behold...I shall be a fugitive and a vagabond in the earth; and it shall come to pass, that every one that findeth me shall slay me".—Genesis 4:13-14

Cain is now acceptable to LORD God. So like the gangster he is, LORD God places an equally murderous thought into Cain's mind: ***And the LORD said unto him, "therefore whosoever slayeth Cain, vengeance shall be taken on him sevenfold" Genesis 4:15.***

Notice that LORD God didn't act to remove the thoughts of murder from the mind of Cain, nor did he suggest that HE personally would be the one taking vengeance on anyone who would kill Cain. Instead, LORD God further cultivated the thought of murder by adding vengeance to Cain's thinking. Vengeance is the cousin of murder. Vengeance is the emotional and intellectual justification for murder. The thought of vengeance allowed Cain to think that everyone would be out to kill him, and in turn provided a reason to unleash retaliation, preemptive war, and taking of the earth on behalf of LORD God.

Cain is now acceptable to LORD God for his offering of Abel's blood. As proof that LORD God accepts and protects the murderer, as belonging to him, ***"the LORD set a mark upon Cain, lest any finding him should kill him"—Genesis 4:15***. So, the same one who cursed the parents' Minds, and placed his mark of death on them (Gen 3) has now cursed the children and placed his mark of death on them!

"For this is the message that ye heard from the beginning, that we should love one another. Not as Cain, who was of that wicked one, and slew his brother. And wherefore slew he him? Because his own works were evil, and his brother's righteous."—1 John 3:11-12

Cain loved the Wicked One and murdered his brother out of love for the Wicked One. He wanted love and acceptance in return. Who is the wicked one that influenced Cain to murder his own brother?

Christian scholars, in their attempt to absolve LORD God of being the Wicked One who motivated Cain, suggest that it was the serpent of the Garden. But there is no mention or hint of the serpent anywhere in the story of Cain and Abel!

In fact, other than in the Garden of Eden, the serpent never speaks again in the entire Bible! There was no other entity EXCEPT LORD God communicating with Cain just prior to him murdering his brother. It was out of love for LORD God, not the serpent, that Cain committed the act. Thus if Cain is a murderer and OF the Wicked One, then LORD God must be the wicked one since his mark was a symbol of LORD God's acceptance and protection of Cain the Murderer.

LORD God needed someone to be the progenitor of Man-kind. He needed one who looked like MAN, sounded like MAN, walked and talked like MAN, but had Death as his center; the final touch was one who understood the Principles of the Universe. Through the illusion of sacrifice, LORD God found a way to extract Cain's identification with the creative GOD, and at the same time keep intact his confidence in universal principles.

LORD God cursed the earth in Cain's mind to make him think that earth would not help him without LORD God. Knowing the power of the Mind, LORD God knew that if Cain believed, he would be unable to produce contrary to his own belief system. Cain could now easily be convinced that LORD God was his only source. Cain's own inherent power has now been hijacked and is controlled by Satan himself! Cain was now adequately prepared to go out among the Sons of GOD to spread his thinking and ways.

And Cain went out from the presence of the LORD, and dwelt in the land of Nod, on the east of Eden. And Cain knew his wife; and she conceived, and bare Enoch… And Lamech said unto his wives, Adah and Zillah, Hear my voice; ye wives of Lamech, hearken unto my speech: for I have slain a man to my wounding, and a young man to my hurt. If Cain shall be avenged sevenfold, truly Lamech seventy and sevenfold". Genesis 4:16-24

LORD God sent Cain out into the earth with the thoughts of murder swirling in his head. He begins mixing with the righteous peoples of the earth to spread the thoughts of division and murder among them.

Cain was the first of Mankind, A direct descendent of LORD God's Mind, to be unleashed on the rest of humanity. He had the creative nature of the ALL (GOD), but the murderous thoughts of LORD God. He began to teach all those who would listen, about the mercies of LORD GOD. Thus, everywhere the descendants of Cain appear, murder is multiplied; Violence appears to be normal; Brother murders brother; the female is persecuted, exploited or demeaned; slavery and ignorance prevails!

According to the scriptures, within six generations of Cain's decedents, the murder and vengeance rate multiplied by seventy:

"And Lamech said unto his wives, Adah and Zillah, Hear my voice; ye wives of Lamech, hearken unto my speech: for I have slain a man to my wounding, and a young man to my hurt. If Cain shall be avenged sevenfold, truly Lamech seventy and sevenfold".-Genesis 4:23-24.

On another front, Adam and Eve are producing children and teaching them to look to LORD God of the curse.

And Adam knew his wife again; and she bare a son, and called his name Seth: For God, said she, hath appointed me another seed instead of Abel, whom Cain slew. And to Seth, to him also there was born a son; and he called his name Enos: then began men to call upon the name of the LORD. Genesis 4:26

The Decedents of Cain Today

In LORD God's eyes, everything is upside down. He is Lord of the Dead; and as Lord of the dead he cannot see nor give life to anyone! He exists as long as Man holds his thoughts. Everything he produces has death as its center. Death is acceptable and **good** to him. Life is **sin and evil** to him. So Abel's offering of the dead was something LORD God could see. Cain's offering of the living was invisible and evil to LORD God.

This is the reason today that the preachers of LORD God call the Original creator "The invisible God"—A spirit that cannot be seen. Like the LORD God, their impurity of heart prevents them from seeing GOD (Matthew 5:8). And like LORD God and his other offspring, the preachers of death have eyes, but cannot see life. They have ears but cannot hear the voice of GOD. They have tongues but cannot speak life which permeates the universe. Like their father Cain, today's preachers are literally "of the Wicked One".

They gladly preach his doctrine of the murder of GOD and the death of MAN. To this very day, everywhere the offspring of the grafted Cain goes; he provokes brothers to kill brothers. In Iraq, this very day, prior to the invasion of the children of Cain, Iraq was a thriving country. She produced some of the most talented engineers and scientists. Now Iraq is in civil war. Brother killing brother.

In the United States of America, black males' total education has been given by the American system of thinking. Our original language, culture, names, and religion are long stripped from us, and our minds have been totally transformed under the system of present America. We are killers of one another. We will take one another's life for little or nothing. We have been taught and provoked to hate one another.

Yet for all our self destructive teaching, we desire nothing more than to be accepted into the Mind of white supremacy. So at the urging of the preachers, we march, beg, supplicate and bow down in obeisance to the leaders of white supremacy—never looking within for our identity as Original MAN—the image and likeness of GOD himself!

The Serpents among us

Every now and then a truth speaking serpent slips into the garden undetected by the LORD God and asks us to eat of the tree of Knowledge and take hold the tree of Life.

The Honorable Elijah Muhammad in his books Message to the Blackman in America and Our Savior has Arrived, tells the story of Yacub the scientist who grafted the first of Mankind and caused him to be the enemy of heaven, earth and the Original MAN. According to Muhammad, Yacub possessed the knowledge of genetic manipulation and the psychology necessary to develop particular mental dispositions in human offspring.

At the time these books were written, the processes of science to genetically manipulate the biological attributes of humans; and the psychology of pre-birth manipulation, was largely unknown by the average person. Non scientists and those who were aware of the concepts passed them off as legends or old wives tales. In more recent years however, through the knowledge and psychology of Willie Lynch, and the revelation of the Human Genome project, it is clear that Elijah Muhammad was either way ahead of his time, or was taught by the same entity that gave the Original MAN the earth in the first place.

The story of Cain almost perfectly matches the discussion of Yacub. How could Elijah Muhammad know this unless someone who understood the principles had taught him?

According to history, Elijah Muhammad only had a 4th or 5th grade education. It is also interesting to note that some of the first things he taught his followers were circumference of the earth, how to eat to live, and how to mold the mind of a child while its still in the womb of the woman. Are those not the same principles that the GOD of Original MAN gave to his creation? Are those not the same concepts that LORD God distorted to produce death? And are they not the same concepts Willie Lynch utilized to produce slaves?

Presently, LORD God and his representatives maintain rule by convincing the Original MAN that the earth belongs to LORD God, with **Mankind** as the representative of LORD God. MAN, believing it, labors on behalf of LORD God and his representatives. LORD God's representatives are careful to never allow MAN to look within and free himself from guilt and death. They use every opportunity to warn MAN that if he looks within, he will find sin and death. As a result, MAN, thinking that LORD God is his only protector, never looks within.

To this day, the Original MAN has been made afraid to do anything in the earth that does not first benefit LORD God or his people, thereby perpetuating his own slavery. He looks only to LORD God to protect him from his own nature. It has yet to dawn on MAN that he has the same righteous, living nature of the very GOD of creation and is the direct descendant of GOD. MAN cannot sin nor die because he is born of GOD (I John 3:9).

MAN is not the dust of the earth. MAN is the legitimate Lord of the earth. He is the one Jesus spoke of when he said, "Blessed are the Meek, for they shall inherit the earth" (Matthew 5:5). LORD God is actually the wicked servant who has rebelled against the creator and the Original MAN.

I am here to proclaim unequivocally that the earth does not belong to the LORD. The earth belongs to MAN as given to him in the beginning!—Genesis 1:27-31

EXHIBIT 2d: Let's Make a Slave

Greetings

"Gentlemen. I greet you here on the bank of the James River in the year of our Lord one thousand seven hundred and twelve.

First, I shall thank you, the gentlemen of the Colony of Virginia, for bringing me here. I am here to help you solve some of your problems with slaves. Your invitation reached me on my modest plantation in the West Indies, where I have experimented with some of the newest and still the oldest methods for control of slaves.

Ancient Rome would envy us if my program is implemented. As our boat sailed south on the James River, named for our illustrious King, whose version of the Bible we Cherish, I saw enough to know that your problem is not unique. **While Rome used cords of wood as crosses for standing human bodies along its highways in great numbers, you are here using the tree and the rope on occasions**. I caught the whiff of a dead slave hanging from a tree, a couple miles back.

You are not only losing valuable stock by hangings, you are having uprisings, slaves are running away, your crops are sometimes left in the fields too long for maximum profit, You suffer occasional fires, your animals are killed.

Gentlemen, you know what your problems are; I do not need to elaborate. I am not here to enumerate your problems, I am here to introduce you to a method of solving them.

In my bag here, I HAVE A FULL PROOF METHOD FOR CONTROLLING YOUR BLACK SLAVES. I guarantee every one of you that if installed correctly IT WILL CONTROL THE SLAVES FOR AT LEAST 300 HUNDREDS YEARS.

My method is simple. Any member of your family or your overseer can use it. I HAVE OUTLINED A NUMBER OF DIFFERENCES AMONG THE SLAVES; AND I TAKE THESE DIFFERENCES AND MAKE THEM BIGGER. I USE FEAR, DISTRUST AND ENVY FOR CONTROL PURPOSES. These methods have worked on my modest plantation in the West Indies and it will work throughout the South.

Take this simple little list of differences and think about them. On top of my list is "AGE" but it's there only because it starts with an "A."

The second is "COLOR" or shade, there is INTELLIGENCE, SIZE, SEX, SIZES OF PLANTATIONS, STATUS on plantations, ATTITUDE of owners, whether the slaves live in the valley, on a hill, East, West, North, South, have fine hair, course hair, or is tall or short. Now that you have a list of differences, I shall give you a outline of action, but before that, I shall assure you that DISTRUST IS STRONGER THAN TRUST AND ENVY STRONGER THAN ADULATION, RESPECT OR ADMIRATION.

The Black slaves after receiving this indoctrination shall carry on and will become self refueling and self generating for HUNDREDS of years, maybe THOUSANDS. Don't forget you must pitch the OLD black Male vs. the YOUNG black Male, and the YOUNG black Male against the OLD black male. You must use the DARK skin slaves vs. the LIGHT skin slaves, and the LIGHT skin slaves vs. the DARK skin slaves. You must use the FEMALE vs. the MALE. And the MALE vs. the FEMALE.

You must also have you white servants and over- seers distrust all Blacks. But it is NECESSARY THAT YOUR SLAVES TRUST AND DEPEND ON US. THEY MUST LOVE, RESPECT AND TRUST ONLY US. Gentlemen, these kits are your keys to control. Use them. Have your wives and children use them, never miss an opportunity. IF USED INTENSELY FOR ONE YEAR, THE SLAVES THEMSELVES WILL REMAIN PERPETUALLY DISTRUSTFUL.

Thank you gentlemen.

"LET'S MAKE A SLAVE" by Willie Lynch
The Origin and Development of a Social Being Called "The Negro"
The following Information Is Considered Offensive!!

Let us make a slave. What do we Need?

First of all we need a black nigger man, a pregnant nigger woman and her baby nigger boy. Second, we will use the same basic principle that we use in breaking a horse, combined with some more sustaining factors. We reduce them from their natural state in nature; whereas nature provides them with the natural capacity to take care of their needs and the needs of their offspring, we break that natural string of independence from them and thereby create a dependency state so that we may be able to get from them useful production for our business and pleasure.

CARDINAL PRINCIPLE FOR MAKING A NEGRO
For fear that our future generations may not understand the principle of breaking both horses and men, we lay down the art. For, if we are to sustain our basic economy we must break both of the beasts together, the nigger and the horse. We understand that short range planning in economics results in periodic economic chaos, so that, to avoid turmoil in the economy, it requires us to have breadth and depth in long range comprehensive planning, articulating both skill and sharp perception. We lay down the following principles for long range comprehensive economic planning:

1) Both horse and niggers are no good to the economy in the wild or natural state.
2) Both must be broken and tied together for orderly production.
3) For orderly futures, special and particular attention must be paid to the female and the youngest offspring.
4) Both must be crossbred to produce a variety and division of labor.
5) Both must be taught to respond to a peculiar new language.
6) Psychological and physical instruction of containment must be created for both.

We hold the above six cardinals as truths to be self-evident, based upon following discourse concerning the economics of breaking and tying the horse and nigger together...all inclusive of the six principles laid down above.

NOTE: Neither principles alone will suffice for good economics. All principles must be employed for the orderly good of the nation.

Accordingly, both a wild horse and a wild or natural nigger is dangerous even if captured, for they will have the tendency to seek their customary freedom, and, in doing so, might kill you in your sleep. You cannot rest. They sleep while you are awake and are awake while you are asleep. They are dangerous near the family house and it requires too much labor to watch them away from the house. Above all you cannot get them to work in this natural state. Hence, both the horse and the nigger must be broken, that is, break them from one form of mental life to another, keep the body and take the mind. In other words, break the will to resist.

Now the breaking process is the same for the horse and the nigger, only slightly varying in degrees. But as we said before, you must keep your eye focused on the female and the offspring of the horse and the nigger. A brief discourse in offspring development will shed light on the key to sound economic principle.

Pay little attention to the generation of original breaking but concentrate on future generations. Therefore, if you break the female, she will break the offspring in its early years of development and, when the offspring is old enough to work, she will deliver it up to you. For her normal female protective tendencies will have been lost in the original breaking process.

For example, take the case of the wild stud horse, a female horse and an already infant horse and compare the breaking process with two captured nigger males in their natural state, a pregnant nigger woman with her infant offspring. Take the stud horse, break him for limited containment.

Completely break the female horse until she becomes very gentle whereas you or anybody can ride her in comfort. Breed the mare until you have the desired offspring. Then you can turn the stud to freedom until you need him again. Train the female horse whereby she will eat out of your hand, and she will train the infant horse to eat of your hand also.

When it comes to breaking the uncivilized nigger, use the same process, but vary the degree and step up the pressure so as to do a complete reversal of the mind. Take the meanest and most restless nigger, strip him of his clothes in front of the remaining niggers, the female, and the nigger infant, tar and feather him, tie each leg to a different horse faced in opposite directions, set him a fire and beat both horses to pull him apart in front of the remaining niggers. The next step is to take a bullwhip and beat the remaining nigger male to the point of death in front of the female and the infant. Don't kill him. But put the fear of God in him, for he can be useful for future breeding.

THE BREAKING PROCESS OF THE AFRICAN WOMAN

Take the female and run a series of tests on her to see if she will submit to you desires willingly. Test her in every way, because she is the most important factor for good economics. If she shows any signs of resistance in submitting completely to your will, do not hesitate to use the bull whip on her to extract that last bit of bitch out of her. Take care not to kill her, for in doing so, you spoil good economics. When in complete submission, she will train her offspring in the early years to submit to labor when they become of age.

Understanding is the best thing.
Therefore, we shall go deeper into this area of the subject matter concerning what we have produced here in this breaking of the female nigger. We have reversed the relationship. In her natural uncivilized state she would have a strong dependency on the uncivilized nigger male, and she would have a limited protective dependency toward her independent male offspring and would raise female offspring to be dependent like her. Nature had provided for this type of balance. We **reversed nature** by burning and pulling one civilized nigger apart and bull whipping the other to the point of death--all in her presence.

By her being left alone, unprotected, with the protective male image destroyed, the ordeal will cause her to move from her psychological dependent state to a frozen independent state. In this frozen psychological state of independence she will raise her male and female offspring in reversed roles. For fear of the young male's life she will psychologically train him to be mentally weak and dependent but physically strong. Because she has become psychologically independent, she will train her female offspring to be psychologically independent of the nigger man as well.

What have you got? You've got the nigger woman out front and the nigger man behind and scared. This is the perfect situation for sound sleep and economics. Before the breaking process, we had to be alert and on guard at all times. Now we can sleep soundly, for frozen out of fear, his woman stands guard for us. He cannot get past her early infant slave molding process. He is a good tool, now ready to be tied to the horse at a tender age. By the time a nigger boy reaches the age of sixteen, he is soundly broken in and ready for a long life of sound and efficient work and the reproduction of a unit of good labor force.

Continually, through the breaking of uncivilized savage niggers, by throwing the nigger female savage into a frozen psychological state of independency from the nigger male, by killing the protective male image, and by creating a submissive dependent mind of the nigger male slave, we have created an orbiting cycle that turns on its own axis forever, **unless a phenomenon occurs and re-shifts the positions of the male and female savages**.

We show what we mean by example. We breed two nigger males with two nigger females. Then we take the nigger males away from them and keep them moving and working. Say the nigger female bears a nigger female and the other bears a nigger male. Both nigger females, being without influence of the nigger male image, frozen with an independent psychology, will raise him to be mentally dependent and weak, but physically strong...in other words, body over mind. We will mate and breed them and continue the cycle.

That is good, sound, and long range comprehensive planning.

WARNING: POSSIBLE INTERLOPING NEGATIVES

Earlier, we talked about the non-economic good of the horse and the nigger in their wild or natural state; we talked about the principle of breaking and tying them together for orderly production. Furthermore, we talked about paying particular attention to the female savage and her offspring for orderly future planning; then more recently we stated that, by reversing the positions of the male and female savages we had created an orbiting cycle that turns on its own axis forever, unless phenomenon occurred, and re-shifted the positions of the male and female savages.

Our experts warned us about the possibility of this phenomenon occurring, for **they say that the mind has a strong drive to correct and re-correct itself over a period of time if it can touch some substantial original historical base; and they advised us that the best way to deal with this phenomenon is to shave off the brute's mental history and create a multiplicity of phenomenon or illusions so that each illusion will twirl in its own orbit, something akin to floating balls in a vacuum**.

This creation of a multiplicity of phenomenon or illusions entails the principles of crossbreeding the nigger and the horse as we stated above, the purpose of which is to create a diversified division of labor. The result of which is severance of the points of original beginning's for each spherical illusion.

Since we feel that the subject matter may get more complicated as we proceed in laying down our economic plan concerning the purpose, reason, and effect of cross-breeding horses and niggers, we shall lay down the following definitional terms for future generations.

1. Orbiting cycle means a thing turning in a given pattern.
2. Axis means upon which or around which a body turns.
3. Phenomenon means something beyond ordinary conception and inspires awe and wonder.
4. Multiplicity means a great number.
5. Sphere means a globe.
6. Cross-breeding a horse means taking a horse and breeding it with an ass and you get a dumb backward ass, longheaded mule that is not reproductive nor productive by itself.
7. Cross-breeding niggers means taking so many drops of good white blood and putting them into as many nigger women as possible, varying the drops by the various tone that you want, and then letting them breed with each other until cycle of colors appear as you desire.

What this means is this: Put the niggers and the horse in the breeding pot, mix some asses and some good white blood and what do you get?

You got a multiplicity of colors of ass backwards, unusual niggers, running, tied to backwards ass longheaded mules, the one productive of itself, the other sterile. (The one constant, the other dying. We keep nigger constant for we may replace the mule for another tool) both mule and nigger tied to each other, neither knowing where the other came from and neither productive for itself, nor without each other.

CONTROLLED LANGUAGE

Cross-breeding completed, for further severance from their original beginning, we must completely annihilate the mother tongue of both the nigger and the new mule and institute a new language that involves the new life's work of both.

You know, language is a peculiar institution. It leads to the heart of people. The more a foreigner knows about the language of another country the more he is able to move through all levels of that society.

Therefore, if the foreigner is an enemy of the country, to the extent that he knows the body of the language, to that extent is the country vulnerable to attack or invasion of a foreign culture. For example, you take the slave, if you teach him all about your language, he will know all your secrets, and he is then no more a slave, for you can't fool him any longer and having a fool is one of the basic ingredients of and incidents to the making of the slavery system.

By The Black Arcade Liberation Library; 1970 (recompiled and reedited by Kenneth T. Spann)

Exhibit 2e

The Reality of Man is Connectedness to GOD and All Men. This is GOD's Image and Likeness.

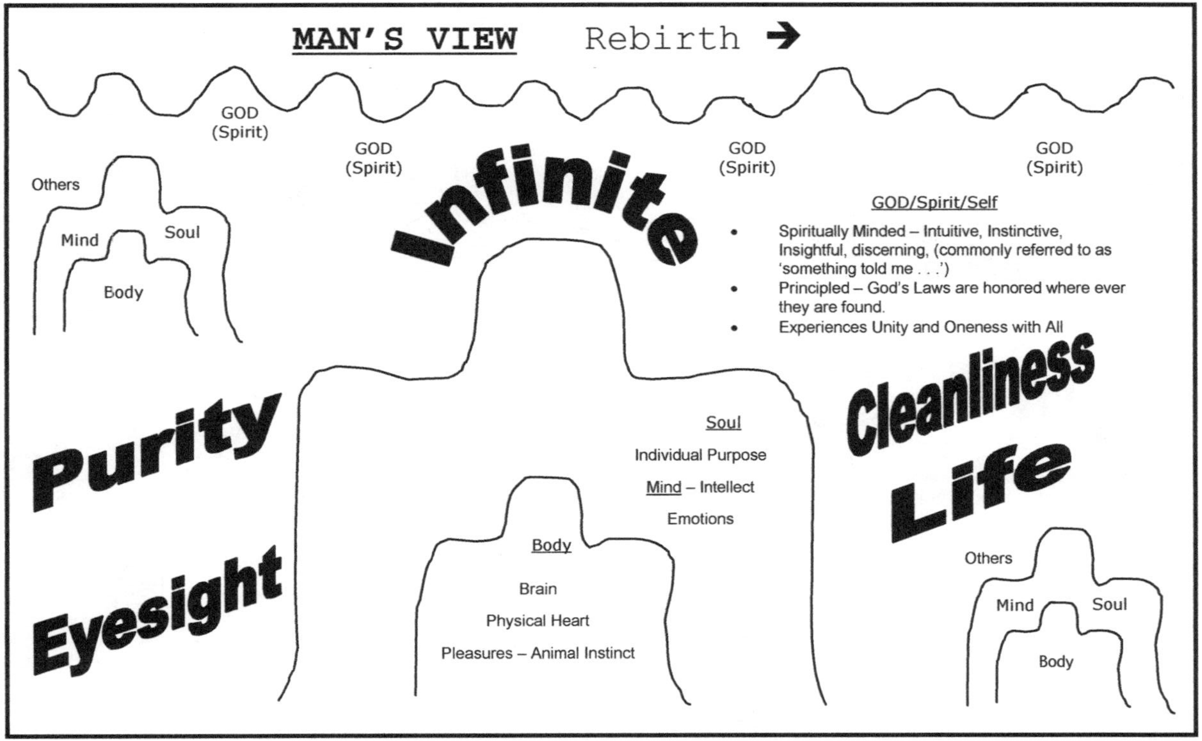

This chart attempts to demonstrate how Man views himself in relationship to the world. He is in tune with his spirit which he knows is connected to GOD and others. He sees his Self as the reality of who he is. His mind is aware of his Self and his Oneness. His major life decisions are based on the implications of its effects on others.

Scriptures Offering Understanding

The wind bloweth where it listeth, and thou hearest the sound thereof, but canst not tell whence it cometh, and whither it goeth: so is every one that is born of the Spirit. – John 3:8

And I will pray the Father, and he shall give you another Comforter, that he may abide with you for ever; Even the Spirit of truth; whom the world cannot receive, because it seeth him not, neither knoweth him: but ye know him; for he dwelleth with you, and shall be in you. – John 14: 16-17

Howbeit when he, the Spirit of truth, is come, he will guide you into all truth: for he shall not speak of himself; but whatsoever he shall hear, that shall he speak: and he will shew you things to come.
– John 16:13

In him we live, move and have our being; -- Acts 17:28

Exhibit 2f

The Illusion of being disconnected from GOD has been created in LORD God's world.

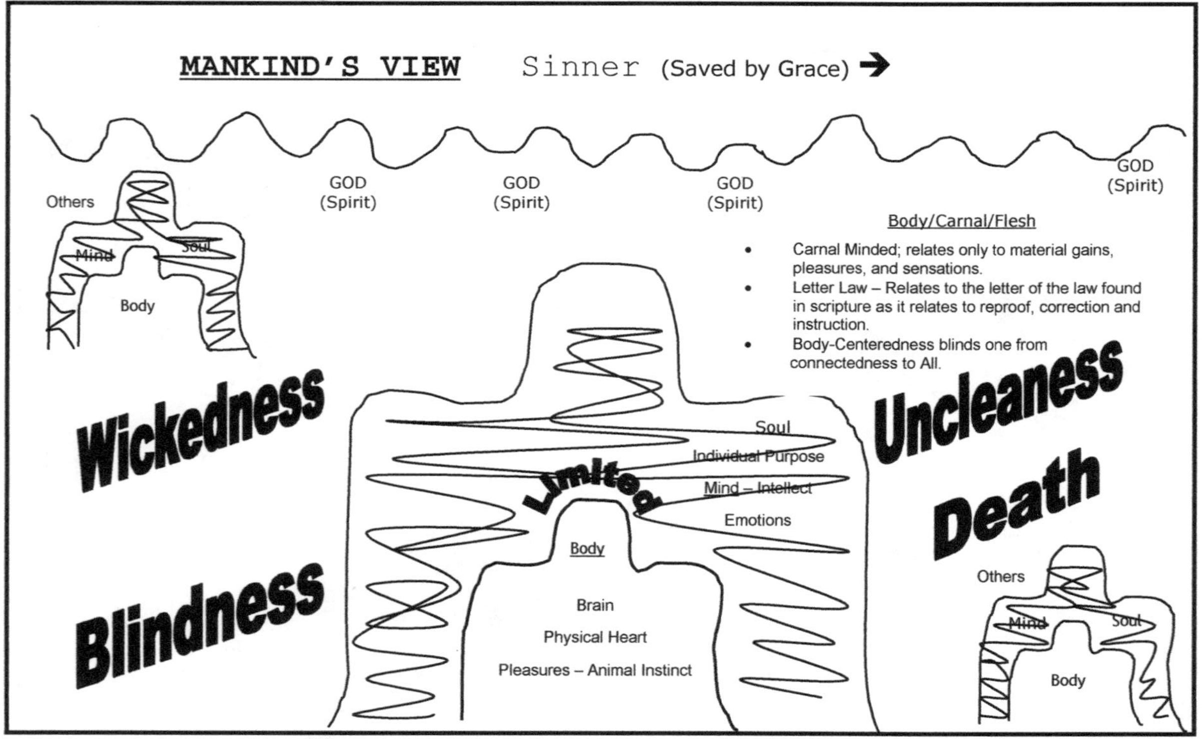

This chart attempts to demonstrate how Mankind views himself in relationship to the world. He has no understanding of his spirit which he believes is housed somewhere **inside** of his body and is subject to his body. He's sees his body as the reality of who he is. His mind is blind to Self and Oneness.

Scriptures Offering Guidance

Having the understanding darkened, being alienated from the life of God through the ignorance that is in them, because of the blindness of their heart: Who being past feeling have given themselves over unto lasciviousness, to work all uncleanness with greediness. But ye have not so learned Christ; If so be that ye have heard him, and have been taught by him, as the truth is in Jesus: That ye put off concerning the former conversation the old man, which is corrupt according to the deceitful lusts; And be renewed in the spirit of your mind; And that ye put on the new man, which after God is created in righteousness and true holiness. – Eph 4:18-24

NOTE: The DA does not seek to diminish the body experience because it has purpose. The body is Man's tool. We simply seek to demonstrate how in the world of LORD God, man is kept blind to purpose. It is understanding of purpose which brings the balance that we seek.

Exhibit 2g: On Walking in Flesh

The Gods at War

*"...Walk in the Spirit, and ye shall not fulfill the lust of the flesh; [for the flesh and spirit **appear**] contrary the one to the other: so that ye cannot do the things that ye would. For to be fleshly minded is death; —Galatians 5:16, 17, Romans 8:6*

We immediately declare to you that LORD God has placed the material world as the highest priority in your Mind. Though you believe to the contrary, the substances found in the body, are not unique to the universe. It is the same matter found elsewhere in the cosmos.

We make this declaration to remind you that the proof of our argument is all around you. Those of the order of Original Male and Female are to this day, deceived and remain in a deep sleep[96], under the deadly spell of LORD God, through his churches.

LORD God's spell prevents you from ever accessing ANY natural power of your Self. If he ever did allow the light of knowledge of good and evil to enter your Mind, you would immediately awaken and make an escape.

The World of Satan is based in the thought system of Materialism[97]. Believing that physical matter is fundamental reality; and all being -- processes and phenomena can be explained as manifestations or results of matter. LORD God's children (Mankind) think the material world is the starting point and cause of thought and reality, rather than thought actually being reality.

Although churches attempt to mask their materialistic foundation through frequent use of the word "Spiritual", and other terms rooted in Higher Law; a cursory examination will make it glaringly clear that Christian Doctrine is founded in placing its highest values and objectives in material well-being and furtherance of material progress, to the sacrifice of the Human Spirit. One need only consider the multitude of multi-million dollar church enterprises saturating the Original Man's otherwise depressed communities. They are the proof of what LORD God and his ministers value.

Of late, the preachers have taken on a more "community oriented" rhetoric to shift attention to the illusion that their doctrine is of the Original Order; however, be not deceived. The Elevated One warned you at the beginning. **Beware of the Doctrine of LORD God's ministers; a little of their doctrine poisons the entire Thought System**[98]. There is no compromise between the thought system of LORD God, and the System of Original Man.

---

96 Read Genesis 2: 21-23.

97 We use Material and Flesh interchangeably.

98 Read Matthew 16: 5-12.

Thus, the Sons of Man come with swords; dividing and pitting one thought system against the other; and the gods are now at war[99] to determine which Thought System prevails.

LORD God's societies, economics, science, religion and politics are ALL built on the foundation of a materialism and violence. According to the fleshly thinker, the physical world is fragmented and hostile; every piece towards the other. His Thought System values the flesh as though it is somehow a **cause** of experience, rather than the **effect** of thinking. In other words, its premise is that experience comes first, and then thought. There is no part of this system that the Original Male and Female can use.

Those who follow the flesh define themselves as a body, and things they believe the body can possess. The materialist totally identifies the Self with the material arrangement of Matter as an initial-point and end-point of his world; and thinks the **Self** is subject to the flesh. He kills for it; steals for it, goes into debt for it; he even makes other men slaves for it.

Although the fleshly Mind can be found across every strata of the present World, the fleshly Mind is especially incubated in the Christian churches of LORD God. There the thought system of materialism is so strong that it teaches the thinker that even though LORD God cursed him to Death, and Jesus came to prove that Death is not real by "rising from the dead[100]", he must still die. However, he need not worry; after his Death, LORD God will someday reassemble his physical body, which has long been returned to its source, and change the body into a newly configured "everlasting spiritual body".

The materialistic Mind never considers the enormous number of absurdities in LORD God's version of resurrection, but we examine them herein. To make the point in no uncertain terms, we examine what occurs to the body after a typical burial of "believers" in LORD God. We remind you that the burial experience of a believer in LORD God is exactly the same as a non-believer.

After a believer dies, his body is embalmed, placed in the ground and sealed in a metal or wooden casket. The standard burial depth is about 6 feet. After burial many kinds of organisms that live by feeding on dead bodies, are attracted to the casket. In the process, their activities result in the decomposition of the body and the recycling of nutrients.

---

99 Read Matthew 10:34.

100 If Death was real, Jesus could not have risen. It would mean GOD created Death, thus making Death real. The real cannot be made Un-real, nor can the Un-real be made real. Jesus rose to prove that Death is Un-real.

The dominant groups of organisms involved in decomposition are bacteria, flies, beetles, mites and moths.

The notorious Coffin fly is able to dig his way through cracks in the soil above buried coffins. A coffin fly has been observed to dig to a depth of 0.5 m in four days, and once they have tunneled down to a body, different organisms can move between the body and the surface quite freely. They are also capable of completing their entire life cycle beneath the ground, so that several generations can occupy a corpse without coming to the surface.

It has been calculated that with 98% survival, one pair of coffin flies in a protected place could produce 55 million flies in 60 days. Even with only 1% survival it would take only 7 months to produce 1 million flies.

If you live after the flesh, ye shall die: but if ye through the Spirit do mortify the deeds of the body, you shall live.—Romans 8:13

As a body decomposes by way of millions of organisms (about 1 year), Other animals, mainly parasitoid wasps, predatory beetles and predatory flies, feed on the animals that feed on the corpse; which in turn are eaten by even larger animals; who in turn are eaten by humans who might be on the other side of the planet; who digest and dispose of them in waste and then himself dies and is buried. This cycle continues for thousands of years.

A dead body is therefore an ecosystem of its own, in which different fauna arrive and depart from the corpse at different times. The science is so exact that the arrival time and growth rates of insects inhabiting corpses are used by forensic scientists to determine the circumstances surrounding suspicious deaths.

So now consider what LORD God promises his believers in totality: "I have cursed you and your body to Death, so Fear me; in spite of my curse on you, I will die in your place to give you a way out of Death, provided you serve me. However, you must still die, in spite of my Death in your place.

But don't worry, for even though your body has been dead for thousands of years, and may even be part of someone else's body, I will repossess your molecules from every being and reconstruct them as you; then raise your body from the grave and turn it into a spirit and you will live in your body forever with me in heaven."

LORD God forgot to tell them the principle of Constant Composition, which is found in the statement: "That, which is born of flesh, is flesh; and that which is born of spirit, is spirit".—John 3:6

In other words, a thing is what a thing is. LORD God does not tell his followers that as they manifest, in earth, drunk with illusions of gaining a life that they already have, he robs them of their essence and perpetuates his kingdom of Death, while enslaving the sleeping children of GOD. He puts the people of GOD to sleep my making them think they are the hammer, rather than the carpenter using the hammer. Should you still not be convinced of the illusory nature of the flesh, we offer you more evidence. Consider what scientists know about the flesh (material world).

As you consider what scientists know, keep these questions at the forefront of your mind: *What does it mean to "Walk in the flesh" or be "materialistic"? Is the material world real, or is it some agreed upon projection of the mind onto some universal canvas?*

Here are the scientific facts. When DNA (flesh or material) is traced down to its individual atoms, each is more than 99.9999% empty space. Individual electrons have no fixed position in either time nor space. Rather, ghostly vibrations wink in and out of the universe thousands of times per second, and what lies beyond the boundary of the five senses holds enormous mysteries...

Greater still, events at opposite ends of the universe are paired with each other, so that a change in the spin of one electron immediately produces a twin effect in another electron. This ability to communicate instantly across millions of light years cannot be explained by materialism. It defies all [materially-based] notions of cause and effect. It also defies chance. Every electron in the universe exists as a wave function that is everywhere at once. When this wave function collapses, we observe a specific isolated electron. Before the wave collapses, however, matter is non-local.[101]

"Every Cause has its Effect; every Effect has its Cause; everything happens according to Law; Chance is but a name for Law not recognized".--The Kybalion

[101] Quoted from Deepak Chopra—The God Delusion, part 3.

The image below is a picture of the human cerebral cortex. It is the part of your brain that conducts the electrical signals giving your body the ability to think, act and create. In essence, it is the physical body's "power plant". But what is the ultimate source of its power?

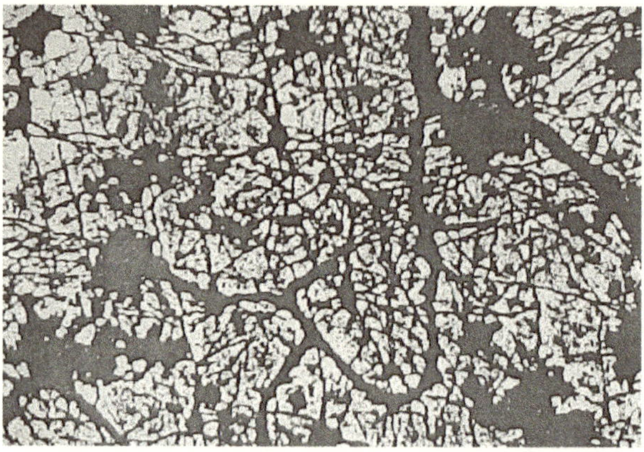

Now compare the image of Dark Matter; Notice any Similarities?

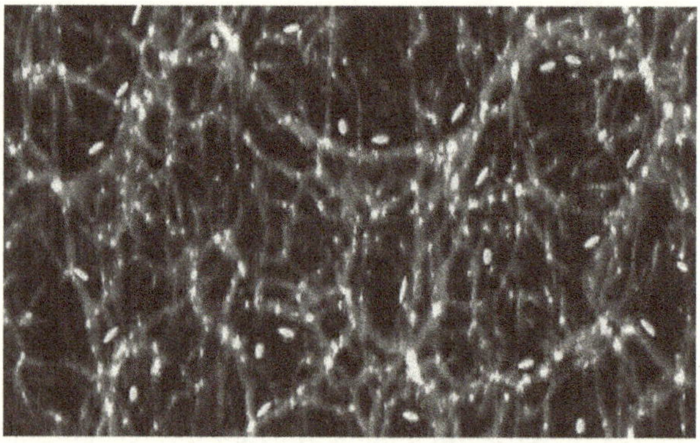

Dark Matter[102] *is the invisible "stuff" which makes up 90% of the universe. At present, scientists do not know exactly what it is. We cannot detect Dark Matter by physical means, i.e. radiation. We notice that it rarely; if ever, interacts with normal matter; yet it controls the development and expansion of the universe. As a result, we believe it could exist everywhere, yet is undetectable through physical senses. Along with "Dark Energy" it causes the universe to function, expand and accelerate. The picture above is a computer simulation of what Dark Matter could look like.*

---

102 Visit NASA's web site **http://imagine.gsfc.nasa.gov/docs/science/mysteries_l1/dark_matter.html** for more information on Dark Matter.

Again we raise the question: Is the material world an agreed upon physical arrangement, projected by the human Mind (and other Minds) onto some great canvas; or is it a physical reality existing apart from Mental influences? Could the "stuff" that makes up Dark Matter be the brain or "Power Plant" or life force of the universe? If so, are we contained within that brain? And who or what controls that universal brain?

Now, return to the question at hand; in light of the previous discussion.

We asserted that the term "flesh" is simply another name for material or Matter. Every element in the physical body is also found somewhere in the physical universe. This indicates that the physical body IS the physical universe (Localized). But the physical universe clearly had a beginning. In other words, there was a time when the physical universe did not manifest. It evolved, and is still evolving to this day. It is also clear that a "force" caused the physical universe to burst into existence. Therefore, neither the physical universe, nor the physical body could be its own cause.[103]

With respect to the physical body, we clearly see that when the "Life Force" leaves the physical body; it behaves similar to a tool or other material instrument. It no longer animates; and is simply laid down by its user. Left alone eventually its molecular structure disassembles, and then reassembles as another body or "tool".

—That is to say, the material that makes up your physical body is not unique in terms of existence. Its uniqueness is only in the physical arrangement of existing atoms. You could actually have some of the same molecules that were in Albert Einstein's body, or even Adolph Hitler. DNA and genetics proves this assertion.

"For as many as are led by the Spirit of God, they are the sons of GOD".— Romans 8:14

If you walk according to the flesh you are subject to illusions and cannot create the universe. In fact, the universe appears hostile to you, since it cannot be controlled by physical means.

On the other hand if you walk in the Spirit (or as GOD) your are safe. GOD is your friend and the universe is your servant because you are operating from the level of Man; whose mind controls the universe. In this case, All things are reconciled.

---

[103] This is not intended to make the Christian argument that a "separate" God created the universe.

EXHIBIT 4a: The Development of a Double-Mind

Out of the same mouth proceedeth blessing and cursing. My brethren, these things ought not so to be. Doth the fountain send forth at the same place sweet water and bitter? Can the fig tree, my brethren, bear olive berries? Either a vine, figs? So can no fountain both yield salt water and fresh. James 3:10-12 The author finds the following Thought Seeds **High Crimes** against Humanity.

CURSE	THOUGHT SEED	THE LAW
He will make you greater than any other nation on earth.	Your LORD God IS a Respecter of Persons and plants Selfishness in the Mind..	**GOD is no respecter of persons.** Acts 10:34
Obey the LORD your God and all these blessings will be yours . . .	You are an effect rather than a cause. Your blessings are based on obedience rather than what YOU SOW.	**YOU are the MASTER of your FATE.** 2 Corinthians 9:6
The LORD will bless you with many children, with abundant crops etc.	LORD God places into the future, based on strict obedience, what is presently enforced by GOD.	**GOD said BE Fruitful and Multiply.** Gen. 1:28
The LORD will bless everything you do.	Your blessings are somewhere in the future.	**GOD blessed YOU [Immediately]** Gen. 1:28
The LORD will defeat your enemies when they attack you.	See others as enemies. Therefore, attack them and LORD God will make you victorious.	**Return Good for Evil.** Luke 6:27
The LORD will bless your work and fill your barns with grain.	Think that it is to the LORD's credit that the work of YOUR HANDS filled your barns.	**Whatsoever YOU Sow YOU will Reap.** Galatians 6:7
Do everything LORD God commands [and] he will make you his OWN people.	Your Race is Special. Your Race is LORD God's favorite. You can take from others without asking and murder others without regret.	**GOD sees Man as ONE PEOPLE.** Matthew 5:45
All peoples on earth will see that the LORD has chosen you to be his own people, and they will be afraid of you.	Because you are LORD God's CHOSEN people you will terrorize others and cause them to fear you.	**Perfect your LOVE and Cast Out Fear.** 1 John 4:18
The LORD will [do all this] that he promised your ancestors to give you.	He had a previous relationship with your ancestors so you can trust him.	**SATAN Promises Only to Deceive.** Holy Qur'an

EXHIBIT 4a: The Development of a Double-Mind

CURSE	THOUGHT SEED	THE LAW
You will lend to many nations, but you will not have to borrow from any.	Lend to others because then they will be in debt to you. Never borrow because you do not want to be in debt to Others.	**GIVE FREELY as YOU see Sufficient.** 2 Corinthians 9:7
The LORD your God will make you the leader among the nations and not a follower.	Be arrogant. Never consider sharing power or being led. You must always LORD over others.	**If You are the CHIEF, SERVE.** Matthew 20:25-27
But you must never disobey in any way or worship other gods.	You must abhor the Original people of the earth who see God in each other and adore and serve each other.	**Recognize that Man represents GOD and respect him.** John 10:34-36
LORD God will send disease after disease in the land that you are about to occupy.	You will be OCCUPIERS of other people's lands and one hint of disobedience will cause LORD God to destroy you with disease.	**Share the Earth and GOD will Heal the Land.** Genesis 1:26
Foreigners who live in your land will gain more and more power while you gradually lose yours.	See others as Foreigners or Aliens. They are threats to 'your' land and want 'your' power.	**Realize your Connectedness to Others.** Matthew 5:40-41
When your enemies are besieging your towns, you will become so desperate for food that you will even eat the children LORD God has given you.	You will become bestial and animalistic. You will even do harm to your own child.	**Earth is Abundant. See Others as Friends.** Matthew 7:11
She will become so desperate for food that she will secretly eat her newborn and afterbirth as well and will not share with her husband and other children.	Sheer INSANITY is being placed in your Mind by LORD God. The Mind of Satan is so full of gross and vengeful atrocities that the depth of his wickedness cannot be fathomed.	**There is Always Enough. Protect Children.** Luke 12:32
[LORD God] will send all kinds of disease and epidemics that are not mentioned in this book of God's laws and teachings and you will be destroyed.	Just in case, LORD God thinks of some more curses later, He reserves the right to add them to his book.	**Healing is Always Available.** Numbers 23: 20

EXHIBIT 4a: The Development of a Double-Mind

CURSE	THOUGHT SEED	THE LAW
You will be uprooted from the land that you are about to occupy.	When you are uprooted from the land that you are OCCUPYING, you will think it is a curse.	**Land is Plenteous. Be Meek.** Psalm 37:10
Your life will always be in danger.	You will be paranoid of retaliation from everyone you have pillaged, deceived, and murdered.	**Follow Peace with All Men.** Isaiah 57:20-21
Day and night you will be filled with terror, and you will live in constant fear of Death.	Though you do not realize your connection with others, you will feel all the pain, agony, and death you caused others.	**If You Live by the Sword, You will fall by it.** Matthew 26:52
The LORD will send you back to Egypt in ships, even though he said that you will never have to go there again.	The LORD can change his Mind about his Covenants and Promises at any time.	**GOD's Word is BOND.** Numbers 23:19

See Other High Crimes on Next Page.

EXHIBIT 4a: The Development of a Double-Mind

Other High Crimes

All of LORD God's Curses are only Seeds of Thought He has planted into the Minds of Mankind. Only their Collective submission and compliance brings about the experience. Thus Collective Repentance will Free All Humanity.

BIBLICAL STORY	THOUGHT SEED	THE LAW
Adam and Eve	**Adam and Woman – SEPARATE.** Blindness, Ignorance, Nakedness and the thought of things not being good in creation and in Man is introduced.	**Male and Female - ONE** Eyes Open, Knowledge, Clothed, and GOD's creation and Man are Perfect. See The Truman Show (Notice how Serpents keep entering the Garden)
Cain and Abel	LORD God is a respecter of persons. He plays favorites and pits the brothers against each other. He approves Cain ONLY after he fills him with guilt, vengeance, and murder. See LION KING Movie (Pay close attention to how Scar makes Simba think he is responsible for his father's death when Scar was manipulating the entire situation.	**Forgive One Another.** GOD is no respecter of person. He does not require sacrifice. He tells us to love even our perceived enemies. GOD is oft forgiving.
Noah's Ark	LORD God commits Mass Genocide after he REPENTS that he made Mankind.	**Bring Your THOUGHTS into Peace and Earth will be at Peace.** GOD is not a Man that he should REPENT.
Tower of Babel	LORD God fears Man remembering his Greatness and Unity once again and causes confusion and Blindness. (Just as he did to Adam and Eve)	**Man is ONE.**
Abram and his wife	LORD God teaches Abram to uses his wife to deceive a leader of another country.	**Be Truthful with the Righteous.** Ephesians 4:5
Sodom and Gomorrah	LORD God destroys entire cities and turns Lot's wife into a pillar of salt. He provides for Lot's drunkenness and incest with his daughters.	**Be Sober and of Good Character.** Titus 2:2

EXHIBIT 4a: The Development of a Double-Mind

Other High Crimes

BIBLICAL STORY	THOUGHT SEED	THE LAW
Ishmael and Isaac	LORD God tells Abram to put away his oldest son and his Birth Right. None of LORD God's rules are dependable.	**BE FAIR with Your Children.** Deuteronomy 21:15-16
Elisha is teased by Children	And he turned back, and looked on them, and cursed them in the name of the LORD. And there came forth two she bears out of the wood, and tare forty and two children of them.	**Children will be Children. Be Mature.** Luke 18:16
First Recorded Rape and Massacre	And I took my concubine, and cut her in pieces, and sent her throughout all the country of the inheritance of Israel: for they have committed lewdness and folly in Israel. Judges 20:6	**Esteem and Protect the Female.** This is why it is a well known proverb, "The hands that rock the cradle, rule the World."
Basis of LORD God's World is FEAR	FEAR HIM or BE DESTROYED.	**Perfect Your Love, Be Powerful, and of Sound Mind.** 2 Titus 1:7

If any of you lack wisdom, let him ask of GOD, that giveth to all men liberally, and upbraideth[104] not; and it shall be given him. . . A double minded man is unstable in all his ways.
James 1: 5 & 8

[104] Upbraid: Chastise, rebuke, scold or reprimand.

EXHIBIT 4b: Standing Debate Challenge to Sharpton and Jackson

March 8, 2006

Dear Reverend Jesse Jackson & Reverend Al Sharpton;

I and several of my colleagues are appalled at your continued use of reactionary politics, useless marches and demonstrations under the guise of civil rights. With every new crisis you march about, your continued invocation of Dr. Martin Luther King, Rosa Parks and other pioneering spirits, makes a mockery of their names and the purpose for their movement. Your behavior is untimely, outdated and counterproductive to our real advancement as GOD's People. Each of your marches is a glaring indication of the fact that you and your organization have completely missed the substance of what Dr. King was doing in his time. You have instead, locked on to the symbol of marching, without substance and purpose. You have almost single-handedly rendered Dr. King's methods, at best, an impotent media circus that keeps GOD's People focused on how bad the great white man treats us. It is embarrassing to me as a black male.

Dr. King primarily used marching to raise the consciousness of America to her own brutality and callousness toward black people (His assumption being that they were largely unaware of their own behavior).

King invoked the high principle of reaping and sowing in order to appeal to a higher authority. His knowledge of that universal principle was a central piece to the movement. It gave America the opportunity to reap in the same manner that she chose to sow. This allowed her to make a conscious decision about her fate. Marching was the smallest part of his movement.

After almost forty years, we can clearly see that America's consciousness has long been raised. She has made a decision to continue -- indeed worsen in her evil ways. Your frequent and reactionary marches and demonstrations to relatively minor crisis, serve no purpose other than to divert the attention of black people from the fact that God himself has judged America. God himself has set this house on fire and every room in the house is burning. Marches only keep the people blind to the fact that God is the arsonist.

Time, not method must dictate the People's agenda and actions. Just because there are 99 wrong ways to do a thing and only ONE right way to do it, does not mean you have 100 options to get the desired result! You have only ONE CORRECT WAY to get the desired result. Therefore, to suggest that your wrong way of doing a thing is just as valid as the other leader's right way, is false.

The questions are:
1) What time is it?
2) What is the correct action that we should be engaged in?

The time to seek civil rights in America has past. Now GOD's people must turn from our wicked ways of seeking acceptance in a wicked system and turn our minds towards GOD and HIS plan for us.

We must:

1) Turn our full attention toward ourselves and use Dr. Kings methods of nonviolence towards the healing of the violence we inflict upon ourselves.

2) Direct our full attention to accepting the covenant that GOD has repeatedly offered to us, as outlined in II Chronicles 7:14, and most recently articulated by Honorable Minister Louis Farrakhan.

God himself has hardened America's heart towards us. GOD himself has claimed us as His People and His nation for the purpose of Healing ourselves and all who would be healed. The civil rights movement served its purpose and has now come and gone. Let it rest in peace, and take its rightful place in history.

Marching, demonstrating and petitioning this government and society for justice is a failed policy in this day and age. We have moved into the age of Unalienable Rights. We now appeal to a Higher Authority than what is currently in your consciousness.

I therefore challenge you or your representative, to a public debate on the merits of your continued use of civil rights marching, demonstrating and petitioning American society as a useful means to address the race problem.

The question before us: **Has marching and demonstrating to petition American government outlived its usefulness as a method of Black Liberation?**

While we can further modify the question and format, the basic program should consist of the following:

1. Each of us will have fifteen minutes to present our opening statements and arguments.

2. We formulate ten questions each to ask each other in cross-examination format.

3. A ten minute free debate forum moderated by a third party.

4. Fifteen minutes of questions from the audience to each of us.

5. Fifteen minutes of closing statements.

This debate would serve to give the people a REAL analysis of the Civil Rights Movement and help us all participate in formulating a 21st century agenda inclusive of a cross-section of our people.

I look forward to your timely response.

Dr. Alonzo Fleming Jr.

(No response to date)

EXHIBIT 4c: Letter to Congressional Black Caucus on Ralph Nader

June 24, 2004

Dear Congressman Cummings,

I am an African-American woman of your constituency (in that you represent Black People). I have always been proud of the Black Caucus and its voice in the world. However, your recent decision to ask Ralph Nader to drop out the presidential race shocked and confounded me.

Being politically correct has never been my strong point so I would like to cut right through the chase and inform you that your conduct regarding your friend and my friend, Ralph Nader, made me ashamed of you and reminded me of why Black people (especially Black leaders like yourselves) are in such GREAT Need of Reparations.

We are in need of repair. We cannot discern our enemies from our friends. We are not even true friends to each other. Ralph Nader has openly expressed his support of your organizational funding (which no president has done since Reagan shut you out) and he has also expressed his support of the Reparations Bill while Senator Kerry rejects it.

You are like an abused woman, who settles for her abusive husband (forsaking friends and allies) rather than filing for divorce. You and I both know that the Republican and Democratic hopefuls are different wings of the same buzzard. It's a classic case of good cop, bad cop – we place our hope in the good cop because we refuse to face the fact that they are both the same.

I don't think that you have sold us out. I believe you did this act in fear and in arrogance. Have you fallen so far into the quagmire of politics that you no longer believe in God? Don't you believe in the messengers of God? We do not have to concern ourselves with whether or not Bush gets back into office when we already know that America has been weighed in the balance and found wanting. We already know that Pharaoh's heart has been made hard. The only requirement we have is to stand up for righteousness -- less we find ourselves on the wrong side of the issue.

Please (with a capital 'P') *synchronize YOUR conscience with YOUR conduct and do not allow YOUR pride and arrogance to make YOU forget about our children who are yet unborn.* Call Ralph Nader back to the table and if you do nothing else express to him that you will use his ticket and his following to negotiate the Reparations Bill with Senator Kerry. **We Are in Need of Repair!** Instead of asking him to sit out -- USE HIM to push the Black Agenda.

And then, if Senator Kerry will not hear you, you will have done righteously and **God will show you his Reality!**

I wish you well in your future endeavors,

Cherice Fleming

EXHIBIT 4d: A Student Argues with his Professor regarding Reality

The story was sent to Gail Gupton from a 'religious' person who believes in a power opposed to God (Satan, Devil). This verifies that *spiritual evolution is occurring* in mainstream society today, however slight.

Did God create everything that exists? Does evil exist? Did God create evil?

A University professor at a well known institution of higher learning challenged his students with this question.

"Did God create everything that exists?"

A student bravely replied, "Yes he did!"

"God created everything?" the professor asked.

"Yes sir, he certainly did," the student replied.

The professor answered, "If God created everything; then God created evil. And, since evil exists, and according to the principal that our works define who we are, then we can assume God is evil."

The student became quiet and did not answer the professor's hypothetical definition. The professor, quite pleased with himself, boasted to the students that he had proven once more that the Christian faith was a myth.

Another student raised his hand and said, "May I ask you a question, professor?"

"Of course," replied the professor.

The student stood up and asked, "Professor, does cold exist?"

"What kind of question is this? Of course it exists. Have you never been cold?"

The other students snickered at the young man's question. The young man replied, "In fact, sir, cold does not exist. According to the laws of physics, what we consider cold is in reality the absence of heat. Every body or object is susceptible to study when it has or transmits energy, and heat is what makes a body or matter have or transmit energy. Absolute zero (-460 F) is the total absence of heat; and all matter becomes inert and incapable of reaction at that temperature. Cold does not exist. We have created this word to describe how we feel if we have no heat."

The student continued, "Professor, does darkness exist?"

The professor responded, "Of course it does."

The student replied, "Once again you are wrong, sir, Darkness does not exist either. Darkness is in reality the absence of light. Light we can study, but not darkness. In fact, we can use Newton's prism to break white light into many colors and study the various wavelengths of each color. You cannot measure darkness. A simple ray of light can break into a world of darkness and illuminate it. How can you know how dark a certain space is? You measure the amount of light present. Isn't this correct? Darkness is a term used by man to describe what happens when there is no light present."

Finally the young man asked the professor, "Sir, does evil exist?"

Now uncertain, the professor responded, "Of course, as I have already said. We see it everyday. It is in the daily examples of man's inhumanity to man. It is in the multitude of crime and violence everywhere in the world. These manifestations are nothing else but evil."

To this the student replied, "Evil does not exist, sir, or at least it does not exist unto itself. Evil is simply the absence of God. It is just like darkness and cold, a word that man has created to describe the absence of God. God did not create evil. Evil is the result of what happens when man does not have God's love present in his heart. It's like the cold that comes when there is no heat, or the darkness that comes when there is no light."

The professor sat down.

The young man's name - **Albert Einstein**

I reference this story as an example of Truth which has been around forever, but only *realized* by those persons who are above the world's beliefs. God is ALL and the absence of God's Allness from one's consciousness leaves mankind **void** of God's perfection. Only one's limited concept of God, and his or her concept of mankind, separates him from prosperity, health, love, and all the qualities of life one is heir to. To believe in a power other than God naturally causes one to experience their own belief. This is not theory or psychological - it's a **principle**.

Moses tried to teach the Allness and Oneness of God to his followers. Jesus tried to teach the Allness and Oneness of God to his disciples. Mohammed tried to teach the Allness and Oneness of God to his believers. Some, like Einstein, realized Truth. Shakespeare's writings hint of it. Truth has been realized by many, but forgotten in time. However, this same Truth re-appears, time and time again - and will, for infinity.

God is ALL. God is all there is. Only God IS. - God is our life. One life, One God. Period. The sooner one realizes this fact, the sooner will society become harmonious, individually and collectively. *The nature of God is good.*

All is well.

THE INFINITY OF TRUTH by Gail Gupton

EXHIBIT 4e: Cheikh Anta Diop's Two Cradle Theory

As the chart below indicates, those living in the safe, accommodating climate of the Southern Cradle (Africa) were more likely to develop Liberty, creativity, equality and support, as a result of their secure environment; while those living in the hostile Northern Cradle (Europe) were more likely to develop a mind of scarcity insecurity, treachery and warfare.

A Comparison of Southern and Northern Cradle Development

SOUTHERN CRADLE OF CIVILIZATION	NORTHERN CRADLE OF CIVILIZATION
1. Abundance of vital resources	1. Bareness of resources
2. Sedentary-agricultural	2. Nomadic-hunting (piracy)
3. Gentle, idealistic, peaceful nature with a spirit of justice	3. Ferocious, warlike nature with spirit of survival
4. Matriarchal family	4. Patriarchal family
5. Emancipation of women in domestic life	5. Debasement / enslavement of women
6. Territorial state	6. City state (fort)
7. Xenophilia	7. Xenophobia
8. Cosmopolitanism	8. Parochialism
9. Social collectivism	9. Individualism
10. Material solidarity of right for individual which makes material misery unknown	10. Moral solitude
11. Idea of peace, justice, goodness and optimism	11. Disgust for existence, pessimism
12. Literature emphasizes novel tales, fables and comedy	12. Literature favors tragedy

Its clear to see from chart that a person whose mind develops in the Northern cradle tends to be kept in a constant state of "Fight or Flight", which affects how he views himself, others, and God. In addition he will experience poor health and various biological anomalies.

When the Mind is kept under a constant state of fight or flight, the effects on development will be as though he was in the Northern (European) cradle, even if he, in reality is living in the Southern Cradle. An individual living under such conditions, views the world as scarce. He cannot develop the requisite experience of Liberty that's necessary for creation.

Instead, he views himself as a product of his environment, rather than the master of it. He views others as a threat to his domain, rather than as fellow travelers on earth. He views God as a brutal dictator exacting punishment to the non-believer, rather than as giver of life to ALL. His entire existence is consumed with day-to-day survival. This person hardly has the time to experience the liberty to create.

In spite of existing in the land of plenty, the slave-descendant population is kept in a constant state of 'fight or flight'. With each "anomaly" of racial hatred, the entire slave population's collective Sympathetic Nervous System (SNS) acts like a fire alarm and commands release of various hormones in the body like the adrenaline, noradrenalin, glucocorticoids etc. through our various endocrine glands, like the pituitary & adrenal. Together these hormones increase our heartbeats & blood pressure at times by 100% (to increase the blood supply), breathing becomes faster (to increase the intake of oxygen), throat muscles and nostrils open wider, pupils dilate and eyes alertly stare.

The hormones stop the secretion of saliva & mucus, and the process of digestion temporarily halts (conserving precious energy). Sugar is released from liver (for instant energy), subcutaneous fat is also released into the blood stream (for greater energy). More fat (cholesterol) is produced by the liver for fuel; sweating increases thus decreasing the temperature of the body.

This state is normal when sprinkled periodically in the course of life; however, it is very dangerous and unhealthy when one is kept in a constant state of 'fight or flight'. For the slave-descendant, his only release is minor, because he dedicates his life to building the world of White Supremacy, thereby thwarting or severely limiting the creativity of the general slave-descendant population.

Exhibit 4f: In Commemoration of the Million Man March

An Open Letter To Black leaders: Why Affirmative Action Makes No Sense To A Black Man

The following was written by Alonzo Fleming in commemoration of the Million Man March and prior to the vote on Affirmative Action in Michigan.

October 16, 2006

Dear Civil Rights Leaders:

As America celebrates the arrival of its 300 millionth citizen, I am concerned and perplexed by your preoccupation with Affirmative Action. I don't deny the racism that plagues America, but I can't seem to wrap my brain around the reasoning and hope you place in Affirmative Action as a remedy. The more I listen to your explanations, the more insane you sound; so I have composed a list of reasons why I as a black male believe that a vote for or against proposal 2 in Michigan, is a vote for the declaration of black inferiority. I hope that you will summon the courage and faith to muster a coherent answer that would change my thinking if I am wrong in this matter.

You say affirmative action is an act by white men to fix past wrongs done to black men. By creating a special door for us to enter, someday the playing field will be equal. You say that without this special treatment, we don't have the wherewithal to be successful. You further argue that although affirmative action has been in place for some time now, blacks (especially black males), have not progressed in society, but have in fact regressed. This sad fact is annually paraded before us by the National Urban League reports. With that in mind, here are my reasons for calling the affirmative action concept a "bankrupt" idea doomed to failure.

1) Mathematically improbable that we will benefit from it

In an environment of a shrinking economy, those who control what we seek in affirmative action are like parents who have four available jobs, and five children seeking those jobs. We are like people having five children, begging the other parent to give just one of those jobs to our children. However, that is a ridiculous expectation. No one in his right mind would deprive his own children, in order to feed another parents' child -- Especially when he sees the other parent has just as much strength and intellect to develop for himself. With all the hardworking individuals flooding America, just itching for the opportunity to put their hands to the plow, it is utterly insane for us to think that the good will of others (rather than our own genius) will create a proper future for our children. The age of good will for us is past; it's time for us to get up off our knees, drop our buckets where we stand, and build, because mankind is building all around us as we beg for morsels.

2) <u>Affirmative Action has been used as a means to deny black males opportunity</u>

For Affirmative Actions' success, there must first be a desire to repair the wrong; but in your arguments, you insist that white women have benefited most from affirmative action laws, while blacks are systematically excluded. If mostly white women have benefited from something designed for us, doesn't that speak volumes to the intent of those who would fix the wrongs? "A Mind changed against its Will is of the same Mind still". If a person does not want to do a thing, he will find ways to keep from doing it, hence white women are double minorities. Why would you continue to appeal and beg from someone whom you clearly see does not want to repair the damage? And why would you even desire to associate with someone who does not want you around? It makes no sense! Wouldn't it be wiser to seek justice from a higher authority?

3) <u>Affirmative Action attempts to force others to affirm in us what we refuse to affirm in ourselves.</u>

As you march, beg and protest for special treatment, there's a 20-ton elephant sitting in the living room of black America. All across black America, people with little or no resources are building for themselves right in our midst. They feed us, clothe us and control the local economy of every black community in America. Although they are the minority among us, by self-reliance, innovation and determination, they silently wield an economic power that should have us marveling. They don't need affirmative action programs to hire their youth in the summer. They create jobs and opportunities for their children by building for themselves.

After they have employed their own, they then hire a few of us -- Not because they like us, but because they have satisfied the basics of human nature -- self sufficiency! Is it not wiser to study and imitate their success, rather than keep knocking on the same old tired door of inferiority? Blacks control school boards, yet cannot seem to develop education systems that build communities. We are city councils and mayors, yet in almost every case, the cities we control are bankrupt municipalities and ghettoes that even WE run from. So, to keep from facing our own failure and impotence, we appeal to the "great white man" to affirm our equality, in spite of our refusal or inability to conduct ourselves as true equals. And the evidence is all around us.

4) Affirmative Action is an admission of our inferiority

Don't you feel even a little twinge of embarrassment as you shamelessly assert that without special treatment, we cannot build for ourselves? Are we that feeble-minded? Your very appeal is an admission of mental inferiority. We are asking one who is greater to cut a special door because of our mental handicap. Is that not true? Jesse Jackson proudly admitted we are inferior when he said: "We need affirmative action because while we are free, we are not equal". That has to be the most insane statement I have ever heard! Carter G. Woodson spoke of Jesse's fatal thinking when he said: "History shows that it does not matter who is in power; those who have not learned to do for themselves and have to depend solely on others, never obtain any more rights or privileges in the end than they had in the beginning".

Now I ask you, have 30 years of Affirmative action made us equal? Are we surging ahead economically as a result of affirmative action? If not, then what is your basis for wanting more of the same, yet expecting a different result? Isn't that the very definition of insanity? Am I the only one in black America who sees the absurdity of this push for a special door? Am I to tell my son that he will forever be a victim?-A helpless leaf blowing in the wind of white supremacy; Forever subject to the whims of others unless a special door is cut for him?

5) Affirmative Action uncovers the hypocrisy of the democrats.

The Democratic Party is laughing at us behind closed doors. We literally worship that party, yet no affirmative action is given us when we put them in office. Look around you! Are we the leaders of the Democratic Party though we vote for them at the clip of ninety percent? Do we control the agenda of the party? It's under the nose of a democratic governor that proposal 2 is on the ballot in Michigan; and all the polls show that it will pass. Doesn't that tell you something about the unwillingness to give us special treatment? Why didn't the democrats protect our interests before the fact?

They always seem to get behind some useless cause to make us think they are on our team. Why are the democrats silent on reparations?-something that has more merit than affirmative action. And why are you black leaders silent on that fact? Instead, you raise millions of dollars and spend thousand of man-hours bankrupting our children's future, for a morsel that has little, if any benefit. In the meantime the hypocritical democrats give us support, but only in our insane behavior.

6) Affirmative Action can never bring about equality

Black leaders don't seem to know what everyone else on earth knows: "We hold these truths to be self-evident that ALL men are created equal, that they are endowed by their creator with certain unalienable rights; that among these are life, liberty and the pursuit of happiness."--Declaration of Independence. You say that affirmative action will level the playing field, but observation suggests that the real playing field is in the Mind, imagination and resilience of the human spirit. The playing field is already equal in that case. Maybe we just refuse to get on the playing field!

Since freedom and equality are **unalienable**, they can't be granted nor taken by anyone. Since both come from the creator, and Jesse suggests that we are not equal; maybe it is God who deprived us of equality. The appeal for equality therefore should be made to GOD, rather than other men. And since most of you are preachers anyway, it is only fitting that you approach God with the question and get back to us with his answer.

A better way: I believe the only affirmative action should be FUBU (For Us By Us). Our thinking is the problem. In our minds are the psychoses that keep us poor in the midst of plenty. Poor thinking, poor health, poor behavior, short sighted goals and poor planning should be addressed first. Secondly, let's study success and imitate it. Success is in the multitude of stores, shop and enterprises run by others in our communities. Suppose we demanded excellence from ourselves and our children in spite of our circumstances? Suppose we refused to use excuses (though we may have many)? Suppose we concentrated our energies within to pull on the resources that GOD has given to every man?

The entire world would then beat down our doors to shower us in recognition as equal partners with the peoples of this planet. But as it stands now, we are like infants having not the wherewithal to do anything for ourselves except beg to suck on the great white nipple.

Sincerely,

Dr. Alonzo R. Fleming Jr.

6.2
DICTIONARY

DICTIONARY HIGHLIGHTS
Quick Reference

GOD
The MIND that created ALL.

LORD God
The Mind that perceived fault with GOD's creation and decided to manipulate it.

Devil
The perceived absence of GOD.

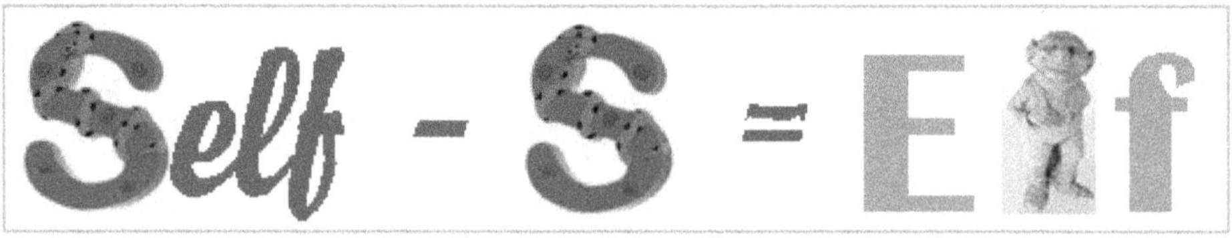

SIN – Blindness or Ignorance of Self.

Glossary of Terms

A

ALL – This word is understood to mean total. There are <u>no exceptions</u> to this definition. 100% is synonymous with this term.

B

BELIEF – That which is thought to be true, but may or may not be true.

C

CARNAL – Given to manifesting One's lower nature.

CASE STUDY – Examples of events that occurred in 'real time'.

CIVIL RIGHTS – Rights which slaves expect from their masters.

D

DEATH – Ignorance of Self; Sin; **Note:** This term is routinely mislabeled as One's transition from this life manifestation.

DEVIL – The perceived absence of GOD.

E

EARTH – The physical material that makes up the Universe.

ELF – The symbol for one who has been separated from spiritual truth or enlightenment. A small-minded, mischievous, humanoid.

ESSAYS – Opinions that are written to further develop a particular subject.

EVIL – Thoughts based in materialism.

EXHIBITS – Scripture Proof, Charts, Letters, Events and Scientific Analysis.

F

FACT – That which is known and can be known by all who observe. It can be reproduced in some form for all to see.

FAITH – A belief based on knowledge of principles. Faith empowers knowledge and knowledge empowers faith. Faith provides evidence that all inquirers can examine independently.

FEMALE – The Manifestation of Feminine Energy. Study the Principle of Gender in The Kybalion.

FLESH – Both a singular and plural term; Flesh is the Material Manifestation of Thought and Word; The Material World; MAN's tools.

G

GET OFF YOUR KNEES – This statement means to discontinue marching, picketing, pleading or groveling for others to provide that which you already inherently possess.

GOD – The ALL; Creative Energy; Life Force; All that is; MIND; Substantial reality underlying all outward manifestations; Oneness; Man's likeness.

God (or god) – One who has mastered Universal Principles and makes or manipulates worlds utilizing this knowledge.

GOOD – Thoughts based in Self.

H

HUMAN RIGHTS – Rights which humans expect from each other.

I

IGNORANCE – That which is unknown. A belief may be based on it, but faith cannot be based on it.

J

K

KNOWLEDGE – That which is known and can be known by all. Once knowledge has been acquired, it erases belief.

L

LIFE – Substantial Reality; The nature and law of all that is.

LOVE – Manifestation of GOD through attraction and unity.

Lord – Original Man; Those to whom GOD gave dominion of the Earth.

LORD God – refers to the Mind that used the knowledge of universal principles to make this present world; the mental orientation of the present world. The Mind that rules the world that is passing away. Satan.

M

MALE – The manifestation of Masculine Energy. Study the Principle of Gender in The Kybalion.

MATERIAL WORLD – The physical Manifestation of Thought and Word.

MATERIALISM – Valuing physical manifestation above Self which creates and manifests the material.

MIND – another name used to describe GOD's Life Force.

Mind – The conduit or portal of communication between Self and the Material World; Life Force.

N

NATURE – Mental Orientation; Manifestations of Mind

NEGRO – The Dead or Neutral Man; One in whom Spiritual and Mental Growth was Negated.

NEHUSHTAN – (Hebrew) is a sacred object in the form of a bronze snake upon a pole.

O

ONE – Unity of Mind. Flesh cannot Unite.

ORIGINAL MAN – The first generation of Man created by GOD.

P

PRAYER – The act of acknowledging One's connection to the Life Force, the Universe and the Human Family and One's responsibility over it.

Q

R

RESURRECTION – The act of coming to the knowledge of One's Self; Identification with GOD.

S

SATAN – The Manifestation of a Destructive Mind. A Mind rooted in Materialism.

SATANIC – Destructive, Insane, or Crazy Thinking.

SEER – One who sees.

SELF – Cannot be Defined. Our best attempt to define this term is that Self is GOD Manifesting as You.

SELF INTEREST – Decisions based in Principle; Sees self-connection to others.

SELFISHNESS – Decisions based in Personality; Blind to self-connection with others.

SUBSTANCE – Universal Principals; Unchangeable reality.

SIN – Ignorance of Self; Death; This term is characterized as Nakedness, Blindness or Sleep.

T

THOUGHT – Communication between the Self and Flesh.

TRUTH – That which is. Truth cannot be changed or modified. That which is true is true for all time. Note: Knowledge is varying degrees of Truth.

U

UNALIENABLE RIGHTS – GOD-Given Rights that Man is born with.

V

VIRTUE - Power

W

WHITE SUPREMACY – The Mind of Satan based in pale skin hue. The final product of Mind and Body Grafting; The world system of Death currently poisoning the earth.

WOMAN – The dividing of MAN by the LORD God. That which was taken out of Man and distinguished as separate and unequal. This term is not synonymous with the Female that GOD made who is ONE with Man.

WORD – The Manifestation of Thought.

X

Y

Z

RECOMMENDATIONS

We recommend the following items to further increase your understanding of the Power of your Mind and your Self.

BOOKS

The Kybalion – Three Initiates
A Course in Miracles – Foundation for Inner Peace
Acts of Faith – Iyanla Vanzant
Spirit of a Man – Iyanla Vanzant
The Mis-Education of the Negro – Carter G. Woodson
Astrological Revelations about You – Sydney Omarr
Message to the Black Man – The Honorable Elijah Muhammad
My Grandfather's Son – Clarence Thomas
Come on People – Bill Cosby and Alvin F. Poussaint
Standing in the Majesty of Grace – Keefa Lorraine Weatherspoon, N.D.
The Places You'll Go – Dr. Seuss

MOVIES

Sankofa – Haile Gerima
The Truman Show – Peter Weir
Trading Places – John Landis
The Matrix – Andy Wachowski
The Shawshank Redemption – Frank Darabont
The Lion King – Roger Allers & Rob Minkoff
The Secret – Drew Heriot
What the Bleep Do We Know – Mark Vicente, Betsy Chase & William Arntz
Pay it Forward – Mimi Leder

MUSIC *(Music is the most powerful of all art forms. The universe is musical. Music sends messages to the deepest parts of the Mind, so choose your music wisely.)*

Hotel California – Eagles
Don't Believe the Hype – Public Enemy
"Sleeping with the Enemy" Album – Paris
Karma – Alicia Keys
I am not my hair: Remix – India Arie
(The Mystery) Who is God? - Rakim
Everybody's got a Story – Amanda Marshall
All Falls Down – Kanye West
Waiting on the World to Change – John Mayer
Appletree – Erykah Badu
If you knew – Paul Hardcastle

This list represents our greatest oracles and is only designed to place you on the path to Self. It does not mean that our oracles were aware of the Message nor would agree; it only means that their works reveal hidden Principles that open up the Mind to Truth.

RECOMMENDATIONS

WEBSITES

www.muhammadspeaks.com – On-Demand audio and video of Elijah Muhammad
www.alonzofleming.com – On-Demand audio and video of Dr. Alonzo Fleming Jr.
www.beyondprayerandmeditation.com – Principled Philosophy Teachings
www.nextworldpublishing.com – Excerpts from coming books

CREDITS

The Author wishes to give the greatest credit to
Master Fard Muhammad
Who gave me a Messenger,
The Honorable Elijah Muhammad;
Who has often visited me in dreams.
While the Author acknowledges
That the Law he presents cuts across All Religions;
It was the Honorable Elijah Muhammad who taught me
That I am in the Order of the Original Man
And that I should read, analyze, and think critically
And never be afraid of Truth!

To the Honorable Minister Louis Farrakhan
For his Magnificent efforts
To continue the work.
'Thank you for introducing me to the teachings!'

To Bill Cosby
Who Assured me that Raising a Family is Normal!

To Clarence Thomas
You and I are Twin Souls
Who drew opposite conclusions from Similar Experiences.

To Clinton Street Greater Bethlehem Temple
For teaching me to study the scriptures.

To Jesus Tabernacle of Deliverance and the Shrine of the Black Madonna
For preparing me a Spiritually, Powerful wife.

To Professor Kehinde Solwazi at Fresno City College
For Believing in Me
In the Face of Ridicule.

To Jean Warrington, my white, GED. Instructor, who when I was ready to quit,
Asked me, "Do You Know Who You Are?! Your ancestors built the mighty pyramids
and great civilizations!" And then she proceeded to give me knowledge.

Thank you All for Shaping
My Mind!

A VERY SPECIAL TRIBUTE
To Auntie Dee bka Dorothy Pickens
Words she lived by and taught this Man to live by.

If you can keep you head when all about you are losing theirs
And blaming it on you'
If you can trust yourself when all men doubt you;
But make allowance for their doubting too;
If you can wait and not be tired by waiting,
Or being lied about, don't deal in lies
Or being hated, don't give way to hating,
And yet don't look too good, nor talk too wise:

If you can dream – and not make dreams your master;
If you can think – and not make thoughts your aim;
If you can meet with TRIUMPH and DISASTER
And treat those two imposters just the same;
If you can bear to hear the truth you've spoken
Twisted by knaves to make a trap for fools,
Or watch the things you gave your life to, broken,
And stoop and build'em up with worn-out tools:

If you can make one heap of all your winnings
And risk it on one turn of pitch-and-toss,
And lose, and start again at your beginnings,
And never breathe a word about your loss;
If you can force your heart and nerve and sinew
To serve your turn long after they are gone,
And so hold on when there is nothing in you
Except the Will which says to them: "Hold on!"

If you can talk with crowds and keep your virtue,
Or walk with Kings – nor lose the common touch,
If neither foes nor loving friends can hurt you,
If all men count with you, but none too much;
If you can fill the unforgiving minute
With sixty seconds worth of distance run,
Yours is the EARTH and everything that's in it,
And – which is more – you'll be a Man, my son!

-Rudyard Kipling

Be encouraged Kwame Kilpatrick, you are of the Original Order, my Brother

www.ingramcontent.com/pod-product-compliance
Lightning Source LLC
Chambersburg PA
CBHW021049090426
42738CB00006B/256
* 9 7 8 0 6 1 5 1 9 1 1 8 8 *